Final = 9-14
20·21

STEPHEN J. KAPLOWITT, Ph.D., University of Pennsylvania, is Associate Professor of German in the Department of Germanic and Slavic Languages at the University of Connecticut. Prior to this appointment he taught for four years at Columbia University.

WOLFGANG PAULSEN, Ph.D., University of Berne, is Professor of German and Head of the Department at the University of Massachusetts. He has also taught at the University of Connecticut, State University of New York at Albany, Smith College, and the University of Iowa. He is the co-author of an elementary grammar and the editor of various text editions of literary works for both American and German publishers.

A GERMAN GRAMMAR

For Review and Reference

STEPHEN J. KAPLOWITT
UNIVERSITY OF CONNECTICUT

WOLFGANG PAULSEN
UNIVERSITY OF MASSACHUSETTS

THE RONALD PRESS COMPANY • NEW YORK

Library of Congress Catalog Card Number: 76–110551

Preface

This second-year grammar is designed to offer the college student who has completed a basic course in German a thorough review of the work generally covered in a first-year course. It presents, in addition, a considerable amount of more advanced material usually encountered on the second-year level or later. The authors have taken into consideration the fact that ability to read German is one of the primary goals of instruction on the second-year level. This book, therefore, always keeps the reading objective clearly in mind and may be easily used by instructors emphasizing the teaching of grammar from the standpoint of reading. On the other hand, the book also presents a comprehensive account of German grammar for those interested in the active use of the language.

With this double objective in mind, the authors have organized their material to appeal both to teachers concentrating on the reading approach and to those emphasizing active grammar. The first five chapters of the book deal with the basic problems of the structure of the German sentence. This presentation focuses the attention of the student on the special problems of word order, an understanding of which is essential to the mastery of the German language. The remaining chapters are devoted to the traditional topics of German grammar, in two major groupings: the various problems of declension and uses of cases, and matters related to conjugation and uses of the verb.

The main body of each chapter contains a detailed discussion of the grammatical material in question. Each chapter concludes with a section, "Special Points," dealing with problems not ordinarily found in review grammars, but commonly encountered by the student in his reading. The basic patterns to be reviewed are presented in the pertinent chapters, so that only an alphabetical listing of the principal parts of strong and irregular weak verbs is included at the back of the book, before the vocabularies.

The exercises for each chapter are divided into two parts—active and recognition exercises. The recognition exercises, consisting of practice sentences to be translated into English, have been designed particularly to aid in developing the skills necessary to read German. The active exercises provide ample opportunity for practice in grammatical problems from the active point of view. This division will make it possible for the book to be used by instructors concerned solely with a reading approach as well as by those who wish their students to obtain additional practice in dealing with the problems of the active use of the language.

STEPHEN J. KAPLOWITT
WOLFGANG PAULSEN

Storrs, Connecticut
Amherst, Massachusetts
  January, 1970

Contents

PART I

Structure of the Sentence

1

Principal Clauses—I

Two Types of Word Order

1. There are two types of word order for declarative statements in principal clauses: normal and inverted. In both, THE FINITE VERB (which is the form of the verb changing in conjugation) IS THE SECOND ELEMENT.

Normal word order

2. In normal word order the subject begins the clause:

> subject   verb
> **Die Kinder** *spielen* den ganzen Tag auf der Straße.
> The children play on the street all day.

Caution. The subject may be enlarged by one or more modifiers:

(1) By adjectives:

> Die **kleinen** Kinder *spielen* auf der Straße.

(2) By dependent clauses, relative or conjunctional:

> Die Kinder, **die nebenan wohnen,** *spielen* auf der Straße.
> The children who live next door are playing on the street.

> Die Meinung, **daß der Platz der Frau in der Küche ist,** *ist* alt.
> The opinion that woman's place is in the kitchen is old.

(3) By infinitive phrases:

> Die Aussicht, **viel Geld zu verdienen,** *ermutigte* ihn.
> The prospect of earning a lot of money encouraged him.

(4) By attributive genitives and prepositional phrases:

3

Die Kinder **der jungen Frau** *spielen* auf der Straße.
The children of the young woman are playing on the street.

Nicht jeder Mann **mit einer roten Nase** *ist* ein Trunkenbold.
Not every man with a red nose is a drunk.

Inverted word order

3. In inverted word order the clause begins with a part of speech other than the subject (and its modifiers), for example, with an object or adverb. This may be done to emphasize the element in first position or merely for stylistic variation. Since the verb must be in second position, THE SUBJECT (together with its modifiers) IS PLACED AFTER THE VERB:

    adverbial phrase   verb   subject (and modifier)
Den ganzen Tag *spielen die Kinder, die nicht zur Schule gehen,* auf der Straße.

Modified objects in first position

4. Although, as a rule, ONLY ONE such part of speech can occupy the initial position in a clause, this part of speech may also be extended by modifiers. Therefore, the verb and the following subject of the principal clause will be more difficult to locate since they do not appear until after the conclusion of the modifying material:

                  object and its modifier   verb subject
Seinen Vater, der ein reicher Arzt in New York ist, *hat*   *er*   um das Geld für einen neuen Wagen.

Since English cannot imitate such a construction, the translation will normally have to begin with the subject.

Same forms with different functions

5. Since neuter singular, feminine singular, and all plural nouns and pronouns have the same forms in the nominative as in the accusative (for details, see Chapter 6), it is often not possible to determine whether the first element of a principal clause is the subject or the object until one has read beyond the verb. The following contrasting sentences will illustrate the difficulties involved:

> **Die Frau,** von der wir reden, kennt meinen Vater nicht.
> The woman we are talking about does not know my father.
>
> **Die Frau,** von der wir reden, kennt mein Vater nicht.
> My father does not know the woman we are talking about.

Words separating subject and verb

6. Locating the subject of a sentence with inverted word order can

also be difficult because the subject is not necessarily the word (or word unit) immediately following the verb. The appearance of the subject may be delayed by objects, adverbs, or prepositional phrases, usually for reasons of sentence rhythm:

> Das *hat* **mir** *der Mann* selbst gesagt.

INSTEAD OF: Das *hat der Mann* **mir** selbst gesagt.

> The man told me that himself.

> Und das *hat* **mit ihrem Singen**/ *die Lorelei* getan.[*]
> And that Lorelei did with her singing.

An diesem Vormittag *trat* **ihr in einem winzigen Zimmer mit vergitterten Fenstern** *ein kleiner, magerer Mann mit schwachem, dunklem Bart* entgegen.[†]	That morning a little emaciated man with a sparse dark beard walked up to her in a tiny room with barred windows.

Dependent clause in first position

7. If a dependent clause begins a sentence, it is treated as the first element of the following principal clause, which therefore has the verb in first position (inverted word order):

> dependent clause   verb   subject
> **Als er endlich nach Hause kam,** *war seine Frau* nicht mehr da.
> When he finally came home his wife was no longer there.

Elements in final position

8. Since the finite verb often expresses only part of the verbal idea, it is imperative to look to the end of the principal clause for the following elements in final position:

(*a*) Infinitives:

> Er wird morgen abend **kommen.**
> He will come tomorrow night.

(*b*) Past participles:

> Er ist gestern abend **gekommen.**
> He came last night.

(*c*) Separable prefixes. ‡

> Er kommt heute abend **an.**
> He will arrive tonight.

[*] Heine, „Die Lorelei."
[†] Brecht, „Der Mantel des Ketzers."
[‡] See Chapter 22, paragraph 3.

(*d*) Predicate adjectives: *

> Er ist in der ganzen Welt dafür **bekannt.**
> He is known for that all over the world.

Caution. Whenever the finite verb is a form of **haben, sein,** or **werden,** check for a possible supplementary verb form at the end of the clause to complete the verbal idea:

$$\text{Er ist} \underline{\hspace{3cm}} \rightarrow \text{angekommen.}$$
$$\text{gestern abend}$$

If the finite verb is an ordinary verb in one of its simple tenses, check at the end of the clause to see if it is modified by a separable prefix:

$$\text{Er kommt} \underline{\hspace{3cm}} \rightarrow \text{an.}$$
$$\text{heute abend}$$

Special Points

Prepositional phrases at end of clauses

1. For emphasis, prepositional phrases may be placed after the infinitive, past participle, or separable prefix which otherwise concludes such a sentence:

> Er ist natürlich nach Hause gekommen **ohne seinen Schirm.**
>
> FOR   Er ist natürlich **ohne seinen Schirm** nach Hause gekommen.
>
> Of course, he came home without his umbrella.

Second part of comparison at end of clauses

2. Similarly, the second part of a comparison is commonly placed after the concluding infinitive, past participle, or separable prefix:

> Du hast das nicht so schnell gesehen **wie ich.**
> You did not see that as fast as I (did).
>
> Er hat das besser gewußt **als sein Bruder.**
> He knew that better than his brother.

Infinitive and past participle in first position

3. Infinitives and past participles may be placed in first position for emphasis:

> **Zwingen** kann ich dich nicht, wenn du nicht willst.
> I cannot force you if you don't want to.

* See Chapter 7, Section A.

Er hat vieles getan, aber **gearbeitet** hat er nicht.

He did a lot of things but work was not one of them.

Introductory *es*

4. Another way in which the appearance of the subject of a principal clause may be delayed is the use of the so-called introductory **es**. This **es** is employed when the author, for one reason or another, does not wish to begin the clause with the grammatical subject. Note that the **es** is often not translated in English, which will normally begin such a sentence with the real subject:

Es sind in den letzten Wochen selt-
subject
same *Erscheinungen* beobachtet worden, die die Fachleute noch nicht verstehen.

Strange phenomena which the experts do not yet understand have been observed in the past few weeks.

Es siegt immer und notwending die *Begeisterung* über den, der nicht begeistert ist.*

Enthusiasm always and inevitably wins out over someone who is not enthusiastic.

Often, particularly when the verb in question is a form of *sein*, English can begin the sentence with *there:*

> **Es** sind im Augenblick nur fünfzehn *Studenten* im Zimmer.

> There are at the moment only fifteen students in the room.

FOR:　At the moment only fifteen students are in the room.

RECOGNITION EXERCISES

A. *Location of the grammatical subject. Translate:*

1. Die Kinder, die gestern auf der Straße gespielt haben, sind heute zur Schule gegangen. 2. Die Kinder, die gestern auf der Straße gespielt haben, haben wir heute noch nicht gesehen. 3. Die alte Frau, der niemand helfen wollte, weil sie so arrogant war, hat meinen Vater gestern wieder besucht. 4. Die alte Frau, der niemand helfen wollte, weil sie so arrogant war, hat mein Vater gestern wieder besucht. 5. Diese Antwort hat mir schon gestern auf dem Weg nach Hause mein Bruder selbst gegeben. 6. Diese Antwort hat mir schon gestern auf dem Weg nach Hause nicht gefallen. 7. Am Abend vor ihrer Abreise besuchte sie in dem kleinen Hotel am Bahnof den alten Mann, den sie seit Jahren nicht gesehen hatte. 8. Am Abend vor ihrer Abreise besuchte sie in dem kleinen Hotel am Bahnof der alte Mann, den sie seit Jahren nicht gesehen hatte. 9. Es wurden gestern von unseren Freunden Dinge gesagt, die uns gar nicht gefallen haben. 10. Es sind in den letzten Tagen einige deutsche Diplomaten in Washington angekommen. 11. Er spricht oft darüber, aber es

---

* Fichte, *Reden an die deutsche Nation.*

hört ihm gewöhnlich niemand zu. 12. Letzte Woche hat mir bei meiner Arbeit in der Bibliothek ein Mann geholfen, den ich noch nie gesehen hatte. 13. Die Behauptung, daß arme Leute arm bleiben, weil sie faul sind, habe ich oft gehört. 14. Die Behauptung, daß arme Leute arm bleiben, weil sie faul sind, ist alt.

B. *Translate, observing how the verbal idea does not become clear until the end of the principal clause has been reached:*

1. Er wollte schon an seinem ersten Tag in Paris die Eltern seiner Freundin besuchen. 2. So etwas kommt zu allen Zeiten und sogar in den besten Familien vor. 3. Sie werden auf diese Weise die unglückliche Mutter des kranken Kindes nie trösten können. 4. Er ist trotz des schlechten Wetters den ganzen Sommer bei seinen Verwandten in Berlin geblieben. 5. Er ist nicht nur bei uns, sondern überhaupt überall in der Welt für seine schönen und amüsanten Kurzgeschichten bekannt. 6. Dem Studenten ist weder gestern zu Hause noch heute in der Klasse die Antwort auf diese einfache Frage eingefallen. 7. Sie hat letzte Woche in allen Buchhandlungen kein einziges Exemplar seines Buches über die Kunst der Renaissance gefunden. 8. Sie hat heute ein grünes Kleid, einen gelben Hut, braune Schuhe und weiße Handschuhe an. 9. Gestern hat sie ein blaues Kleid, einen braunen Hut, schwarze Schuhe und weiße Handschuhe gekauft; sie ist wahrscheinlich vollkommen farbenblind. 10. Er war nicht nur letzten Winter, sondern auch noch den ganzen Frühling und einen Teil des Sommers krank. 11. Sie wird erst am Ende des Sommers mit ihrer Seminararbeit über den Gebrauch von ,,und" in Goethes *Faust* fertig. 12. Sie wird erst am Ende des Sommers mit ihrer Seminararbeit über den Gebrauch von ,,und" in Goethes *Faust* anfangen.

ACTIVE EXERCISES

A. *In this exercise sentences are given with normal word order. Rewrite each sentence three times, using inverted word order and placing each time a different element* (a, b, c, *below*) *in first position:*

1. Ich habe letzten Sommer in Deutschland viele Bücher gekauft.
   a. Letzten Sommer . . .
   b. In Deutschland . . .
   c. Viele Bücher . . .
2. Wir werden morgen früh bestimmt die Wahrheit erfahren.
   a. Morgen früh . . .
   b. Die Wahrheit . . .
   c. Bestimmt . . .
3. Sie wird sich nächste Woche ein neues Kleid kaufen, wenn sie das Geld dafür hat.
   a. Nächste Woche . . .
   b. Ein neues Kleid . . .
   c. Wenn sie das Geld dafür hat, . . .

B. *Translate into German:*

1. The woman with the big hat is my sister.
2. She stayed at home all day. (*Place adverbial expression of time in first position.*)
3. We get up every morning at seven o'clock.
4. He will arrive tomorrow evening. (*Use future tense.*)
5. She went home yesterday. (*Place adverb of time in first position.*)
6. The meeting will take place next week. (*Use present tense.*)
7. If I have time I shall go downtown.
8. Tomorrow we are going to visit our uncle. (*Use future tense.*)
9. Yesterday my wife bought a new dress. (*Use present perfect.*)
10. Last evening she really sang very beautifully. (*Use present perfect tense.*)
11. She sang much better than her sister. (*Use present perfect tense.*)
12. He can understand that as well as you.
13. We now have to work every evening.
14. This morning I met my friend on the street. (*Use present perfect tense.*)
15. He is known for his beautiful songs.
16. The mountain is visible only in (**bei**) good weather.
17. The children were really very sick two days ago.
18. In this case the answer is very simple.
19. He has often done it better than I.
20. When I arrived she was no longer here.

2

Principal Clauses—II

A. Position of Objects and Adverbs

Objects

1. The relative position of objects is essentially: INDIRECT BEFORE DIRECT IF THE DIRECT OBJECT IS A NOUN:

indirect   direct
Die Frau gibt **dem Kaufmann das Geld.**
The woman gives the merchant the money.

indir.   direct
Die Frau gibt **ihm das Geld.**
The woman gives him the money.

This rule applies also if the direct object is a demonstrative pronoun or if it is abbreviated to 's (for **das** or **es**):

Die Frau gibt **ihm das.**   Die Frau gibt **ihm's.**

On the other hand, if the direct object is a personal pronoun it precedes the indirect object:

Die Frau gibt **es ihm.**   Die Frau gibt **es dem Kaufmann.**

Adverbs of time and place

2. A great deal of flexibility exists with regard to the relative position of adverbs or adverbial phrases, but by and large ADVERBS OF TIME PRECEDE ADVERBS OF PLACE:

time   place
Er ist **heute morgen in der Schule.**
He is in school this morning.

Note that in English the order of the adverbs is reversed.

Adverbs of manner

3. The adverb of manner can in most instances either precede or follow adverbs of time or place:

BEFORE ADVERB OF TIME:
> Er hat **am besten** *immer* zu Hause gearbeitet.

BEFORE ADVERB OF PLACE:
> Er hat immer **am besten** *zu Hause* gearbeitet.

AFTER ADVERB OF PLACE:
> Er hat immer *zu Hause* **am besten** gearbeitet.
> He always worked best at home.

Relative position of objects and adverbs

4. When a sentence contains a noun object (or noun objects) and an adverb (or adverbs), the position of the objects in relation to the adverbs is also flexible; the last element in the sentence tends to carry the emphasis:

> Er hat *gestern* **seinem Freund** *im Büro* **das Geld** gegeben.
> Er hat *gestern im Büro* **seinem Freund das Geld** gegeben.
> Er hat **seinem Freund** *gestern im Büro* **das Geld** gegeben.
> Er hat **seinem Freund das Geld** *gestern im Büro* gegeben.
> Er hat **seinem Freund** *gestern* **das Geld** *im Büro* gegeben.

> He gave his friend the money yesterday in the office.

Note that although the relative position of adverbs and noun objects is flexible, the relation of adverbs to one another (time before place) is maintained, as is that of the noun objects (indirect before direct). But if the object, on the other hand, is a pronoun it must precede the adverbs:

> Er hat **ihm** *gestern* im Büro das Geld gegeben.

Ich kann **sie** *jetzt* nicht sprechen.   Er möchte **es** *morgen* haben.
I can't talk to her now.   He would like to have it tomorrow.

Position of *nicht*

5. The position of **nicht** is determined by the part of speech which is being negated. If the idea of the verb is negated, **nicht** is placed at the end of a principal clause provided the verb is used in a simple tense form and has no separable prefix:

Ich gebe ihr das Buch **nicht**.   Er sah mich **nicht**.
I won't give her the book.   He didn't see me.

> Ich verstehe das **nicht**.
> I don't understand that.

nicht, however, precedes a separable prefix, a past participle, or an infinitive, any of which normally must be in final position:

> Ich habe ihr das Buch **nicht** *gegeben.*
> I did not give her the book.

Ich gehe heute **nicht** *aus.*   Ich will es ihr **nicht** *geben.*
I am not going out today.   I don't want to give it to her.

Specific negation

6. If any element other than the verb is negated, **nicht** immediately precedes it:

> **Nicht** *sie,* sondern ihre Schwester hat den Brief geschrieben.
> Not she but her sister wrote the letter.

> Ich habe **nicht** *den Titel,* sondern den Autor gemeint.
> I didn't mean the title but the author.

In view of this use of **nicht** for specific negation, **nicht** tends to precede the following grammatical elements:

(*a*) Predicate adjectives and predicate nominatives:

Ich bin wirklich **nicht** *müde.*   Berlin ist **nicht** *die Hauptstadt.*
I am really not tired.   Berlin is not the capital.

(*b*) Prepositional phrases, particularly those serving as adverbial expressions of time or place:

> Ich gehe heute **nicht** *zur Universität.*
> I am not going to the university today.

> Man lernt die deutsche Grammatik **nicht** *in einer Woche.*
> One doesn't learn German grammar in one week.

(*c*) Most adverbs:

TIME:

> Er steht **nicht** *früh* auf.
> He doesn't get up early.

PLACE:

> Er wohnt **nicht** *hier.*
> He doesn't live here.

MANNER:

> Er arbeitet **nicht** *gerne.*
> He doesn't like to work.

Note that a few common adverbs (such as **heute, morgen,** and **gestern**) are not normally preceded by **nicht** because it is the idea of the verb which is then negated and not that of the adverb:

> Er kommt heute **nicht**.   Er sah uns gestern wohl **nicht**.
> He isn't coming today.   He probably didn't see us yesterday.

Caution.   **nicht** will precede the above parts of speech (*a, b, c*) even if the clause ends with a dependent infinitive, past participle, or separable prefix:

> Ich bin heute **nicht** zur Universität gegangen.
> I didn't go to the university today.
>
> Er wird wohl **nicht** hier wohnen.
> He probably doesn't live here.

B. Interrogative Clauses

Formation

1. Simple questions which do not contain an interrogative (pronoun, adjective, or adverb) are formed by placing the verb in first position:

> **Hast** du den Mann gesehen?
> Did you see the man?

Position of interrogative

2. If the question uses an interrogative, the interrogative begins the sentence and is followed by the finite verb. However, if an interrogative is used with a preposition, the preposition precedes it:

> **Was** hast du da gesagt?   *Mit* **wem** hat er gesprochen?
> What did you say there?   With whom did he speak?
>
> *Mit* **welchem** Recht sagen Sie das?
> What right do you have to say that?

Position of subject

3. Although the subject usually follows directly after the verb, as can be seen in the above examples, other elements are sometimes found between the verb and the subject:

>   verb   subject
> Was *hat* dem armen Mann nun **all die Mühe** genützt?
>
> OR   Was *hat* nun **all die Mühe** dem armen Mann genützt?
>
> OR   Was *hat* **all die Mühe** nun dem armen Mann genützt?
>
> Of what use was all this trouble to the poor man?

C. Coordinating Conjunctions

1. Two principal clauses may be connected by a coordinating conjunction. The following simple coordinating conjunctions stand outside the structure of the clause which follows and hence do not affect its word order:

aber (but, however)

> Er möchte kommen, **aber** er hat keine Zeit.
> He would like to come but he has no time.

Note that **aber**, like English *however*, can occur later on in the clause:

> Er möchte kommen, er hat **aber** keine Zeit.
> Wir möchten kommen, er **aber** hat keine Zeit.

allein (but, yet, however)

> Er möchte kommen, **allein** er hat keine Zeit.

Although **aber** and **allein** have the same general meaning, **allein** is less frequently used and is more emphatic.

Caution. Do not confuse the conjunction **allein** with the adverb **allein** (*alone*) when it appears in first position. The adverb is then always followed by the verb; the conjunction is not:

> **Allein** *möchte* er nicht kommen.
> He would not want to come alone.

denn (for, because)

> Er konnte ihr das nicht sagen, **denn** er hat sie kaum gekannt.
> He couldn't say that to her because he scarcely knew her.

Caution. Occasionally, for greater emphasis, **denn** may be omitted. The clause then begins with the finite verb and contains a **doch,** by which the construction can be easily identified. The greater emphasis can often be expressed in English by inserting the phrase *after all:*

> Er konnte ihr das nicht sagen, hat er sie **doch** kaum gekannt.
> He couldn't say that to her, for (after all) he scarcely knew her.

oder (or)

> Kann er kommen, **oder** muß er arbeiten?
> Can he come or does he have to work?

sondern (but, but rather)

> Er will nicht kommen, **sondern** (er will) arbeiten.
>
> He does not want to come but (rather) wants to work.

Note that **sondern** is used after a negative statement which is to be contradicted.

und (and)

> Er will morgen kommen, **und** morgen habe ich keine Zeit.
>
> He wants to come tomorrow and tomorrow I have no time.

2. In the conjunctional construction **entweder . . . oder** (*either . . . or*) only the **oder** is, strictly speaking, a conjunction and acts as such. **entweder** can be followed either by normal word order or inverted word order:

> **Entweder** *kommst du,*⎫
> **Entweder** *du kommst,*⎭ **oder** du kommst nicht.
>
> Either you come or you don't come.

In the related construction **weder . . . noch** (*neither . . . nor*) both parts function as adverbs, and if they introduce a clause inversion must be used:

> **Weder** *kenne ich* ihn, **noch** *will ich* ihn kennen.
>
> I neither know him, nor do I want to know him.

Special Points

Punctuation

1. In German it is permissible to have a series of independent clauses which are separated by commas from one another. The equivalent clauses in English would be separated either by a semicolon or by a period:

Ich schlich durchs Tor der Gerberei in den Gerbergarten, es war Feierabend und niemand zu sehen.*

I slipped through the gate of the tannery into the tanner's garden. It was after hours and nobody was to be seen.

Adverbs as coordinating conjunctions

2. In addition to the simple coordinating conjunctions, some ordinary adverbs, especially **doch** (*but, yet*), but occasionally also **bloß** (*only*) and **nur** (*only*) can serve as coordinating conjunctions and introduce a principal clause without disturbing its word order:

* Hermann Hesse, *Knulp.*

Ich möchte kommen, **doch** (**bloß, nur**) ich habe keine Zeit.
I would like to come, but (only) I have no time.

Verb first in exclamations

3. The word order normally used in questions (verb first) can also be found in such exclamations as those expressing amazement or disbelief. Often the adverb **aber, doch,** or **ja** is then added:

Ist die **aber** dumm!	Bin ich heute müde!
Is she stupid!	Am I tired today!

Habe ich dir das **doch** (**ja**) schon tausend Mal gesagt!
Oh, I have told you that a thousand times!

RECOGNITION EXERCISES

A. *Translate:*

1. Er hat sein Bestes getan, allein er konnte mit dieser Aufgabe nicht fertig werden. 2. Er hat sein Bestes getan, aber allein konnte er mit dieser Aufgabe nicht fertig werden. 3. Er möchte heute gerne mit uns ins Theater gehen, aber er hat leider keine Zeit. 4. Er will heute nicht ins Theater gehen, sondern den Abend gemütlich zu Hause verbringen. 5. Meine Frau fährt heute weder mit Ihnen in die Stadt, noch bleibt sie allein zu Hause. 6. Entweder fahre ich morgen mit Ihnen in die Stadt, oder ich bleibe allein zu Hause. 7. Erst muß meine Arbeit fertig sein, dann kann ich zu Bett gehen. 8. Erst muß meine Arbeit fertig sein, denn ich kann unmöglich vorher zu Bett gehen. 9. Er muß schon mit seiner Arbeit fertig sein, denn er ist eben zu Bett gegangen. 10. Er muß schon mit seiner Arbeit fertig sein, ist er doch eben zu Bett gegangen! 11. Ich möchte heute noch mit meiner Aufgabe fertig werden, doch ich habe einfach nicht genug Zeit dafür. 12. Obwohl er die alte Frau schrecklich langweilig fand, wollte er sie nicht kränken, hat sie doch so viel für ihn getan, als er noch klein war. 13. Entweder geht mein Freund mit mir ins Kino, oder er macht einen langen Spaziergang, aber er geht bestimmt aus, denn er hat keine Lust, noch einen Abend allein zu Hause zu bleiben. 14. Weder gehen wir heute abend ins Kino, noch machen wir unseren gewöhnlichen Spaziergang durch den Park, sondern wir gehen mit Schmidts ins Theater. Dann, wenn wir hungrig sind, essen wir in einem kleinen, aber guten Restaurant in der Ludwigstraße.

B. *Translate:*

1. Hat sie ihm wirklich ihre Meinung gesagt? 2. Hat sie ihm aber ihre Meinung gesagt! 3. Ist sie wirklich so ungeschickt, oder tut sie nur so? 4. Ist sie aber ungeschickt! Sie tut bestimmt nicht nur so. 5. Hat er tatsächlich diesen dummen Fehler gemacht? 6. Hat er einen dummen Fehler gemacht! 7. Er hat den Soldaten den Bauern beschrieben, den sie suchten. 8. Wer hat ihn den Soldaten beschrieben? 9. Herr Schmidt hat ihn ihnen beschrieben.

10. Wer hat den Bauern den Soldaten beschrieben, der ihnen das Pferd gestohlen hatte? 11. Der Junge, der sich hinter dem Haus versteckt hatte, hat ihn den Bauern beschrieben. 12. Hat er ihnen den Soldaten deutlich beschrieben? 13. Ja, dieses Pferd wird dem Soldaten den Kopf kosten. 14. Ich wollte meinen Kollegen meinen alten Schulkameraden vorstellen. 15. Warum wollten Sie ihn Ihren Kollegen vorstellen? 16. Ich wollte ihnen meinen Schulkameraden vorstellen, weil ich ihn ihnen so oft genannt hatte. 17. Ich wollte meinen alten Schulkameraden meinen Kollegen vorstellen. 18. Er schickte seinen Assistenten den Studenten, der Hilfe brauchte. 19. Um ihnen zu helfen, schickte er seinen Studenten den Assistenten zu. 20. Hat Marie der Katze die Milch schon gegeben? 21. Ja, sie hat ihr eben die Milch gegeben. 22. Schade, ich wollte sie ihr geben. 23. Mein Onkel hat das alte Haus am anderen Ende der Stadt, das ihm schon so lange gefallen hatte, endlich gekauft. 24. Mein Onkel hat das alte Haus am anderen Ende der Stadt, das ihm schon so lange gefallen hatte, endlich nach langen Überlegungen doch nicht gekauft, denn es war zu teuer. 25. Mein Onkel hat nicht dieses alte Haus gekauft, sondern eine Villa am Fluß. 26. Nicht mein Onkel hat das alte Haus gekauft, sondern sein Partner—bloß um ihn zu ärgern!

ACTIVE EXERCISES

A. Change the following sentences into negative statements by inserting **nicht** in its appropriate place:

1. Er schreibt eine solche Geschichte. 2. Er hat diese Geschichte geschrieben. 3. Sie will die Aufgabe machen. 4. Wir gehen heute. 5. Wir gehen heute aus. 6. Das kleine Mädchen ist hübsch. 7. Mein Bruder ist hier. 8. Mein Bruder ist hier gewesen. 9. Seine Schwester reist diesen Sommer nach Deutschland. 10. Ich will zu Hause arbeiten. 11. Kommen Sie heute abend? 12. Kommt er morgen nach Hause?

B. Rewrite the following sentences, using normal word order:

1. Gestern ist er ins Kino gegangen. 2. Einem armen Mann haben wir Geld gegeben. 3. Das Buch haben sie vor zwei Tagen in der Stadt gekauft. 4. Am Rhein findet man immer irgendwo einen guten Wein. 5. Einen langen Brief hat er seinen Eltern geschrieben. 6. Mir hat er neulich ein großes Paket geschickt. 7. Letzten Sommer ist mein Vater in Frankreich gewesen. 8. In einer kleinen Stadt kann man abends nicht ausgehen. 9. Meiner Mutter wird er so etwas nicht sagen. 10. Das hat er mir gestern abend erzählt.

C. Translate into German:
1. The girl with the red hair is really not my girl friend.
2. He can write such a letter easily, for he has done it very often.
3. He gave her a new dress yesterday.
4. Why did he give it to her?
5. He showed me a picture of his daughter.

6. I am going downtown now. Are you coming along?
7. He wants to read the newspaper outside in the garden.
8. Why does he want to read it there?
9. Are you ready or must I go alone?
10. Either I'll go to the movies tonight or I'll write letters.
11. Is he lucky that I am here!
12. She did not go to bed early but (rather) read a good book.
13. She went to bed but she could not fall asleep.
14. He spoke for a long time but he did not say very much.
15. Did you see her last evening?
16. She is driving alone to New York this summer, and I'll meet her there.
17. He bought a watch and sent it to his mother.
18. He did not write to his uncle but to his aunt.
19. Did he write this letter or did he not write it?
20. With whom do you want to go to the movies this evening?

3

Conjunctional Clauses

Transposed word order

1. IN DEPENDENT CLAUSES THE FINITE VERB STANDS LAST; this is called transposed word order. In all other respects, the word order is the same as in principal clauses:

Ich glaube, daß die Kinder den ganzen Tag draußen gespielt **haben.**
I think that the children played outside all day.

Subordinating conjunctions

2. There are two general types of dependent clauses: conjunctional and relative. Conjunctional dependent clauses are introduced by subordinating conjunctions. These conjunctions are listed alphabetically in Table A, at the end of this chapter. They are basic from the point of view of vocabulary and should be under complete control. As far as grammar is concerned, it is necessary to discuss only the following troublesome conjunctions:

als

als means *when* if it refers to a SINGLE ACTION IN THE PAST;

Als er endlich kam, war ich nicht mehr zu Hause.
When he finally arrived I was no longer at home.

als may also be used as a comparative conjunction meaning *than* to introduce either a complete or an abbreviated dependent clause or an infinitive phrase:

Er hat das *besser* gemacht, **als** ich erwartet habe.
He did that better than I expected.

Er hat das *besser* gemacht **als** ich (i.e., es gemacht habe).
He did that better than I (did it).

19

Ich habe *etwas Besseres* zu tun, **als** mir seinen Unsinn anzuhören.

I have something better to do than to listen to his nonsense.

After an **um so** which is followed by a comparative the conjunction **als** means *since, because:*

Das Interesse war **um so** *größer*, **als** das Problem ganz neu war.

The interest was all the greater since the problem was quite new.

Caution. (1) **als** followed by a verb, usually in the subjunctive, is the shortened form of **als ob** (*as if*) and should not be confused with the foregoing uses of **als** (see Chapter 18, Section B):

Es scheint, **als** *hätte* er mich nicht verstanden.

It seems as if he did not understand me.

(2) Do not confuse the subordinating conjunction **als** (verb at the end!) with the connective **als**, meaning *as, as a* (verb in second position!), when the latter begins a clause:

Als der reiche Mann schließlich zurückkehrte, erkannte man ihn nicht.

When the rich man finally returned one did not recognize him.

Als reicher Mann kehrte er schließlich zurück.

As a rich man he finally returned.

da

The conjunction **da** occurs most frequently in a causal sense to mean *since:*

Da ich heute keine Zeit habe, kann ich nicht kommen.

Since I have no time today I cannot come.

However, after an expression of time, **da** can also be used in a temporal sense; it can then be translated by *when* or *that,* whichever applies in English:

Das war die Zeit, **da** wir alle noch jung waren.

That was the time when we were all still young.

Jetzt, **da** ich sie gut kenne, bewundere ich sie nicht mehr so sehr.

Now that I know her well I no longer admire her so much.

Caution. The conjunction **da** must not be confused with the adverb **da** (meaning *then* or *there*), which can also begin a clause. Whenever **da** is an adverb in first position, the finite verb follows immediately after it:

Da *griff* er nach der Flasche und fand sie leer.

Then he reached for the bottle and found it empty.

damit

The conjunction **damit,** *so that* (verb at the end!), should not be confused with the **da**-compound **damit** (*with it, with that, with them*) when it begins a clause and the verb is in second position:

> Ich kaufe mir eine Schaufel, **damit** ich im Garten arbeiten kann.
> I am buying myself a shovel so that I can work in the garden.

But:

> **Damit** *kann* ich im Garten arbeiten.
> I can work with it in the garden.

indem

The conjunction **indem** (not to be mistaken for **in** followed by the article or relative pronoun **dem,** always written in two words!) generally expresses simultaneousness of action or explains how something happened or was done. In the former usage, it is best translated by while or as:

> **Indem** er das sagte, trat seine Mutter ins Zimmer.
> As (while) he said that, his mother entered the room.

In its other usage, an **indem**-clause is usually translated with *by* plus a gerund:

> Er lernte Deutsch, **indem** er jeden Tag eine deutsche Zeitung las.
> He learned German by reading a German newspaper every day.

Occasionally **indem** can be found in the causal sense of *since, because:*

Solche Talente machen uns oft ungeduldig, indem man selten von ihnen erlangt, was man augenblicklich wünscht.* / Such talents often make us impatient because one rarely receives from them what one wishes at that moment.

ob

The conjunction **ob** (*whether, if*) is used only to introduce an indirect question when the direct question upon which it was based did not begin with an interrogative (see Chapter 2, Section B):

> Ich möchte wissen, **ob** sie kommt.   (Direct: Kommt sie?)
> I'd like to know if (whether) she is coming.

An **ob**-clause can be found also without an introductory principal clause, in which case a phrase like *I wonder* must be supplied in English:

> **Ob** sie wohl kommt?   *I wonder* whether she'll come.

* Goethe, *Gespräche mit Eckermann.*

Note that such an **ob**-clause standing by itself commonly contains the adverb **wohl**, which is not translated.

seit, seitdem

Both **seit** and **seitdem** are conjunctions which express the idea of *since* in a temporal sense (for the use of tenses in clauses in which this construction occurs, see Chapter 15, Section A, paragraph 9):

> **Seit** (**seitdem**) ich ihn kenne, tut er das.
> Since I have known him he has been doing that.

Caution. (1) Do not confuse the conjunction **seit** (verb at the end!) with the preposition **seit** when it happens to begin a clause (verb in second position!):

> **Seit** drei Jahren kenne ich ihn.
> I have known him for three years.

(2) The conjunction **seitdem** should likewise not be confused with the adverb **seitdem** (*since then*) at the beginning of a clause:

> **Seitdem** sehe ich ihn jeden Tag.
> Since then I have seen him every day.

während

Be careful to distinguish between the conjunction **während** (*while*) and the preposition **während** (*during*) when it begins a clause. Again, the position of the verb will clarify the issue:

> **Während** ich im Garten *war,* ist mein Onkel angekommen.
> While I was in the garden my uncle arrived.

But:

> **Während** meiner Abwesenheit *ist* mein Onkel angekommen.
> During my absence my uncle arrived.

wenn

When the conjunction **wenn** is used to introduce a condition, it means *if:*

> **Wenn** ich Geld habe, kann ich im Sommer nach Deutschland fahren.
> If I have (the) money I can go to Germany this summer.

wenn can also be employed in a temporal sense to mean *when* in a present or future situation:

> **Wenn** ich in die Stadt fahre, nehme ich meinen Koffer mit.
> When I go downtown I'll take my suitcase along.

Finally, **wenn** can express the idea of repeated action in the past or present, meaning *when* in the sense of *whenever:*

> **Wenn** ich ihn besuche (besuchte), ist (war) er immer müde.
> When(ever) I visit (visited) him he is (was) always tired.

Caution. (1) Distinguish carefully between the use of **als** and **wenn** in reference to past time: **als** refers to a single action in the past, whereas **wenn** expresses repeated action. Although both may be translated by *when,* **wenn** means *when* here only in the sense of *whenever:*

> **Wenn** ich ihn besuchte, war er *immer* müde.
> When(ever) I visited him he was always tired.

But:

> **Als** ich ihn *gestern* besuchte, war er müde.
> When I visited him yesterday he was tired.

(2) The interrogative **wann** means *when,* but it can occur only in direct or indirect questions:

> **Wann** besuchst du mich?   When will you visit me?

> Ich weiß nicht, **wann** er mich besuchen will.
> I don't know when he wants to visit me.

Splitting of conjunctions

3. Some conjunctions can be split so that their parts are separated in the sentence:

(*a*) The second element of the concessive conjunctions **obgleich, obschon, obwohl** (rare also: **obzwar**), **wenngleich,** and **wennschon,** all meaning *although,* can be found separated from the first without change of meaning:

Dieser Mensch muß ein Mörder sein, welchen die Rache nicht leben läßt, **ob** er **gleich** (FOR: obgleich er) dem Meer entgangen ist.°

No doubt this man is a murderer, whom, though he hath escaped the sea, yet vengeance suffereth not to live.

(*b*) The **auch** of the conjunction **wenn auch** (*even if, even though*) often does not follow immediately after **wenn.** It may occur in any of several positions without affecting the meaning in any way:

> Wenn **auch** der Vater seinem Sohn das Geld gern gibt, . . .
> Wenn der Vater **auch** seinem Sohn das Geld gern gibt, . . .

° From Luther's translation, Die Apostelgeschichte, of the book of the Bible known in English as The Acts.

Wenn der Vater seinem Sohn **auch** das Geld gern gibt, . . .
Wenn der Vater seinem Sohn das Geld **auch** gern gibt, . . .
Even if the father gives the money gladly to his son, . . .

wenn and **auch,** however, MUST be separated if the subject or the object(s), or both, are pronouns:

Wenn er es ihm **auch** gern gibt, . . .   Even if he gives it gladly to him . . .

Note that in **auch wenn,** which is identical in meaning with **wenn auch,** the parts cannot be separated:

Auch wenn er es ihm gern gibt, . . .

Exceptions to transposed word order

4. Contrary to the basic rules concerning word order in dependent clauses, transposed word order is NOT USED in the following instances:

(*a*) When the conjunction **daß** is omitted the clause ceases to act as a dependent clause and the word order is that of a principal clause:

Ich glaube, { **daß** die Kinder auf der Straße gespielt haben.
{ die Kinder haben auf der Straße gespielt.

I believe (that) the children have been playing on the street.

(*b*) The conjunction **wenn** is frequently omitted, in which case the finite verb moves into first position and is followed by the subject:

Wenn ich Zeit habe, komme ich.

or:

Habe ich Zeit, (so, dann) komme ich.
If I have time I'll come.

Caution. Do not confuse the **wenn**-clause in which the **wenn** is omitted with the other constructions beginning with the verb: i.e., questions (see Chapter 2, Section B, paragraph 1), exclamations with interrogative word order (see Chapter 2, Special Points 3), commands (see Chapter 16, Section D), and the omitted **denn** (see Chapter 2, Section C). When the **wenn** has been omitted, the following principal clause usually is introduced by either **dann** or **so,** which is, in turn, a safe indication that the preceding clause is a **wenn**-clause of the type described:

Geht man am Strande spazieren, *so* gewähren die vorbeifahrenden Schiffe einen schönen Anblick. **Haben sie** die blendend weißen Segel aufgespannt, *so* sehen sie aus wie vorbeiziehende, große Schwäne.*

If one goes for a walk on the beach, (then) the ships passing by provide a beautiful sight. If they have put up their sparkling white sails they look like large swans passing by.

* Heinrich Heine, *Die Nordsee.*

(*c*) For word order with double infinitives in dependent clauses, see Chapter 19, Section A, paragraph 8.

Special Points

Interrogatives as subordinating conjunctions

1. The interrogatives in German (**wer, was, wann, wo, wie,** and others), which are followed by the finite verbs in direct questions (see Chapter 2, Section B), function as if they were subordinating conjunctions (verb at the end!) in indirect questions:

DIRECT	INDIRECT
Wann *kommst* du?	Ich weiß, **wann** du *kommst.*
When are you coming?	I know when you are coming.
Wer *hat* das gesagt?	Ich weiß, **wer** das gesagt *hat.*
Who said that?	I know who said that.

Interrogatives in concessive statements

2. The interrogatives likewise act as subordinating conjunctions when they are used, in concessive statements, in combination with **auch, auch immer** (or occasionally only with **immer**) in the sense of *no matter who* (or *whoever*), *no matter what* (or: *whatever*), *no matter when* (or: *whenever*). The **auch** here has the same flexibility of position as the **auch** in the conjunction **wenn auch** (see paragraph 3b, above). Observe also that the principal clause following the dependent clause usually DOES NOT have inverted word order:

Was auch (immer) seine Argumente sein mögen,⎫
Was immer seine Argumente sein mögen, ⎭ *seine Theorie ist* falsch.
No matter what his arguments are, his theory is wrong.

Wen du **auch** bitten wirst, *niemand wird* dir helfen.
No matter whom you ask, no one will help you.

Wann er **auch** kommt, *es wird* schon zu spät sein.
No matter when he comes, it will be too late.

Wie er es **auch** macht, *er wird* es falsch machen.
No matter how he does it, he will do it wrong.

When **wie** is followed by an adverb or adjective in a concessive statement of this type, **so** can be used in its place:

Wie (OR: **so**) sehr er sich **auch** anstrengt, *er wird* nicht fertig.
No matter how he exerts himself, he will not finish.

TABLE A
Major Subordinating Conjunctions

als, when; than	ohne daß, without . . . –ing
als ob, als wenn, as if	seit, seitdem, since
auch wenn, even if	selbst wenn, even if
bevor, before	sobald, as soon as
bis, until	so daß, so that
da, since; when	sofern, as far as
damit, so that	solange, as long as
daß, that	so oft, as often as
ehe, before	soviel, as far, as much as
falls, in case, if	soweit, as far as, if
indem, while, as; by . . . ing	sowie, as soon as; just as
insofern, insoweit, in so far as	trotzdem °, although, in spite of
je nachdem, according to whether	während, while, whereas
nachdem, after	weil, because, since
ob, whether	wenn auch, even if, even though
obgleich, obschon, obwohl, obzwar,	wenngleich, wennschon, although
although	zumal, especially since

RECOGNITION EXERCISES

A. *Translate:*

1. Er sagte viel mehr, als wir wissen wollten. 2. Er sagte nicht viel, als wir ihn fragten, wo er gewesen war. 3. Er sagte umso mehr, als er sah, daß wir gar nichts wissen wollten. 4. Er sagte das, als glaubte er wirklich, wir wollten es wissen. 5. Als der reiche Kaufmann nach vielen Jahren in seine Heimat zurückkehrte, erkannte ihn niemand mehr. 6. Als reicher Kaufmann kehrte er nach vielen Jahren in seine Heimat zurück, aber niemand erkannte ihn mehr. 7. Sie gab dem armen Kind etwas, da es so hungrig aussah. 8. Als sie das arme Kind sah, mußte sie an die Zeit denken, da sie selbst auch so arm gewesen war. 9. Sie hielt dem armen Kind das Geld hin, da griff es sogleich danach. 10. Ich möchte das Geld haben, damit ich mir einen neuen Wagen kaufen kann. 11. Ich möchte das Geld haben, damit kann ich mir einen neuen Wagen kaufen. 12. Indem er vorsichtig die Tür öffnete und leise in das Zimmer trat, hörte er jemanden weinen. 13 Er öffnete vorsichtig die Tür und trat leise in das Zimmer, in dem jemand weinte. 14. Er trat leise in das Zimmer, indem er vorsichtig die Tür öffnete. 15. Seitdem ich zweimal die Woche zum Psychiater gehe, geht es mir viel besser. 16. Seitdem geht es mir viel besser. 17. Wenn er mich um etwas Geld bat, habe ich es ihm immer gegeben. 18. Als er mich um etwas Geld bat, habe ich es ihm sofort gegeben. 19. Ich möchte nur wissen, wann er mich jetzt wieder um Geld bitten wird.

° Usually, and by the orthodox grammarian, still considered an adverb; but it has been more and more accepted in modern German as a conjunction synonymous with **obgleich.**

B. *Translate:*

1. Wenn ich ihm nicht helfen kann, wird es ihm in den nächsten Wochen sehr schlecht gehen. 2. Wenn ich ihm auch nicht helfen kann, wird er doch immer noch genug zu essen haben. 3. Kommen Sie morgen mit mir in die Stadt, Herr Schmidt? 4. Kommen Sie morgen mit mir in die Stadt, Herr Schmidt! 5. Kommen Sie morgen mit mir in die Stadt, Herr Schmidt, dann können wir zusammen zu Mittag essen. 6. Während ich auf der Universität in München war, ist meine Familie in ein neues Haus gezogen. 7. Während meiner Studienzeit in München ist meine Familie in ein neues Haus gezogen. 8. Was hat er gestern gesagt? Ich weiß nicht, was er gestern gesagt hat. 9. Was er gestern auch gesagt hat, er wird heute bestimmt nicht kommen. 10. Ich möchte wissen, wie er die Arbeit gemacht hat. 11. Wie er die Arbeit auch gemacht hat, er hat bestimmt alles falsch gemacht. 12. Wissen Sie, wo er hingegangen ist? 13. Wo er auch hingegangen ist, ich werde ihn schon finden. 14. Ich weiß nicht, wann er hier ankommen wird. 15. Wann immer auch er hier ankommt, man wird ihn freundlich begrüßen. 16. Kannst du die Fragen beantworten? 17. Kannst du die Fragen beantworten, dann brauchst du die Geschichte nicht noch einmal zu lesen.

ACTIVE EXERCISES

A. *Connect the following statements with the German equivalent of the English conjunctions given in parentheses; use the listing of the major subordinating conjunctions on the facing page.*

1. Ich werde das Buch lesen. Ich habe einen freien Abend. (as soon as) 2. Er geht zur Universität. Er will Arzt werden. (because) 3. Er studiert Deutsch. Er kann Goethes *Faust* im Original lesen. (so that) 4. Er war nicht mehr da. Sie kam endlich nach Hause. (when) 5. Er ist nie zu Hause. Sie will ihn sprechen. (when) 6. Sie haben mich nie besucht. Ich wohne hier. (since) 7. Ich werde ihm Ihren Scheck geben. Ich sehe ihn morgen. (if) 8. Wir haben unser Haus vermietet. Wir waren letzten Sommer in Europa. (while) 9. Sie muß ihre Schulaufgaben machen. Sie darf ins Kino gehen. (before) 10. Er sagt selten etwas. Er ist sehr intelligent. (although)

B. *Proceed as in Exercise A above, but note that here both subordinating and coordinating conjunctions are involved:*

1. Ich werde zu Bett gehen. Er ist nach Hause gekommen. (after) 2. Sie geht in die Stadt. Er bleibt zu Hause. (and) 3. Er kann nicht mitgehen. Er hat heute keine Zeit. (for) 4. Sie müssen zurückkommen. Ich kann nach Hause gehen. (before) 5. Soll ich heute ins Theater gehen? Soll ich zu Hause bleiben? (or) 6. Er kommt mit. Er ist mit seiner Arbeit nicht fertig. (even if) 7. Wir müssen warten. Unsere Mutter kommt aus der Stadt zurück. (until) 8. Ich weiß nicht. Er hat das Buch gelesen. (whether) 9. Er hat die Aufgabe noch nicht gemacht. Ich bin schon damit fertig. (but) 10. Er kann nicht arbeiten. Sie ist im Zimmer. (as long as)

C. *Rewrite the following direct questions as indirect questions introduced by the clause* **Ich möchte wissen,:**

1. Warum sind Sie gestern so spät gekommen?
2. Wollen Sie morgen mit mir in die Stadt fahren?
3. Wo wird er nächstes Jahr studieren?
4. Warum hat sie sich den neuen Wagen gekauft?
5. Wer hat Ihnen schon von dem reizenden Mädchen erzählt?
6. Was werden Sie mit all dem Geld machen?
7. Wessen Kind ist im Krankenhaus?
8. Mit wem ist er nach Paris gereist?
9. Wie gefällt Ihnen unser neues Haus?
10. Ist er gestern oder vorgestern angekommen?

D. *Translate into German:*

1. When I explain something to him he never understands it.
2. When I explained it to him he understood it immediately.
3. I must go on working (= **weiterarbeiten**) until I have learned these rules.
4. Since he had not learned these rules, he found the sentences very difficult.
5. As far as I know he is not coming.
6. Since I gave him the money I have not heard from him.
7. We can get more light by opening the curtains.
8. After he had said that, I was convinced that it was not true.
9. I know I shall see him before he leaves (the) town.
10. Even if we give him the money he will not be satisfied.
11. She will return the book as soon as she can come.
12. As long as she gets her pension she will not starve.
13. He did not feel very well because he had eaten too much.
14. He must work this summer so that he can study in the fall.
15. If my wife does not want to come along I'll go alone.
16. While he was working in the library it began to rain.
17. Although he did not do his assignment very well, he did it better than we had expected.
18. Give him this message in case you see him.
19. I shall give it to him when he comes.
20. When he said that they all laughed.

4

Relative Clauses

Two Types of Relative Clauses

1. The second major type of dependent clause is the relative clause, which begins with either a definite or an indefinite relative pronoun; but if the relative pronoun is used with a preposition, the preposition precedes the relative pronoun:

> Es gibt kaum Kinder, **die** gerne in die Schule gehen.
> There are scarcely any children who like to go to school.

> Das sind die Kinder, **mit denen** sie immer spielt.
> Those are the children with whom she always plays.

> Das ist alles, **was** ich zu sagen habe.
> That is all (that) I have to say.

Definite relative pronouns

2. The definite relative pronouns are: **der, die, das,** and **welcher, welche, welches** (*who, which*), and they are declined as follows:

	SINGULAR			PLURAL		SINGULAR			PLURAL
Nom.	der	die	das	die		welcher	welche	welches	welche
Gen.	dessen	deren	dessen*	deren		dessen	deren	dessen	deren
Dat.	dem	der	dem	denen		welchem	welcher	welchem	welchen
Acc.	den	die	das	die		welchen	welche	welches	welche

There is no distinction in meaning between these two sets of relative pronouns; the **der**-forms are more common than the **welcher**-forms.

Agreement

3. The relative pronoun agrees in gender and number with its antecedent, but its case depends on its function in its own clause:

* Old form: **des.**

29

masc.   nom.
sing. (subj.)

Wir haben einen Hund, **der** jeden Fremden anbellt.

We have a dog who barks at every stranger.

fem.   dat.
sing. (obj.)

Kennen Sie die Frau, **der** wir eben begegnet sind?

Do you know the woman whom we just met?

dat.
after
plural   **mit**

Wo sind die Kinder, *mit* **denen** du spielen willst?

Where are the children with whom you want to play?

For the use of **wo–** as a substitute for relative pronouns, see Chapter 13, Section B.

Caution. (1) Watch out for the long forms in the genitive and dative which are in heavy type in the table on page 29; they differ distinctly from the corresponding forms of the definite article.

(2) The set of **welcher, welche, welches** has no genitive forms of its own but makes use of the corresponding forms of **der, die, das.**

(3) THE RELATIVE PRONOUN IS NEVER OMITTED IN GERMAN as it so often is in English: *The book I am reading* = **Das Buch,** *das* **ich lese.**

ich, der ich . . .

4. If the antecedent of a relative pronoun is a personal pronoun of the first person, the personal pronoun may be repeated after the relative pronoun and the verb is made to agree with it:

Ich, der kein Geld *hat,*
OR   } bin doch immer zufrieden.
Ich, der *ich* kein Geld *habe,*

I who have no money am nevertheless always satisfied.

Das Geld gibt er **uns,** die (*wir*) es gar nicht brauchen.

He gives the money to us who do not need it at all.

If the antecedent is a personal pronoun of the second person, the pronoun MUST be repeated:

Du, der **du** so viel gesehen hast, . . .

You who have seen so much . . .

Indefinite relative pronouns

5. The indefinite relative pronouns are **wer** (*he who, whoever*) and **was** (*what, that, which*) and are declined as follows:

	REFERS TO PEOPLE	REFERS TO THINGS
Nom.	wer	was
Gen.	wessen	wessen (*old form:* wes)
Dat.	wem	—
Acc.	wen	was

wer

6. The indefinite relative pronoun **wer** differs from the definite relative pronoun **der** in that it can never have an antecedent. The subordinate clause that it introduces (verb at the end!) is followed by a principal clause which usually begins with a demonstrative pronoun:

> **Wer** nicht mitkommen will, *der* soll zu Hause bleiben.
> He who does not want to come along is to (can) stay home.

Whenever the demonstrative pronoun is not the subject of the principal clause, the translation into English almost invariably must begin with the principal clause and often has to paraphrase the German statement:

> **Wer** das nicht versteht, *dem* können wir nicht helfen.
> LITERALLY: He who does not understand this, him we cannot help.
> We cannot help anyone who does not understand this.

> **Wer** nicht arbeiten will, *den* läßt er durchfallen.
> LITERALLY: He who does not want to study, him he'll fail.
> He'll fail anyone who does not want to study.

The demonstrative pronoun in such a sentence may be (and commonly is) omitted if it is in the nominative, but never if it is in any other case form:

> **Wer** zuletzt lacht, lacht am besten.
> He who laughs last laughs best.

was

7. The indefinite relative pronoun **was** is used when the antecedent is:

(*a*) The demonstrative pronoun **das** which, however, is frequently understood and hence omitted (unless it is emphasized):

> **Was** (*Das, was*) ich nicht habe, kann ich nicht verlieren.
> I can't lose what I don't have.

> Ich weiß (*das*), **was** du nicht weißt.
> I know what (something that) you don't know.

But with emphasis:

> Wer *das* verlor,/ **was** du verlorst, macht nirgends halt.*
> Whoever lost/ What you lost will rest nowhere.

(*b*) An indefinite neuter pronoun such as **alles, einiges, etwas, manches, nichts, vieles:**

> Ich habe *alles* vergessen, **was** sie gesagt hat.
> I forgot everything (that) she said.

(*c*) An adjective in the superlative which is used as a noun, such as **das Beste:**

> Das war *das Beste* (*Dummste*), **was** ich je von ihm gehört habe.
> That was the best (dumbest) thing (that) I ever heard from him.

(*d*) A whole clause, in which case **was** is translated by a phrase like *a fact which, something that,* or simply *which:*

> *Ich bin heute früh aufgestanden,* **was**   I got up early today, something that
> ich gar nicht gerne tue.   (which) I do not like to do at all.

> *Er hat mir nicht geschrieben,* **was** ich nicht verstehen kann.
> He did not write to me, which I cannot understand.

Caution. (1) **Was** may be an abbreviation for **etwas** (*something*) and should not be confused with the indefinite relative or with the interrogative pronoun:

> Ich weiß **was** (= **etwas**), was du nicht weißt.
> I know something that you don't know.

> **Was** Besseres weiß ich nicht.
> I know nothing better.

2. Occasionally, **welches** will be found in place of the indefinite relative pronoun **was:**

> Denn ach! du bist der Dreizehnte bei   For, oh! you are the thirteenth at
> Tisch, **welches** immer bedenklich   table, which is always risky.
> ist.†

Punctuation

8. Dependent clauses are normally set off by commas. A comma, therefore, may be a possible indication of the beginning or the end of a dependent clause:

---

* From a poem by Friedrich Nietzsche.
† Heine, *Reisebilder.*

Ich glaube, daß die Kinder jetzt in der Schule sind.
I believe that the children are now in school.

„Das ist alles, was ich zu sagen habe", erklärte er.
"That is all I have to say," he declared.

Special Points

Omission of *sein*

1. German writers, especially of the nineteenth century, frequently drop forms of the verb **sein** or the auxiliary in perfect tenses in dependent clauses. These forms will have to be supplied in translation:

Es gibt Leute, welche den Vogel ganz genau zu kennen glauben, weil sie das Ei gesehen, woraus er hervorgekrochen.*	There are people who believe they surely know the bird because they *have* seen the egg from which he came (lit.: **has** crawled).

"Split" clauses

2. In a German sentence a dependent or principal clause may contain within itself other idea units, such as appositives, dependent clauses, and infinitive or participial phrases. Since the interrupting elements which thus split a clause in two are usually set off by commas, the appearance of a comma before an idea unit has been completed generally indicates that the flow of thought is going to be interrupted, to be resumed only after the inserted material has been concluded. Therefore, never attempt to translate a complete sentence without first having understood the inter-relationship of the various parts. Two examples follow.

Sie hatte die unglaubliche Nachricht kaum gehört, *als sie schon,* **ohne sich auch nur die Zeit zu nehmen, einen besseren Rock umzulegen,** *in das Gebäude des Heiligen Offiziums lief.†*	She had scarcely heard the incredible news when she ran to the building of the Headquarters of the Inquisition without even taking time out to put on a better skirt.

In the example above, the dependent clause which begins with **als sie** is interrupted by two infinitive phrases (in heavy type), before it concludes with **in das Gebäude des Heiligen Offiziums lief.**

. . . *von dem kleinen schmalen Kanapee an der Querwand sprang mit halber und verlegener Mun-*	. . . the young housewife jumped up from the small narrow sofa on the opposite wall with a kind of

* Heine, *Gedanken und Einfälle.*
† Bertolt Brecht, „Der Mantel des Ketzers."

terkeit, **als sei sie in einem Schlummer gestört worden** und **wolle es nicht merken lassen,** *die junge Hausfrau auf.**	half-hearted and embarrassed cheerfulness, as if she had been caught taking a nap and didn't want anyone to know it.

In this example, the appearance of the subject (**die junge Hausfrau**) of the principal clause, in which inverted word order is used, is delayed by the insertion of the dependent clauses (in heavy type) from **als sei sie** to **lassen.**

RECOGNITION EXERCISES

A. *Translate the following sentences and explain the gender, number, and case of the relative pronoun used:*

1. Die Frau, die Sie gestern auf der Straße gesehen hat, hat Sie nicht erkannt. 2. Die Frau, die Sie gestern auf der Straße gesehen haben, haben Sie nicht erkannt. 3. Die Frau, der der Junge das Geld gegeben hat, braucht es weniger als er. 4. Die Frau, deren Jungen er das Geld gegeben hat, braucht es weniger als er. 5. Die Frauen, deren Jungen das Geld bekommen haben, brauchen es weniger als wir. 6. Die Jungen, deren Mütter das Geld bekommen haben, gehen noch in die Schule. 7. Der Junge, der der Frau das Geld gegeben hat, ist mein Vetter. 8. Den Jungen, der das gesagt hat, verstehe ich nicht. 9. Den Jungen, die das gesagt haben, glauben wir nicht. 10. Der Junge, den die Frau gesprochen hat, war sehr frech. 11. Die Jungen, denen die Frau begegnet ist, waren sehr frech. 12. Das Kind, das das Mädchen zur Schule bringt, weint immer noch. 13. Das Kind, das das tote Kätzchen auf dem Arm hält, weint immer noch. 14. Das Kind, dessen Geschwister in der Schule sind, spielt allein im Garten. 15. Freunde, auf die sie sich verlassen kann, hat sie leider nicht.

B. *Definite and indefinite relative pronouns. Translate:*

1. Wer nicht auf uns hören will, dem können wir nicht helfen. 2. Was ich nicht habe, kann ich nicht verlieren. 3. Wer nicht gehorchen will, den können wir nicht brauchen. 4. Wenn du auch vieles weißt, was ich nicht weiß, weiß ich doch was, was du nicht weißt. 5. Wer getan hat, was Sie getan haben, hat etwas geleistet, was nicht jeder leisten kann. 6. Der Professor mußte der schönen Studentin eine schlechte Zensur geben, was er nicht gerne tat. 7. Was er jetzt nicht lernt, wird er nie lernen. Ob er das nicht versteht? 8. Die schlechten Zensuren, die sie bekommen hat, haben ihren Vater sehr enttäuscht. 9. Sie hat schlechte Zensuren bekommen, was ihren Vater sehr enttäuscht hat. 10. Sie bekommt immer schlechte Zensuren, die ihren Vater sehr enttäuschen.

C. *Translate, noting carefully the interruptions of dependent and principal clauses by other clauses, infinitive phrases, etc.:*

1. Als er sich, anstatt zur Universität zu gehen, wo er Medizin studieren

---

* Hermann Hesse, *Knulp.*

sollte, mit einer Schauspielerin verheiratete, sagte sich seine Familie von ihm los. 2. Sie sang, indem sie sich vor dem Spiegel die Haare kämmte, ein Lied, das mir sehr bekannt vorkam. 3. In der vorigen Woche, als der Streik, den eigentlich niemand gewollt hatte, gerade anfing, die ganze Industrie zu paralysieren, fanden die ersten Demonstrationen statt. 4. Kommt er abends, nach einem langen und anstrengenden Tag in der Stadt, müde nach Hause, setzt er sich, um sich ein wenig auszuruhen, mit der Zeitung in den Garten. 5. Das Kind, das immer nur allein im Garten spielen wollte, weil es zu schüchtern war, mit anderen Kindern zu reden, sah ich heute mit den Nachbarskindern auf der Straße spielen. 6. Dem Jungen, der so faul ist, daß er immer, wenn er seine Aufgaben machen soll, entweder ins Kino geht oder Fußball spielt, wird der Lehrer eine schlechte Zensur geben. 7. In einem Geschäft, in dem man die Kunden, die nicht aussehen, als ob sie viel Geld hätten, schlecht behandelt, kaufe ich nicht gern.

ACTIVE EXERCISES

A. *Substitute the appropriate German form of the relative pronoun for the English form in parentheses:*
    1. Ich habe alles getan, (which) er von mir verlangt hat. 2. Die Zensuren, (which) wir bekommen haben, sind nicht sehr gut. 3. (He who) nicht kommen will, braucht nicht zu kommen. 4. Die Bücher, (which) auf dem Tisch liegen, habe ich noch nicht gelesen. 5. Sie lächelt immer, wenn sie mich sieht, (which) ich gar nicht verstehen kann. 6. Er gab es dem Mann, (who) uns gestern besucht hat. 7. (Whoever) schon fertig ist, darf nach Hause gehen. 8. Der Freund, (with whom) ich nach Deutschland fahre, lebt in Boston. 9. (Whoever) das getan hat, (what) du getan hast, hat guten Grund, sich zu schämen. 10. Die Frau, (to whom) er das Geld gegeben hat, ist schon fort. 11. Er hat etwas getan, (that) mir gar nicht gefallen hat. 12. Die Kinder, (to whom) ich den Ball gegeben habe, sind schon wieder vor der Tür. 13. Er hat nichts getan, (that) mich beunruhigt hat. 14. Der Mann, (whose) Buch ich habe, ist ein Deutscher. 15. Ist das das Beste, (that) Sie zu antworten haben? 16. Die Studentin, (whose) Schönheit mich damals so bezaubert hat, ist eine dicke Hausfrau geworden. 17. Die Studenten, (whose) Eltern nicht viel Geld verdienen, werden von der Regierung unterstützt. 18. Die Frau, (who) mich eben angelächelt hat, kenne ich nicht. 19. Das Buch, (which) ich letzte Woche gekauft habe, habe ich noch nicht gelesen. 20. Das Haus, (which) neben der Schule steht, hat einen schönen Garten.

B. *Translate into German:*
    1. The books which we read for this course are not very interesting.
    2. The student who is sitting next to the door fell asleep.
    3. He criticizes everything I do.
    4. The street on (*use* in) which we live is not far from the university.
    5. The car we want to buy costs too much.
    6. The students whose marks were unsatisfactory had to repeat the course.

7. The cigarettes he buys are very expensive.
8. I saw the girl he wants to marry.
9. Who is the girl who is smiling at you?
10. The woman whose son won the prize also has a daughter.
11. The father whose daughter never works in (*the*) school will talk to her teacher.
12. He smokes too much, which often disturbs me.
13. Whoever did this work did not do it very well.
14. That is the best I can do.
15. That is something we will never forget.
16. The children who were playing on the street yesterday are in (*the*) school today.
17. The people to whom we gave the clothes were very grateful.
18. Do you know the man with whom I was talking?
19. Did you forget what I asked you?
20. The woman whose picture is on the table is my aunt.

5

Infinitive and Participial Phrases

1. Infinitives and participles may either stand alone or take objects and be modified by adverbs or adverbial phrases:

INFINITIVE ALONE:

> Er weigerte sich *zu* gehen.
> He refused to go.

INFINITIVE WITH OBJECT AND ADVERB:

> Er weigerte sich, so früh das Wirtshaus *zu* verlassen.
> He refused to leave the inn so early.

PARTICIPLE ALONE:

> Singend ging er die Straße entlang.
> He went down the street singing.

PARTICIPLE WITH OBJECT AND ADVERBIAL PHRASE:

> Aus vollem Hals ein Volkslied *singend,* ging er nach Hause.
> He went home singing a folksong at the top of his voice.

An infinitive or a participle, together with its object and/or modifier of any kind, is generally spoken of as an infinitive phrase or a participial phrase. Such phrases are usually set off by commas.

Position of infinitive

2. Infinitive phrases pose a problem in reading German primarily because the infinitive stands at the end, whereas in English it generally begins the phrase. Thus, if the infinitive phrase in question is of considerable length, it may not be immediately recognizable as such:

Es ist nicht immer leicht, in einem verwickelten deutschen Satz das Subjekt und das Verb *zu finden*.	It is not always easy *to find* the subject and the verb in a complicated German sentence.

Anticipating infinitive phrases

3. In the above example, the sense of the introductory clause, **Es ist nicht immer leicht,** should prepare the reader for the following infinitive construction. In general, verbs or verbal expressions which are followed by infinitive phrases in English are also followed by infinitive phrases in German. The problem of recognizing the construction is simplified if one can get in the habit of anticipating such phrases on the basis of the introductory clause:

> Er **versuchte,** nach dem Abendessen seine Hausaufgabe *zu machen.*
> He **tried** *to do* his homework assignment after dinner.
>
> Sie **wagte nicht,** ihrem alten Lehrer ins Auge *zu sehen.*
> She **did not dare** *to look* her old teacher in the eye.
>
> Wir **haben keine Lust,** heute abend ins Kino *zu gehen.*
> We **have no desire** *to go* to the movies this evening.

Caution. There may not always be an introductory statement to lead one to suspect the presence of an infinitive phrase. In the following sentence, for example, the infinitive phrase stands first and actually functions as the subject of the principal clause which concludes the sentence:

> Den Vater zu so später Stunde *zu finden,* wird kaum möglich sein.
> *To find* the father at this late hour will hardly be possible.

When the reader begins this sentence it is not immediately clear that he is dealing with an infinitive phrase, since the first element, **Den Vater,** could be taken for a direct object of a principal clause. But as soon as it becomes evident that the verb is not the second element, he should begin to think in terms of an infinitive construction (or participial phrase; see below).

Translating German infinitive by English gerund

4. Not all infinitives in German can be translated by infinitives in English. Once one is aware of this fact, however, it is essentially a matter of knowing which English expression to use. The German infinitive in itself cannot offer a clue to the corresponding English idiom. In many instances the German infinitive is to be rendered by an English gerund:

> Es wird ihr nie gelingen, so etwas *zu verstehen.*
> She will never succeed *in understanding* such a thing.

The translation of the German infinitive by the English gerund is particularly common when the verb in the preceding clause is used with a da-compound (see Chapter 13, Section A, paragraph 3).

Ich hatte nie **daran** gedacht, ihm *zu helfen.*
I had never thought of *helping* him.

Es handelt sich **darum,** so viel Geld wie möglich *zu bekommen.*
It is a matter of *getting* as much money as possible.

Infinitive phrases translated by that-clauses

A few German infinitive constructions, such as those following the verbs **meinen** or **glauben** (to think, believe), are best rendered in English by *that*-clauses, the subject of which will be the same person as the subject of the introductory verb:

Er meinte, vor dieser Gefahr sicher *zu sein.*
He thought (*that*) he was safe from this danger.

Sie glaubte, die Aufgabe machen *zu können.*
She believed (*that*) she could do the assignment.

In such constructions the perfect infinitive (past participle and infinitive of the auxiliary verb) may also be encountered:

Sie glaubte, die Aufgabe richtig *gemacht zu haben.*
She believed *that* she had done the assignment correctly.

Infinitive phrases introduced by prepositions

5. There are three special kinds of infinitive phrases which are introduced by the prepositions **um, ohne,** and **anstatt:**

(*a*) **um . . . zu,** *in order to,* expressing purpose. Note, however, that the phrase *in order* is not always needed in English:

Ich fahre oft nach New York, *um* in die Oper *zu gehen.*
I often go to New York (*in order*) *to go* to the opera.

Caution. The infinitive phrase with **um . . . zu** occurs sometimes even where purpose is not involved. In such instances English cannot use the phrase *in order to* but merely *to:*

Er ist jetzt wütend genug, *um* etwas dagegen *zu unternehmen.*
He is now furious enough to do something about it.

So schieden wir vor seiner Haustür, um uns niemals wiederzusehen.*
Thus we said good-bye in front of his door, never to see each other again.

* Goethe über Schiller.

(b) **ohne . . . zu,** *without:*

> Er ging fort, *ohne* ein Wort *zu sagen.*
> He left *without saying* a word.

(c) **anstatt . . . zu,** *instead of:*

> *Anstatt* in die Bibliothek *zu gehen,* ging er ins Kino.
> *Instead of going* to the library he went to the movies.

Observe that in the **ohne . . . zu** and **anstatt . . . zu** phrases the infinitives must be rendered in English as gerunds.

Caution. The prepositions used in these phrases do not function as prepositions taking objects (in the accusative with **um** and **ohne,** in the genitive with **anstatt**). Often it may not be immediately clear which function is involved:

PREPOSITION:

> Um das Haus wachsen die schönsten Blumen.
> Around the house grow the most beautiful flowers.

INFINITIVE PHRASE:

> Um das Haus kaufen *zu* können, mußte er Geld borgen.
> He had to borrow money to be able to buy the house.

PREPOSITION:

> Ohne seinen Vater wollte er nicht fortgehen.
> He did not want to leave without his father.

INFINITIVE PHRASE:

> Ohne seinen Vater *zu* sehen, wollte er nicht fortgehen.
> He did not want to leave without seeing his father.

PREPOSITION:

> Anstatt seines Vaters nahm er seine Mutter mit.
> Instead of his father he took his mother along.

INFINITIVE PHRASE:

> Anstatt seines Vaters Freund *zu* besuchen, ging er spazieren.
> Instead of visiting his father's friend he went for a walk.

Word order in infinitive phrases

6. Aside from the fact that the infinitive is in final position, all other elements of the phrase (objects and adverbial modifiers) will normally follow the same rules of word order as in principal clauses (see Chapter 2):

ADVERB OF TIME BEFORE ADVERB OF PLACE:

> Er wagte nicht, **vor sechs Uhr** *nach Hause* zu gehen.
> He did not dare to go home before six o'clock.

INDIRECT OBJECT BEFORE DIRECT OBJECT:

> Ich denke nicht daran, **diesem Gauner** *das Geld* zu geben.
> I wouldn't think of giving the money to this swindler.

Participial phrases

7. Participial phrases are used much the same way in German as they are in English. But since the participle in German is usually found at the end of the phrase, the same difficulty arises in reading as with infinitive phrases: it may not be evident until the end of the phrase has been reached which construction is involved. In translating participial phrases in English, begin with the participle:

> Mit seiner Freundin am Tisch *sitzend,* hörte er mich nicht eintreten.
> *Sitting* at the table with his girl friend, he did not hear me come in.

> Von dem Mädchen sorgsam *begleitet,* ging die alte Dame nach Hause.
> *Accompanied* carefully by the girl, the old lady went home.

Occasionally it will be necessary to translate a past participle in German with one in English preceded by *having:*

Spät in der kleinen Stadt *angekommen,* konnte er kein Hotelzimmer finden.
Having arrived late in the small town, he could not find a hotel room.

Special Points

Split infinitive and participial phrases

1. Like principal and subordinate clauses (see Chapter 4, Special Point 2), infinitive and participial phrases may be split into two parts by clauses which interrupt the flow of the phrases. Since the infinitive or participle is found at the end of the phrase, the interrupting material further delays the appearance of the verbal idea. In translating such a construction, remember that the infinitive or participle idea comes first in English:

Ja, den Kasten umwoben eine Menge so verlockender Vorstellungen, daß man sich gewöhnt hatte, **den Augenblick,** wo man ihn würde öffnen können, **als den Höhepunkt seines Lebens zu betrachten.***

Indeed, so many enticing ideas were connected with the box that they had gotten used to considering the moment when they would be able to open it as the high point of their lives.

* Gerhart Hauptmann, *Fasching.*

Sie drehten sich auf den Hacken um und gingen weg, **dem Volk,** das draußen stand, **auf die Füße tretend.** *	They turned on their heels and left, stepping on the feet of the people who were standing outside.

Infinitive phrases as subject and predicate nominative

2. With the verbs **heißen, bedeuten,** and similar verbal phrases (like **so viel sein wie, gleichbedeutend sein mit,** *to amount to*) infinitive phrases may function as the equivalent of the subject and predicate nominative. In this use the infinitives are usually encountered without a **zu.** Hence it may be difficult at first to recognize the construction as an infinitive phrase:

Anständiges Benehmen von ihm erwarten, heißt **mehr von ihm verlangen,** als er hat.	To expect respectable behavior from him is to demand more than he can give.

Participle in first position

3. Occasionally, participial phrases may be found in which the participle is, as in English, in first position:

Gegen zehn Uhr nachts drängte sie sich, **begleitet** vom Mann ihrer Schwester, durch das Getümmel. †	About ten o'clock at night she pushed her way through the crowd, accompanied by her sister's husband.

RECOGNITION EXERCISES

A. *Translate:*

1. Er wagte nicht, dem Mann, den er kaum kannte, seine Meinung zu sagen. 2. Dem Mann, den er kaum kannte, sagte er seine Meinung nicht. 3. Dem Mann, den er kaum kannte, seine Meinung zu sagen, hatte er nicht den Mut. 4. Die Leute, die er lange nicht gesehen hatte, freundlich zu grüßen, war nicht seine Absicht. 5. Die Leute, die er lange nicht gesehen hatte, freundlich grüßend, trat er ins Zimmer. 6. Die Leute, die er lange nicht gesehen hatte, grüßte er freundlich, als er ins Zimmer trat. 7. Er versuchte, das Problem, mit dem sich die Experten seit Jahren beschäftigt hatten, auf eine neue Weise zu lösen. 8. Um dieses Problem, mit dem sich die Experten so sehr beschäftigen, handelt es sich hier nicht. 9. Um dieses Problem, mit dem sich die Experten so sehr beschäftigen, genauer untersuchen zu können, hat er seine Lehrtätigkeit aufgegeben. 10. Um den Garten, den er im Sommer gerne pflegt, steht eine hohe Mauer. 11. Um den Garten, den er im Sommer gerne flegt, mehr ge-

* Bertolt Brecht, *Der verwundete Sokrates.*
† Bertolt Brecht, *Der Augsburger Kreidekreis.*

nießen zu können, baut er sich jetzt eine Veranda. 12. Ohne die Hilfe seines Assistenten, der ihm bei seiner Forschung sehr geholfen hat, auf irgendeine Weise zu erwähnen, erklärte er, daß er das Problem gelöst habe. 13. Ohne die Hilfe seines Assistenten, der ihm bei seiner Forschung sehr geholfen hat, wäre er mit der Arbeit nie fertig geworden. 14. Anstatt seine Mutter, die ihn das ganze Jahr nicht gesehen hat, während der Ferien zu besuchen, wird er eine kleine Reise in die Berge machen. 15. Anstatt seiner Mutter, die keine Lust hat, zu dieser Jahreszeit eine so große Reise zu machen, wird er seinen Vater mitnehmen.

B. *Translate:*

1. Das Mädchen, das er seit seiner Kindheit nicht gesehen hatte, wiederzufinden, war jetzt sein Ziel. 2. Das Mädchen, das er seit seiner Kindheit nicht gesehen hatte, immer noch suchend, kam er in seiner Heimatstadt an. 3. Von der Richtigkeit seiner Gedanken über dieses Phänomen überzeugt, veröffentlichte er seine Theorie in einer bekannten Zeitschrift. 4. Von der Richtigkeit seiner Gedanken über dieses Phänomen, mit dem auch ich mich lange beschäftigt hatte, war ich gar nicht überzeugt. 5. Den Brief, der die gute Nachricht gebracht hatte, immer noch in der Hand haltend, ging er zum Telefon, um seine Mutter anzurufen. 6. Den Brief, der die gute Nachricht gebracht hatte, hatte er immer noch in der Hand, als er zum Telefon ging, um seine Mutter anzurufen. 7. Er glaubte, auf diese Weise eine Lösung des Problems, mit dem er sich lange beschäftigt hatte, endlich gefunden zu haben. 8. Er glaubte, auf diese Weise eine Lösung des Problems, das er lange studiert hatte, endlich finden zu können. 9. Sie meint, in diesem Lande, wo niemand sie kennt, vor ihren Feinden sicher zu sein. 10. Mehr von diesem Manne verlangen, als er schon gegeben hat, heißt mehr von ihm erwarten, als er leisten kann. 11. Diesem Mann, der so viel für uns getan hat, will er nicht einmal danken. 12. Diesem Mann, der so viel für uns getan hat, nicht danken, würde bedeuten, der ganzen Welt unsere Undankbarkeit zu demonstrieren.

ACTIVE EXERCISES

A. *Complete the following sentences by rearranging the words in parentheses to form infinitive phrases:*

1. Er versuchte, (nach Hause . . . zu kommen . . . so früh wie möglich). 2. Sie wagte nicht, (zu sagen . . . die Wahrheit . . . ihrem Vater). 3. Wir fahren nach New York, (zu gehen . . . ins Theater . . . um). 4. Sie verließ die Stadt, (Abschied zu nehmen . . . ohne . . . von ihren Freunden). 5. Wir gingen nach Hause, (ins Kino . . . anstatt . . . am Abend . . . zu gehen). 6. Ich dachte nicht daran, (zurückzugeben . . . das Buch . . . meinem Freund). 7. Sie war endlich bereit, (bei der Arbeit . . . zu helfen . . . mir). 8. Ich war entschlossen, (ihm . . . sofort . . . zu geben . . . es). 9. Er hat keine Lust, (in die Stadt . . . zu gehen . . . heute). 10. Er ist nicht imstande, (eine Antwort . . . zu geben . . . mir).

B. *Translate into German:*

1. It is not easy to find an answer to (auf) this question.
2. He tried to help us as much as possible.
3. We went downtown in order to go to the movies.
4. Having arrived in the city, he went directly to his hotel.
5. Accompanied by his wife, the old man entered the room.
6. He began to tell us an interesting story.
7. It is not my intention to wait for him all day.
8. He left the room without saying a word.
9. Instead of staying at home yesterday he went to the (ins) theater.
10. It is difficult to find an apartment in this city.
11. She did not dare to come home so late.
12. We are learning German in order to be able to read Kafka in the original.
13. He will go to (in) the city without visiting his friend.
14. They drank beer instead of doing their assignment.
15. Sitting alone in a corner he read the newspaper.
16. He refused to lend me ten dollars.
17. They seem to be very satisfied with their new car.
18. My friend does not have the courage to tell his mother the whole story.
19. We plan to go to a restaurant after the concert.
20. I have no time now to explain it to you.

PART II

Declension

6

Articles and Nouns

A. Articles

Declension

1. The definite and indefinite articles are declined as follows:

	Definite Article				Indefinite Article		
	SINGULAR			PLURAL	SINGULAR		
Nom.	der	die	das	die	ein	eine	ein
Gen.	des	der	des	der	eines	einer	eines
Dat.	dem	der	dem	den	einem	einer	einem
Acc.	den	die	das	die	einen	eine	ein

der-words

2. The so-called **der**-words, which are declined much like the definite article, are:

dieser, this, that	**mancher,** many a (pl., *some*)
jeder (pl., **alle**), each, every	**solcher,** such (a) (rare in singular)
jener, that	**welcher,** which, what

Note that ordinarily **jener** is not used by itself but only in pointing out a contrast between **dieser** (*this*) and **jener** (*that*):

> **dieser** Mann hier und **jene** Frau da
> this man here and that woman there

All of these **der**-words have the same basic case forms as **dieser:**

	SINGULAR			PLURAL
Nom.	dieser	diese	*dieses	diese
Gen.	dieses	dieser	dieses	dieser
Dat.	diesem	dieser	diesem	diesen
Acc.	diesen	diese	*dieses	diese

* These two forms are often shortened to **dies.**

47

ein-words

3. The so-called **ein**-words, which are declined exactly like the indefinite article, are

    kein, no

and the possessive adjectives:

mein, my	**unser,** our
dein, your (informal)	**euer,** your (informal, pl.)
sein, his, its	**ihr,** their
ihr, her, its	**Ihr,** your (formal, sing. and pl.)

Unlike the indefinite article, these **ein**-words do have plural forms which have the same endings as the **der**-words in the plural:

keine, keiner, keinen, keine

Importance of basic forms

4. Mastery of these basic forms is clearly necessary for active use of German. It is also indispensable for acquiring a reading knowledge because the peculiarities of German word order often make it difficult to locate the subject and the object of the verb. Since the first element of a principal clause does not have to be the subject, the reader must be able to determine the function of the element in question primarily on the basis of his knowledge of case forms. In the following sentence, for example, the word order alone reveals nothing about the relationship between the two nouns:

Diesen Professor kennt jeder Student.

A knowledge of the grammatical forms, however, tells us immediately that the first element cannot be the subject and must be the object, since it is in the accusative singular masculine. Furthermore, the second noun with its preceding **der**-word can only be in the nominative singular masculine.

Forms with multiple uses

5. Of course, the situation is not always as clear as in the example above. Most of the basic forms of the articles and their related words have more than one declensional function. The following table will illustrate the possibilities of **der, den, die,** and **das:**

	der				den				die				das			
	M.	F.	N.	Pl.	M.	F.	N.	Pl.	M.	F.	N.	Pl.	M.	F.	N.	Pl.
Nom.	der									die	die				das	
Gen.		der		der												
Dat.		der						den								
Acc.					den					die	die				das	

Being aware of these possibilities will avoid many pitfalls. Thus, even in the simple sentence:

> Das Kind kennt jeder Lehrer.

the reader will realize that he cannot make up his mind at once about the case of the first element, because the noun could be in the accusative as well as in the nominative. Here, a decision can only be made on the basis of the third element. Since **jeder Lehrer** can be a nominative but not an accusative form, *every teacher* must be the subject, and *the child* the direct object, in the accusative.

Definite article in German

6. The definite article, on the whole, is used in German as it is in English:

> Das hübsche Mädchen sitzt immer in der ersten Reihe.
> The pretty girl always sits in the front row.

There are, however, a considerable number of instances in which German employs the definite article where English does not. The most important of these uses are given below.

The definite article is used in German:

(*a*) With the names of the months, the seasons, and the days of the week:

> **Der** Frühling ist die schönste Jahreszeit.
> Spring is the most beautiful season.

Im* Sommer regnet es nicht viel.   **Der** Februar ist ein kalter Monat.
In summer it does not rain much.   February is a cold month.

> **Der** Sonntag ist der letzte Tag der Woche.
> Sunday is the last day of the week.

Im* April haben wir Ferien.   **Am*** Samstag haben wir keine Schule.
In April we have vacation.   On Saturday we have no school.

Days of the week, on the other hand, may also be used adverbially without either article or preposition: **Samstag** (instead of **am Samstag**) **haben wir keine Schule.**

(*b*) Generally with abstract nouns (such as **Liebe, Treue, Musik, Gesellschaft, Wissenschaft**) and concrete nouns used in a generalizing sense, particularly when they are the subject:

---

* Note that article and preposition are ALWAYS contracted in these adverbial phrases.

ABSTRACTS:

Die Liebe macht blind.   Die Mathematik liegt mir nicht.
Love makes one blind.   Mathematics is not for me.

CONCRETE WORDS IN A GENERALIZING SENSE:

Der Mensch ist sterblich.   Das Gold ist ein Metall.
Man is mortal.   Gold is a metal.

Der Stahl ist ein wichtiges Produkt dieses Landes.
Steel is an important product of this country.

On the other hand, the article is commonly omitted when the noun is the object of a verb or a preposition:

Er studiert Philosophie.   Sie interessiert sich nicht für Mathematik.
He is studying philosophy.   She isn't interested in mathematics.

Sie taten es aus Liebe.   Dieser Schreibtisch ist aus Stahl.
They did it out of love.   This desk is made of steel.

(c) With names of streets:

Sie wohnen nicht in der Hauptstraße, sondern in der Ludwigstraße.
They don't live on Main Street but on Ludwig Street.

In giving an actual address, however, the article is not used:

Hotel Habis, München, Skellstraße 4.

(d) With the names of countries which are feminine or which are used in the plural only, such as: **die Schweiz** (*Switzerland*), **die Türkei** (*Turkey*), and **die Tschechoslowakei** (*Czechoslovakia*); **die Niederlande** (*The Netherlands, Holland*):

Waren Sie je in der Türkei?
Were you ever in Turkey?

Note that most countries are neuter and do not normally require the article. When they are modified by an adjective, though, the definite article is used: *das* schöne Frankreich, *beautiful France.* This also applies to city names, which are neuter: *das* schöne Paris, *beautiful Paris.*

(e) With the names of meals: dative

Was gibts zum Frühstück?   Was machen Sie nach dem Abendessen?
What's for breakfast?   What are you doing after dinner?

(f) Where English uses the indefinite article with expressions of unit measure in the sense of "per":

Er verdient 90 Dollar die Woche.   Das kostet zwei Dollar das Pfund.
He earns 90 dollars a (per) week.   It costs 2 dollars a (per) pound.

(*g*) Instead of the possessive adjective, in referring to parts of the body or to articles of clothing:

> Sie nahm **den** Mantel ab.
> She took off her coat.

If the possessor is not the subject of the clause, he is indicated by the dative of the personal pronoun:

> Sie nahm *ihm* **den** Mantel ab.
> She took off his coat.

(*h*) In many idiomatic expressions which do not fit into any of the above patterns and which have to be learned by experience, such as:

Fritz geht in **die** Schule.	Die ganze Familie ist in **der** Kirche.
Fritz goes to school.	The whole family is in church.

Indefinite article

7. The indefinite article is also generally used in German where it is in English; but here, too, there are a few instances in which the usage in German differs from the English:

(*a*) The indefinite article is not used with a predicate nominative which indicates a profession, a nationality, or a religion:

Er ist Rechtsanwalt.	Mein Freund ist Mohammedaner.
He is a lawyer.	My friend is a Moslem.

If the predicate nominative is modified by an adjective, on the other hand, the indefinite article is also used in German:

> Er ist **ein** geschickter Rechtsanwalt.
> He is a clever lawyer.

(*b*) The indefinite article is not used after the connective **als** (meaning *as*):

> Er ist nicht nur als Arzt, sondern auch als begabter Dichter bekannt.
> He is known not only as a physician but also as a talented poet.

B. Declension of Nouns

1. Review the following basic rules for the declension of nouns:

Singular

(*a*) Most masculine and neuter nouns add –s (or –es, if the noun is of one syllable) in the genitive singular: **der Bruder, des Bruders; der Mann, des Mannes; das Kind, des Kindes.**

(*b*) Most masculine and neuter nouns which have only one syllable MAY add an –e in the dative singular: **dem Mann** or **dem Manne; dem Kind** or **dem Kinde.**

(*c*) In the singular, feminine nouns have no case endings: **die Frau, der Frau, der Frau, die Frau.**

Plural

(*d*) Since it is not always possible to tell how a plural will be formed by looking at the singular of a noun, the best way to master the plurals of nouns is to learn the plural formation of each noun as it is encountered. There are, however, four major different ways of forming plurals, and a knowledge of these ways can be helpful in reading to determine whether a noun is singular or plural:

(1) No SPECIAL ENDING IN THE PLURAL—umlaut sometimes on the stem vowel: **der Wagen, die Wagen; der Garten, die Gärten; die Tochter, die Töchter; das Zimmer, die Zimmer.**

(2) THE ENDING –e is ADDED—sometimes umlaut: **der Arm, die Arme; der Arzt, die Ärzte; die Hand, die Hände; das Jahr, die Jahre.**

(3) THE ENDING –er IS ADDED—umlaut whenever possible: **der Mann, die Männer, das Kind, die Kinder.**

(4) THE ENDING –n (OR –en) IS ADDED—the umlaut is never used: **die Frau, die Frauen; die Blume, die Blumen; das Bett, die Betten; der Staat, die Staaten.**

In addition to these four main groups, there are two minor ones:

(1) A small number of nouns borrowed from other languages add –s in the plural: **das Radio, die Radios; das Auto, die Autos; das Hotel, die Hotels.**

(2) A few nouns of Latin derivation ending in –um form their plurals by dropping the –um and adding –en: **das Museum, die Museen; das Studium, die Studien.**

So-called weak nouns

(*e*) A small group of masculine nouns (sometimes called "weak" nouns) does not add an –s (or –es) in the genitive singular. Instead these nouns use the ending –n (or –en) not only in the genitive singular, but also in the dative and accusative singular as well as throughout the plural:

der Student	die Student–en
des Student–en	der Student–en
dem Student–en	den Student–en
den Student–en	die Student–en

Some very common words belong to this group, such as **der Mensch,** **der Junge, der Held** (*hero*), **der Soldat, der Paragraph.**

–n ending in dative plural

(*f*) With the exception of those few nouns with plurals in –s, an –n is added to the dative plural of all nouns unless the nominative plural already ends in –n: **die Männer** (nominative), **den Männern** (dative); but: **die Blumen** (nominative), **den Blumen** (dative).

Recognition of case form

2. A knowledge of the case forms in the singular and in the plural of nouns can be as valuable in reading German as it is essential to using the language actively. Since a single form of the article can have several possible case functions, recognizing the case form of the noun in question will often clarify the situation:

Den Schülern, die immer zu spät kommen, hat er eine schlechte Note gegeben. He gave a bad mark to the pupils who always arrive late.

In this sentence, for example, the article could at first sight be taken to be either an accusative masculine singular or a dative plural in form, but the noun **Schülern** with the added –n should reveal immediately that the forms in question are dative plural, not accusative singular.

Identical case forms

3. The case forms of nouns, however, do not always make the function clear. Confusion may arise with nouns which have the same forms in the singular as in the plural:

Diese Dichter kennt jeder Leser.
Every reader knows these poets.

Here, the form of the noun **Dichter** does not indicate whether it is singular or plural, but the **der**-word **diese** shows clearly that more than one poet is involved.

There are situations, however, where neither the article nor the noun indicates the function immediately. When a weak noun is used, for instance, the case and number can be determined only on the basis of the context. Compare the following examples:

Diesen Menschen habe ich noch nie gesehen.
I have never seen this person before.

Diesen Menschen habe ich noch nie etwas gegeben.
I have never before given anything to these people.

Special Points

manch ein, solch ein, welch ein

1. Instead of the **der**-words **mancher, welcher,** and **solcher,** the expressions **manch ein** (*many a*), **welch ein** (*what a*), and **solch ein** (*such a*) may be used in the singular; the words **manch, welch,** and **solch** are then indeclinable, and only the **ein** is declined:

> **manch eine Frau,** many a woman
> **solch ein Mann,** such a man
> **welch ein Kind,** what a child

ein solcher

There is yet another variation for the expression *such a:* **ein** may precede **solch,** in which case **solch** is declined like an adjective, not like a **der**-word:

> Was macht man mit einem solchen (OR: solch einem) Mann?
> What does one do with such a man?

Caution. This variation does not apply to **manch** and **welch.**

was für ein

2. The idea of *what a* or *what kind of a* can be expressed in German with **was für ein.** In this phrase the **für** does not function as a preposition governing the accusative, so that the **ein** is declined according to the function of the noun with which it belongs.

> Was für **eine** Frau ist das?
> What kind of woman is that?

> *Mit* was für **einer** Frau ist er verheiratet?
> To what kind of a woman is he married?

RECOGNITION EXERCISES

A. *Translate, paying careful attention to the case forms of articles and nouns:*
1. Das Kind mit den roten Haaren kennt der neue Lehrer noch nicht. 2. Das Kind mit den roten Haaren kennt den neuen Lehrer noch nicht. 3. Den neuen Schüler aus Kalifornien habe ich noch nicht kennengelernt. 4. Den neuen Schülern aus Kalifornien hat der Lehrer heute eine Prüfung gegeben. 5. Die Blumen, die sie eben gepflückt hat, steckt sie in eine kleine Vase. 6. Die Blumen, die sie eben gepflückt hat, wachsen in ihrem Garten. 7. Diese Dichter kennt man noch nicht in den Vereinigten Staaten. 8. Dieser Dichter kennt

seine amerikanischen Kollegen noch nicht. 9. Diesen alten Wagen muß man zu oft reparieren lassen. 10. Diese alten Wagen kann man nicht mehr reparieren lassen. 11. Der Schüler, der jetzt bei Herrn Schmidt Latein lernt, wird seinen alten Lehrer nie vergessen. 12. Der Schüler, die vor zehn Jahren in seiner Klasse waren, erinnert sich der alte Lehrer immer noch. 13. Den Jungen mit den langen Beinen habe ich noch nie gesehen. 14. Den Jungen mit den roten Mützen habe ich den Ball zurückgeworfen. 15. Den Studenten, der seine Klassen immer schwänzt, wird der Professor durchfallen lassen. 16. Dem Studenten, der in der Klasse immer aufpaßt, wird der Professor eine gute Zensur geben. 17. Das Buch, das sie letzte Woche gekauft hat, hat sie noch nicht gelesen. 18. Das Buch, das sie letzte Woche gekauft hat, hat sie sehr enttäuscht. 19. Die alte Dame, die nur ein sehr kleines Einkommen hat, hat das Geschenk von ihrer Freundin sehr gefreut. 20. Die alte Dame, die nur ein sehr kleines Einkommen hat, hat das Geschenk von ihrer Freundin gerne angenommen. 21. Den Soldaten mit der schlimmen Verwundung mußte man in ein größeres Krankenhaus schicken. 22. Den Soldaten mit den schlimmen Verwundungen mußte man sofort Penicillin geben.

B. *Translate, noting carefully the use of articles,* **der**-words *and* **ein**-words:
1. Welches Buch benutzen Sie in dieser Klasse? 2. Welch ein schlechtes Buch! Wir werden es nicht wieder benutzen. 3. Manche Frau möchte einen solchen Mann haben. 4. Nicht jeder Mann hat eine solche Frau, aber alle Männer möchten eine solche haben. 5. E.T.A. Hoffmann war nicht nur Dichter, sondern auch Komponist, aber als Komponist ist er heute überhaupt nicht mehr bekannt. 6. Die Werke mancher Komponisten des achtzehnten Jahrhunderts werden heute immer noch gespielt, aber viele andere, die damals sehr beliebt waren, sind jetzt fast ganz vergessen. 7. Sie hat ihr Haus vermietet. 8. Sie haben ihr Haus vermietet. 9. Haben Sie Ihr Haus vermietet? 10. Ich kenne diese Stadt und ihre Umgebung sehr gut. 11. Ich habe diesen Dichter einmal persönlich kennengelernt, aber ich habe sein neues Buch noch nicht gelesen. 12. Das Buch hat mir sehr gefallen, aber seinen Titel mag ich nicht. 13. Habt ihr euer Auto schon verkauft? 14. Meine Tante will ihr Auto loswerden. Habt ihr ihr Auto einmal gesehen? 15. Was für ein Auto ist es? 16. Das Kind steckt die Hand in die Tasche. 17. Das Kind steckt die Hand in meine Tasche. 18. Sie hat den Hut abgenommen. 19. Sie hat dem Kind den Hut abgenommen. 20. Manche Leute verdienen immer noch weniger als neunzig Dollar die Woche.

ACTIVE EXERCISES

A. *Supply the correct German equivalent of the English word in parentheses within each sentence. Then restate the sentence, substituting the correct German equivalent of the English word in the parentheses added after each sentence:*
1. Er hat (his) Buch verloren. (her) 2. Sie hat (my) Auto gekauft. (our)

3. Wir sind mit (your) Mutter spazierengegangen. (her) 4. Wer hat (my) Geschichte gelesen? (our) 5. Ich habe (his) Vater besucht. (their) 6. Ich kenne (your) Onkel nicht. (her) 7. (My) Kind geht noch nicht zur Schule. (his) 8. (His) Bild hängt an der Wand. (our) 9. (Your) Frau kennt mich nicht. (his) 10. (My) Uhr geht nach. (her) 11. (This) Frau sollte das wissen. (every) 12. (Many a) Mann kann das nicht. (this) 13. Was halten Sie von (my) Freund? (his) 14. Ich kenne (that) Frau nicht. (such a) 15. (This) Kind kann das lernen. (every) 16. Was macht man mit (such a) Kind? (this) 17. Die Mutter (of this) Kindes habe ich neulich kennengelernt (of such a) 18. Ich möchte den Anfang (of his) Geschichte noch einmal lesen. (of their) 19. Das Haus (of my) Onkels hat zwanzig Zimmer. (of their) 20. Um (our) Haus steht eine hohe Mauer. (his)

B. *Translate into German:*

1. This year we have our exams in June.
2. We are going to the movies on Sunday.
3. Spring came very late this year; May was as cool as April.
4. My friends intend to visit their aunt and their uncle in July.
5. Loyalty is unknown among (**bei**) such people.
6. My friend has never been in Switzerland.
7. After dinner I usually read the newspaper.
8. People who earn only ninety dollars a week cannot buy meat which costs two dollars a pound.
9. I have the money in my hand and not in my pocket.
10. My friend, who is a doctor, is a Moslem.
11. As a student I have met some interesting people.
12. We don't know the student who answered her question.
13. He told the story to the men but not to the women.
14. What a woman! She will surely find the husband she deserves.
15. Many a man has tried to find such a wife.
16. What kind of music would you like to hear?
17. Every teacher has had such pupils in his class.
18. The answer to (**auf**) their question you will not find in any book.
19. If you do not have your pencil, Mr. Smith, you may (**dürfen**) use her pen.
20. Children, have you brought (**mit-bringen**) your money for lunch?

7

Adjectives and Adverbs

A. Adjectives

Predicate adjectives

1. Adjectives not immediately preceding nouns (= predicate adjectives) do not have endings indicating case, number, or gender:

Diese Frau ist **hübsch.**	Mein Vater ist **krank.**	Das Kind war **hungrig.**
This woman is pretty.	My father is sick.	The child was hungry.

Caution. Predicate adjectives in German tend to appear in final position in principal clauses. Thus, if the predicate is of sufficient length, the adjective which completes the verbal idea will be separated from the finite verb by other elements in the clause, and the reader will have to reach the end of the clause before encountering the decisive supplementary word (i.e., the predicate adjective):

Die Firma *wurde* nicht nur durch ihre guten Beziehungen, sondern auch durch eine geschickte Geschäftspolitik und nicht zuletzt durch eine Reihe von glücklichen Zufällen **sehr einflußreich.**

The company *became very influential* not only because of its good connections but also through clever business policies and, last but not least, through a series of lucky coincidences.

Attributive adjectives

2. When adjectives stand in front of the nouns which they modify (attributive position), THEY MUST HAVE ENDINGS. The endings to be used depend on what precedes them:

Preceded by der-words

(*a*) If the adjective is preceded by a **der**-word, it is declined as follows (i.e., it takes the so-called weak adjective endings):

SINGULAR

der gut–*e* Vater   die gut–*e* Mutter   das gut–*e* Kind
des gut–*en* Vaters   der gut–*en* Mutter   des gut–*en* Kindes
dem gut–*en* Vater   der gut–*en* Mutter   dem gut–*en* Kind
den gut–*en* Vater   die gut–*e* Mutter   das gut–*e* Kind

PLURAL

die gut–*en* Kinder
der gut–*en* Kinder
den gut–*en* Kindern
die gut–*en* Kinder

Note carefully the phrases in heavy print in the table above: IN THESE FIVE POSITIONS (= all the nominatives singular and the accusative singular feminine and neuter) THE ADJECTIVE ENDING is –**e.** In all other cases, singular as well as plural, the ending is –**en.**

Preceded by *ein*-word

(*b*) If the adjective is preceded by an **ein**-word, it is declined as follows (i.e., it takes the so-called mixed adjective endings):

SINGULAR

kein gut–*er* Vater   keine gut–*e* Mutter   kein gut–*es* Kind
keines gut–*en* Vaters   keiner gut–*en* Mutter   keines gut–*en* Kindes
keinem gut–*en* Vater   keiner gut–*en* Mutter   keinem gut–*en* Kind
keinen gut–*en* Vater   keine gut–*e* Mutter   kein gut–*es* Kind

PLURAL

keine gut–*en* Kinder
keiner gut–*en* Kinder
keinen gut–*en* Kindern
keine gut–*en* Kinder

Observe carefully the endings of the forms in heavy print. They are the same five cases which had an –*e* ending in the table above. All other positions, singular and plural, have –*en.*

Not preceded by *der*- or *ein*-word

(*c*) If the adjective is preceded by neither a **der**-word nor an **ein**-word, it is declined as follows (i.e., it takes the so-called strong adjective endings):

SINGULAR   PLURAL

gut–*er* Kaffee   gut–*e* Milch   gut–*es* Bier   gut–*e* Biere
gut–*en* Kaffees   gut–*er* Milch   gut–*en* Bieres   gut–*er* Biere
gut–*em* Kaffee   gut–*er* Milch   gut–*em* Bier   gut–*en* Bieren
gut–*en* Kaffee   gut–*e* Milch   gut–*es* Bier   gut–*e* Biere

Note that, except for the genitive singular masculine and neuter, the endings added to the adjective in these cases are the same as the endings of **dieser.**

Caution. andere (*other*), **einige** (*some, several*), **mehrere** (*several*), **viele** (*many*), and **wenige** (*few*) are neither **der**-words nor **ein**-words; consequently, adjectives following these words have the so-called strong endings:

Ich habe einige gute Bücher. Andere gute Bücher sind billiger.
I have several good books.   Other good books are cheaper.

Several adjectives

3. Several adjectives modifying one noun have the same endings:

Folgen Sie den **verschiedenen roten** Zeichen.
Follow the various red markings.

Adjectival nouns

4. Any adjective in German can, theoretically, function as a noun. It is then capitalized and declined exactly like an attributive adjective, i.e., it is treated as if a noun followed it:

Der Alte ist heute krank. **Die Kleine** versteht das nicht.
The old man is sick today. The little girl doesn't understand that.

Er hat immer **das Richtige** getan. **Ihr Kleiner** hat den Schnupfen.
He always did the right thing. Her little boy has a cold.

Note that masculine and feminine adjectival nouns designate male and female beings, respectively, while neuters usually denote concepts (or things). The English translation of such phrases will often have to supply the appropriate noun: **der Kleine** (*the little boy*), **die Kleine** (*the little girl*), **das Gute** (*that which is good, the good thing*).

Adjectives with neuter pronouns

5. Adjectives modifying neuter pronouns such as **etwas, nichts, viel,** and **wenig** follow them and are treated as neuter adjectival nouns:

etwas Gutes   **nichts Besseres**   **wenig Interessantes**
something good   nothing better   little (that is) interesting

Relative importance of adjectival endings

6. A good knowledge of adjective endings is obviously important for active use of German. It is not essential, however, for mere recognition purposes since the adjective endings after **der-** and **ein**-words do not offer

reliable criteria for determining the case, number, or gender of nouns. In reading, a knowledge of these adjective endings will prove to be really helpful only to distinguish between the nominative singular and the genitive plural of masculine nouns which have the same form in the singular and the plural (see Chapter 6):

NOMINATIVE SINGULAR:

> **Der schlimmste Fehler** befindet sich gleich auf der ersten Seite.
> The worst mistake is right on the first page.

GENITIVE PLURAL:

> **Der schlimmsten Fehler** war er sich durchaus bewußt.
> He was quite aware of the worst mistakes.

Comparison of adjectives

7. The comparative of most adjectives is formed by adding **–er** to the stem of the adjective:

> Marie ist hübsch**er** als Anna.
> Marie is prettier than Anna.

If the comparative form of the adjective is used in a position where it must have declensional endings, these are added after the comparative **–er:**

> Ein hübsch**eres** Mädchen habe ich noch nie gesehen.
> I have never seen a prettier girl.

Formation of superlative

8. The superlative of most adjectives is formed by adding **–st** to the stem of the adjective. Again, the necessary endings are added after the superlative **–st:**

> Er ist der faul**ste** Bursche, den ich kenne.
> He is the laziest fellow I know.

However, if the adjective stem ends in **d, t,** or an **s**-sound and the last syllable of the adjective is stressed, **–est** is added to form the superlative:

> Heute hatten wir wohl den hei**ßesten** Tag des Sommers.
> Today was probably the hottest day of the summer.

> Goethe ist der bekann**teste** deutsche Dichter.
> Goethe is the best known German poet.

On the other hand, if the last syllable is unstressed, only **–st** is used; this applies particularly to present or past participles used as adjectives:

Sie ist die *reizend*ste Frau unter meinen Bekannten.
She is the most charming woman among my acquaintances.

Krebs ist heute wohl die *gefürchtet*ste Krankheit.
Today cancer is probably the most dreaded disease.

Superlative in predicate

9. Unlike the positive and the comparative, the superlative does not appear undeclined in any position. Thus even in the predicate the superlative has declensional endings. There are two constructions for the superlative in the predicate:

(*a*) The definite article precedes the adjective (as it does in English) if a noun could be supplied:

Von allen Blumen in meinem Garten sind die Rosen **die schönsten** (*Blumen* COULD BE SUPPLIED).

Of all the flowers in my garden the roses are the most beautiful.

Unser Haus ist **das älteste** (*Haus* COULD BE SUPPLIED) im Dorf.

Our house is the oldest in the village.

(*b*) **am** precedes the superlative adjective in the dative when a noun cannot be supplied; English then normally uses the superlative without article:

Unsere Rosen sind im Juli **am schönsten.**
Our roses are **most beautiful** in July.

Irregularities: adjectives in –e

10. Adjectives ending in –e (such as **müde** or **böse**) add only –r to form the comparative, and –st to form the superlative: **böser, der (die, das) böseste; müder, der (die, das) müdeste.**

Umlaut

11. A small number of one-syllable adjectives of common occurrence have an umlaut in the comparative and superlative:

alt	älter	der (die, das) älteste
lang	länger	der (die, das) längste

Some of the more important one-syllable adjectives which take the umlaut are: **arm, alt, hart, jung, kalt, klug, krank, kurz, lang, scharf, schwach, schwarz, stark,** and **warm.**

A few other one-syllable adjectives may be encountered either with or without umlaut: **rot—roter** or **röter; naß—nasser** or **nässer,** and others.

gut, viel

12. The adjectives **gut** and **viel** employ different stems in the comparative and superlative:

gut	besser	der (die, das) beste
viel	mehr	der (die, das) meiste

Caution. In the singular, **viel** and **mehr** are not declined, but their superlative forms are:

Dafür habe ich nicht **viel** Zeit.   Er hat **mehr** Zeit dafür als ich.
I don't have much time for that.   He has more time for that than I.

Hans hat **die meiste** Zeit dafür.
Hans has the most time for that.

In the plural, the positive **viel** and its superlative form are declined, while the comparative **mehr** is not:

Viele Leute haben den Film gesehen.   **Mehr** Männer als Frauen waren da.
Many people have seen the picture.   More men were there than women.

Die meisten Leute würden den Film gern noch einmal sehen.
Most people would like to see the film again.

Note in the last example that the definite article is used in this construction in German but not in English.

hoch, nah(e)

13. The adjectives **hoch** and **nah(e)** show consonant changes in the comparative or superlative as follows:

ho*ch*	hö*h*er	der (die, das) hö*ch*ste
na*h*(e)	nä*h*er	der (die, das) nä*ch*ste

The **-ch** in **hoch** is also changed to **-h-** in the positive when the adjective is declined:

Die Berge im Osten sind nicht sehr **hoch.**
The mountains in the East are not very high.

BUT:

Jede Religion hat ihre **hohen** Feiertage.
Every religion has its high holidays.

groß

14. The adjective **groß** is irregularly compared, the superlative adding only a **t** to the final **ß**:

groß	größer	der (die, das) größte

B. Adverbs

Formation

1. Adverbs are normally not inflected in German:

Sie hat **schön** gesungen.	Wir haben **gut** gegessen.
She sang beautifully.	We ate well.

Adjectives used as adverbs, therefore, look like uninflected adjectives:

ADJECTIVE:

Seine Stimme ist **schön.**   His voice is beautiful.

ADVERB:

Er hat das **schön** gesagt.   He said that beautifully.

Caution. Adverbs modifying adjectives should be carefully distinguished from the adjectives:

adj. adj.	adv. adj.
eine gute gebratene Gans	eine gut gebratene Gans
a good roast goose	a well-roasted goose

Note that the adverb has no ending, while the adjective in attributive position has.

Comparison

2. Many adverbs, because of the idea they express (such as time or place), do not have comparative and superlative forms. Adverbs which do allow of comparison, however, form the comparative and the superlative like adjectives, except that only the **am . . . -sten** construction is used for the superlative:

Sie fährt **vorsichtig.**	Er fährt **vorsichtiger.**
She drives carefully.	He drives more carefully.

Ich fahre **am vorsichtigsten.**
I drive most carefully.

gern

3. The commonly occurring adverb **gern** (used to express the idea of *to like to*) is irregular in its comparison:

gern(e)   lieber   am liebsten

Ich esse **gern(e)** Eier.	Ich esse **lieber** Fisch.
I like to eat eggs.	I prefer to eat fish.

Ich esse Fleisch am liebsten.

I like to eat meat best of all.

Special Points

so . . . wie, als

1. When the persons (or things) compared are represented as being equal, German uses **so . . . wie** (*as . . . as*), with the adjective in the positive degree:

Sie ist **so** intelligent **wie** er.

She is as intelligent as he.

When two persons (or things) involved in a comparison are not equal, the comparative of the adjective is followed by **als** (*than*):

Sie ist intelligenter **als** er.

She is more intelligent than he.

je . . . je, je . . . desto (um so)

2. **je** and a comparative form of an adjective or an adverb may be used to introduce two successive clauses corresponding to the English construction *the . . . the. . . .*

Je *länger* ich arbeite, **je** *müder* werde ich.

The longer I work the more tired I get.

Note that the first **je** acts as a subordinating conjunction (verb at the end of the clause), while the second **je** with its adverb or adjective functions as the first unit of a principal clause (verb in second position). **desto** or **um so** are commonly substituted for the second **je**:

Je älter sie wird, **desto** (**um so**) mehr verliert sie ihre Schüchternheit.

The older she gets, the more she loses her shyness.

immer before comparatives

3. **immer** is placed before a comparative (adjective or adverb) to indicate a continuous increase in the quality denoted by the comparative form. English expresses this idea by merely repeating the comparative:

Es wird **immer kälter.**

It is getting colder and colder.

Absolute use of comparative

4. Comparative forms are sometimes used in German to express a fairly high degree of something rather than an actual comparison:

Eine **ältere** Dame saß mir gegenüber.   Sie saß **längere** Zeit dort.
A rather old (elderly) lady was sit-   She sat there a rather long time (for
ting opposite me.   quite a while).

Emphatic superlative adverb

5. A special emphatic form of the superlative of an adverb (**aufs . . . -ste**) may be found expressing an extremely high degree of the manner in which something is done:

> Er ist **aufs schnellste** abgereist.
>
> He departed in the quickest manner possible (as fast as he could).

äußerst, höchst

6. The indeclinable superlative forms **äußerst** and **höchst** are commonly used as adverbs meaning *extremely, very*:

> Das ist eine **äußerst** (**höchst**) interessante Geschichte.
>
> That is an extremely interesting story.

*colder and colder =
immer
kälter*

RECOGNITION EXERCISES

A. *Translate:*

1. Er ist ein intelligenter Junge. 2. Seine Schwester ist auch intelligent, aber er ist intelligenter als sie. 3. Sie ist so intelligent wie ihre Mutter. 4. Er wurde durch seine vielen Erzählungen, die in den besten Zeitschriften erschienen, in den meisten Ländern Europas bekannt. 5. Er wurde durch seine vielen Erzählungen, die in den besten Zeitschriften erschienen, in weniger als fünf Jahren höchst wohlhabend. 6. Er hat immer die besten Äpfel. 7. Seine Äpfel sind nicht immer die besten. 8. Seine Äpfel sind im September am besten. *at their best an are best* 9. Er weiß das sicher am besten. 10. Du hast das Beste gewählt. 11. Etwas Besseres gibt es nicht. 12. Man arbeitet am leichtesten mit etwas Gutem im Magen. 13. Er hat einen äußerst interessanten Essay über das Komische bei Goethe geschrieben. 14. Das Alte ist nicht immer das Beste. 15. Der Alte war so schwach, daß er sein Bett kaum verlassen konnte. 16. Die Alte ging, ohne ein Wort zu sagen, an den spielenden Kindern vorbei. 17. Als er in Deutschland war, war er noch ein jüngerer Mann. 18. Als jüngerer Mann war er in Deutschland. 19. Er war jünger als ich, als er in Deutschland war. 20. Manche Frauen werden immer jünger! 21. Der beste Schüler der Klasse erinnerte sich noch in späteren Jahren gern seines alten Lehrers. 22. Der besten Schüler der Klasse erinnerte sich der alte Lehrer noch in späteren Jahren gern. 23. Ich gehe gern ins Kino; sie geht lieber ins Theater; am liebsten aber gehe ich in die Oper.

B. *Translate:*

1. Diese Dame ist älter als meine Mutter, aber sie ist keineswegs eine ältere Dame. 2. Von allen Sängerinnen, die wir gehört haben, hat diese am schönsten

gesungen. 3. Sie hat das wunderbare Lied von Schubert aufs eindrucksvollste gesungen. 4. Der Physiker untersuchte das neue Phänomen aufs genaueste, bevor er einen längeren Bericht darüber veröffentlichte. 5. Er hat die ganze interessante Geschichte noch einmal erzählt. 6. Er hat die ganz interessante Geschichte noch einmal erzählt. 7. Je mehr man ißt, desto dicker wird man. 8. Je älter er wird, um so mehr merkt man, wie dumm er eigentlich ist. 9. Es ist ein teurer Anzug, aber ich habe mir schon einmal einen noch teureren gekauft. 10. Als er noch ein Kind war, wollte er immer ein reicher Geschäftsmann werden. 11. Als guter Geschäftsmann wird er jetzt immer reicher. 12. Einen erfolgreicheren Mann als ihn kenne ich nicht. 13. Das ist eine unglaubliche und komplizierte Situation. 14. Das ist eine unglaublich komplizierte Situation. 15. Die Kinder armer Leute bleiben oft arm. 16. Manche werden sogar immer ärmer. 17. Die Kinder reicherer Leute gehen gewöhnlich auf die Universität. 18. Solche Kinder findet man bei Reichen und Armen. 19. Dem Reinen ist alles rein. 20. Ich möchte lieber ins Kino gehen als den ganzen Abend allein zu Hause sitzen. 21. Er ist durch seine höchst eigenartigen Romane, die viele seiner Leser gar nicht verstehen können, am meisten bekannt. 22. Er ist durch seine höchst eigenartigen Romane, die die meisten seiner Leser gar nicht verstehen können, reich geworden.

ACTIVE EXERCISES

A. *Complete the following sentences by substituting the correct form of the German adjective equivalent to the English words in parentheses:*

1. Er wohnt in einem (old) Haus. 2. Ein (new) Haus wird hier an der Ecke gebaut. 3. Ein (young) Mann hat mich eben um eine Auskunft gebeten. 4. Sie hat einen sehr (young) Mann geheiratet. 5. Eine (rich) Witwe wohnt allein in diesem (large) Haus. 6. Wir haben diese (old) Dame heute gesehen. 7. Was haben Sie mit Ihrem (new) Hut gemacht? 8. Er ist mit der (pretty) Schauspielerin ausgegangen. 9. Er hat sich ein (beautiful new) Auto gekauft. 10. Das Auto des (poor) Lehrers fährt nicht sehr gut.

B. *Restate the following sentences, changing all indefinite articles to definite articles:*

1. Ein intelligenter junger Mann hat eben mit mir gesprochen. 2. Er hat ein interessantes Buch gelesen. 3. Sie hat sich einen neuen Mantel angezogen. 4. Er ist mit einer hübschen Studentin ins Kino gegangen. 5. Einem armen Mann habe ich etwas Geld gegeben. 6. Eine kranke Frau wurde ins Krankenhaus gebracht. 7. Wir fahren heute im Wagen einer deutschen Studentin. 8. Ein kleines Kind steht vor der Tür und weint. 9. Sie erzählte eine spannende Geschichte. 10. Ein dicker Mann sitzt am Tisch und ißt Schlagsahne.

C. *Translate into German:*

1. This talented artist is very popular in the larger German cities.
2. A good mother must often be strict with her small children.

3. This intelligent boy asks many interesting questions.
4. We gave our old car to a poor student.
5. The famous professor is going to speak about an interesting book he has just published.
6. My younger brother lives in a large house in a rather small city.
7. I went out with my older sister (*in order*) to visit several old friends.
8. He is as old as I, but I am much taller than he.
9. Of all the gardens on this street your garden is the most beautiful.
10. Your little garden is most beautiful in July.
11. I work better in the morning, but my wife works best at night.
12. July is hotter than June, but August is the hottest month of the year.
13. She is the prettiest girl I have ever seen.
14. We have many German books, but they have more French books than we.
15. I like to drink cold beer, but my wife prefers to drink hot coffee.
16. Most children like to drink cold milk best of all.
17. Since it is getting warmer and warmer we want to drink something cold.
18. That was extremely interesting, Robert. Do you also have something interesting to tell, Barbara?
19. The young physicist explained his new theory most convincingly.
20. The longer I know her, the more I love her.

8

Modified Adjective Construction

1. In German, attributive adjectives modifying nouns can themselves be modified in various ways, with the modifying elements preceding the adjective. If the noun thus qualified is used with a **der**-word or an **ein**-word, the modifiers of the adjective appear between the **der**-word or the **ein**-word and the adjective. Thus, in the phrase **ein berühmter Dichter** (*a famous poet*), the adjective **berühmt** might be modified, for example, by the prepositional phrase **in Deutschland,** telling where the poet was famous, and this prepositional phrase would be found between **ein** and **berühmt:**

ein *in Deutschland* berühmter Dichter . . .

Translating it into English

2. English usually cannot follow the German pattern of a modified adjective construction. In English the article must first be connected with a noun: *a poet.* Then the idea expressed by the adjective and its modifiers can best be rendered by a relative clause, the verb of which is often a form of the verb *to be:*

a poet who is (was) famous in Germany . . .

More than one modifier

3. In principle, any number of elements can modify the adjective in this way. The phrase under discussion could, for example, be further expanded by inserting the prepositional phrase **im achtzehnten Jahrhundert,** telling when the poet in question was famous:

ein *im achtzehnten Jahrhundert* in Deutschland berühmter Dichter . . .
a poet who was famous in Germany in the eighteenth century . . .

Participles as modified adjectives

4. Most frequently, the adjectives modified in such constructions are present or past participles functioning as adjectives:

das mit seinen Freunden auf der Straße **spielende** Kind . . .
the child who is playing in the street with his friends . . .

diese im neunzehnten Jahrhundert bereits **entwickelte** Theorie . . .
this theory, which was already developed in the nineteenth century . . .

Caution. Although usually the modifying elements are adverbs or adverbial phrases, present participles in modified adjective constructions may have noun or pronoun objects as their modifiers:

> der *das Experiment* **ausführende** Wissenschaftler . . .
> the scientist who is conducting the experiment . . .

Recognizing modified adjective constructions

5. A large part of the difficulty involved in handling modified adjective constructions is caused by the reader's failure to recognize the construction immediately. It can therefore be extremely helpful to realize that there are several clues which may indicate the presence of a modified adjective construction:

(*a*) A **der**-word or an **ein**-word is not immediately followed by what one would normally expect in English, i.e., a noun, or an adjective and then a noun:

> der *gestern* angekommene Gast . . .
> the guest who arrived yesterday . . .

(*b*) A prepositional phrase which follows a **der**-word or an **ein**-word:

> sein *im Jahre* 1830 vollendeter Roman . . .
> his novel which was completed in 1830 . . .

Modified nouns without articles

6. Modified adjective constructions are more difficult to recognize when the noun in question occurs without a **der**-word or an **ein**-word, as is often the case in the plural:

In den Bergen lebende Menschen sind an kalte Winter gewöhnt.
People who live in the mountains are accustomed to cold winters.

Über offenem Feuer gebratene Würstchen schmecken am besten.
Sausages which are grilled over an open fire taste best.

More than one modified adjective

7. A noun may be used with more than one modified adjective construction. In such cases, it is more difficult to locate:

dieses deutsch **geschriebene** und in zehn Sprachen **übersetzte** Buch . . .
this book, which was written in German and translated into ten languages . . .

Er suchte ein von den meisten Touristen wenig **besuchtes** und trotzdem mit allem Komfort **ausgestattetes** Hotel.	He looked for a hotel which was little frequented by most tourists and yet was equipped with all modern conveniences.

Unmodified adjectives in modified adjective constructions

8. The noun in a modified adjective construction may also be combined with unmodified adjectives. These unmodified adjectives may precede and/or follow the modified adjective:

dieser **ausgezeichnete** und in der ganzen Welt bekannte **deutsche** Pianist . . .
this excellent German pianist who is known throughout the world . . .

Note how in English all unmodified adjectives come before the noun, while the modified adjective is rendered by a relative clause and placed after it.

Kennen Sie das **reizende,** mitten in den Bergen liegende **kleine** Dorf?	Do you know the charming little village which is situated right in the mountains?

Dependent genitives and prepositional phrases after a noun

9. The noun in a modified adjective construction may be followed by an element dependent on it, either another noun in the genitive or a prepositional phrase. In English, such dependent genitives or prepositional phrases must be translated together with the noun BEFORE the modified adjective is approached:

die von den meisten Gelehrten abgelehnte **Theorie** *dieses Autors* . . .
the theory of this author which is (was) rejected by most scholars . . .

sein im Jahre 1900 veröffentlichtes **Buch** *über die deutsche Sprache* . . .
his book on the German language which was published in 1900 . . .

Adjectival nouns in modified adjective constructions

10. Adjectival nouns (i.e., adjectives functioning as nouns; see Chapter 7, Section A, paragraph 4) may also be encountered in modified adjective constructions. In most instances the adjectival nouns thus employed are neuters denoting abstract concepts or things. Particularly common are past participles as adjectival nouns. Note in the following examples that the adjectival noun, as its name implies, serves as both the adjective being modified and the noun in question:

Das auf Seite zehn **Gesagte** wollen wir hier nicht wiederholen.	We don't want to repeat here that which (what) was said on page ten.

Ich habe **das** im vorigen Kapitel **Besprochene** nicht verstanden.	I have not understood that which (what) was discussed in the previous chapter.
Das an diesem Phänomen **Auffallende** ist das folgende.	That which is striking (the striking thing) about this phenomenon is the following.

In translating these constructions into English, one does NOT use the same procedure as in other types of modified adjective situations. First the adjectival noun (with its article) is translated: **das . . . Gesagte,** *that which is said.* Then the modifying element(s) follow(s) directly WITHOUT the use of a relative clause: *that which (what) was said on page ten.*

Special Points

A present participle with **zu** may be encountered as the adjective in a modified adjective construction. It can best be translated in English by *to be* plus the PAST participle:

das in diesem Kapitel **zu besprechende** Gedicht . . .

the poem (which is) to be discussed in this chapter . . .

die noch **zu beantwortende** Frage . . .

the question (which is) yet to be answered . . .

RECOGNITION EXERCISES

A. *Translate:*

1. Dieser im achtzehnten Jahrhundert beliebte Komponist ist heute in Deutschland kaum noch bekannt. 2. Viele heute nach Europa reisende Amerikaner kennen ihr eigenes Land kaum. 3. Dieses von Sartre nach dem Krieg geschriebene Buch wurde auch in den Vereinigten Staaten viel gelesen. 4. Das gestern abend im Staatstheater aufgeführte Stück hat den Kritikern nicht gefallen. 5. Die meisten Zeitungen haben seinen im September erschienenen Roman noch nicht besprochen. 6. Er beschäftigt sich mit einem bis jetzt von nur wenigen Wissenschaftlern untersuchten Problem. 7. Der dieses neue Buch über Goethe besprechende Autor ist selbst ein berühmter Goethe-Forscher. 8. Der den verlorenen Krieg bedauernde Redner fand bei seinem Publikum großen Anklang. 9. Die von uns Hilfe verlangende Frau ist uns völlig unbekannt. 10. Die Idee einer Toleranz übenden Politik stammt aus dem achtzehnten Jahrhundert. 11. Diese im neunzehnten Jahrhundert oft gespielte und in der Gesellschaft sehr beliebte Komödie sieht man heute kaum noch im Theater. 12. Er hat einen Artikel über dieses kürzlich von verschiedenen Wissenschaft-

lern beobachtete, aber von keinem völlig erklärte Phänomen geschrieben. 13. Dieser vor vierzig Jahren in England geborene, in München an der Kunstakademie ausgebildete und jetzt in Madrid lebende Künstler ist besonders für seine Aquarelle bekannt. 14. In ihrem in einem hübschen Vorort gelegenen und mit einem weißen Zaun umgebenen Häuschen besuchte er seine alte Tante. 15. Auf dem Lande aufgewachsene Leute suchen oft Arbeit in einer großen Stadt. 16. An kalte Winter und kühle Sommer gewöhnte Menschen können gewöhnlich nicht lange in den Tropen leben. 17. Von der Mutter zu Hause gebackenes Brot schmeckt immer am besten. 18. In Deutschland von der Firma Zeiss hergestellte Kameras sind in Amerika sehr begehrt.

B. *Translate:*

1. Diese alte, zur Zeit der Römer gebaute Brücke wird heute immer noch benutzt. 2. Die junge und in ganz Europa bekannte französische Pianistin macht diesen Winter eine Konzertreise nach Amerika. 3. Wir besuchen morgen ein berühmtes, am rechten Ufer des Rheins gelegenes mittelalterliches Schlößchen. 4. Wir suchen für unsere Deutschklasse einen guten, von einem deutschen Dichter unseres Jahrhunderts geschriebenen humoristischen Roman. 5. Sein im Jahre 1900 veröffentlichtes Buch über den deutschen Roman des achtzehnten Jahrhunderts ist immer noch lesenswert. 6. In dieser vor drei Jahren in Berlin erschienenen Geschichte der deutschen Literatur des neunzehnten Jahrhunderts finden Sie ein ausgezeichnetes Kapitel über Heinrich Heine. 7. Seine um die Mitte des vorigen Jahrhunderts aufgestellte Theorie über die Entstehung der Nibelungensage wird heute von den meisten Gelehrten abgelehnt. 8. Die im ersten Teil des Buches gegebene Darstellung der Entwicklung der Faustlegende hat überall großen Anklang gefunden. 9. Das auf Seite fünfzehn Gesagte wird fast wörtlich auf Seite fünfzig wiederholt. 10. Das im zweiten Kapitel Besprochene scheint dem im ersten Kapitel Gesagten zu widersprechen. 11. Das an diesem Gerücht Interessante ist der Umstand, daß bis vor kurzem niemand davon gehört hat. 12. Wir halten das in diesem Aufsatz über Heines *Buch der Lieder* Behauptete für eine völlig falsche, von keinem ernsten Gelehrten annehmbare Interpretation. 13. Wir interessieren uns besonders für das im ersten Experiment zunächst zu untersuchende Problem. 14. Die in diesem Aufsatz zu behandelnde Erzählung wurde schon im Jahre 1800 geschrieben. 15. Die hier zu erklärende Theorie wurde im Jahre 1900 zum ersten Mal entwickelt.

ACTIVE EXERCISES

Since students in their second or even third year of German are generally not expected to use modified adjective constructions, no active exercises have been included in this chapter.

fantastic

9

Uses of Nominative and Genitive

A. The Nominative

Case of the subject

1. The nominative is, first of all, the case of the subject of a clause or sentence:

> **Der Junge** geht in die Schule.
> The boy goes to school.

> Ich weiß, daß **der Junge** in die Schule geht.
> I know that the boy goes to school.

Predicate nominative

2. The nominative is also used in the predicate (= predicate nominative) with the intransitive verbs **sein** (*to be*), **werden** (*to become*), **bleiben** (*to remain*), and **heißen** (*to be called*):

Herr Schmidt ist **unser Lehrer.**   Er soll **ein guter Lehrer** sein.
Mr. Schmidt is our teacher.   He is supposed to be a good teacher.

> Napoleon wurde **der erste Kaiser** von Frankreich.
> Napoleon became the first emperor of France.

> Er blieb nicht lange **der erste** in der Klasse.
> He did not remain the top student (the first) in the class for long.

Less frequent is the occurrence of the predicate nominative with transitive verbs of naming in the passive (such as: **genannt werden,** *to be called;* **geheißen werden,** *to be called;* **getauft werden,** to be christened; **gescholten werden,** *to be called, scolded;* **geschimpft werden,** *to be called, scolded*):

Der Herzog wurde von allen **Heinrich der Stolze** genannt.
The duke was called Henry the Proud by everyone.

B. The Genitive

Attributive use

1. The genitive most frequently has the function of modifying a noun. In such an attributive position it may express a wide variety of relationships, the most common of which are possession (**das Geld** *meines Vaters, my father's money*), the idea of "belonging to" (**das Kind** *dieser Frau, the child of this woman*), and the relationship of the part to the whole (**die Ecke** *des Zimmers, the corner of the room*). No matter what situation is involved, the German genitive attribute is almost always the equivalent in English of the possessive or a prepositional phrase with *of*.

Position of genitive attribute

2. Genitive attributes usually follow the noun they qualify: **das Haus** *meines Vaters, the house of my father, my father's house;* **die** Regierung *Friedrichs des Großen, the rule of Frederick the Great.*

In poetry and elevated prose the genitive modifier may be found before the noun, replacing the article: *meines Vaters* **Haus,** *Friedrichs des Großen* Regierung. Such use is avoided in everyday speech. Only proper names in the genitive normally DO PRECEDE the nouns they modify. They can then also take the ending **–s,** irrespective of gender: *Annas* **Vater,** *Ottos* **Bruder,** *Goethes* **Werke.** But if a name in the genitive is preceded by an article (as in colloquial usage: *der Fritz* **ist schon hier,** *Fritz is here already,* or when modified by an adjective: *die kleine Anna, little Anna*), it must follow the noun and does not have the ending **–s:** **das** Buch *der Anna, Anna's book,* **die** Werke *des jungen Goethe, the works of young Goethe.*

Verbs with genitive objects

3. A number of verbs require an object in the genitive. A very few have ONLY a genitive object, such as **bedürfen** (*to need*), or **gedenken** (*to remember, think of* [in a solemn way], *to honor the memory of*):

> Diese Krankheit bedarf **einer radikalen Kur.**
> This sickness needs a radical cure.
>
> Heute gedenken wir **der Gefallenen** des letzten Krieges.
> Today we commemorate those who died in the last war.

A large number of verbs have an accusative as well as a genitive object. Of these there are two major groups:

(*a*) Reflexive verbs with the reflexive pronoun in the accusative, such as: **sich annehmen** (*to take care of*), **sich bemächtigen** (*to take possession of*), or **sich bedienen** (*to make use of*):

> Er hatte sich **meiner alten Großmutter** angenommen.
> He had taken care of my old grandmother.

> Der Feind bemächtigte sich **der Küstenstädte.**
> The enemy took possession of the coastal cities.

> Er bediente sich oft **altmodischer Ausdrücke.**
> He often used old-fashioned expressions.

(*b*) Verbs which express the idea of "to accuse" (or "to suspect, convict," and similar meanings) somebody of something, such as: **anklagen** (*to accuse*), **beschuldigen** (*to accuse*), or **verdächtigen** (*to suspect*), as well as verbs conveying the idea of "depriving somebody of something," such as: **berauben** (*to rob*), or **verweisen** (*to exile, expel*). These verbs take an accusative object of a person but a genitive object of the thing:

> Man hatte *ihn* **seines ganzen Besitzes** beraubt.
> He had been robbed of all his possessions.

> Man hatte *ihn* **des Landes** verwiesen.
> He had been expelled from the country.

Substitutes for genitive objects

4. It is important primarily for reading purposes to be aware of the fact that certain verbs have genitive objects, because most of these verbs are encountered mainly in literary German. In everyday usage they occur relatively infrequently since alternate constructions with either accusative objects or prepositional phrases have developed:

> Ich erinnere mich **an ihn** (FOR: **seiner**).
> I remember him.

> Er hat **ihn** (FOR: **seiner**) geschont.
> He spared him.

Er schämt sich **wegen seiner Vergangenheit** (FOR: **seiner Vergangenheit**).
He is ashamed of his past.

Position of genitive objects

Caution. Like any object of a verb, the genitive object may be found in first position in a main clause and may therefore often be separated by intervening elements from the verb:

Des Gemäldes, das ich vor vielen Jahren in Madrid gesehen habe und das damals einen großen Eindruck auf mich gemacht hatte, **erinnere ich mich** heute immer noch sehr genau.	I still remember today exactly the painting I saw in Madrid years ago and which had made a great impression on me at that time.

Thus, if a genitive is encountered which does not appear to be used attributively with a noun, there is a possibility that it is a genitive object.

Genitives with adjectives

5. Certain adjectives are used with the genitive case. Some adjectives govern only the genitive. The most common of these are: **bewußt** (*conscious of, aware of*), **fähig** (*capable of*), **gewiß** (*certain of*), **sicher** (*sure of*), and **würdig** (*worthy of*). The dependent genitive usually precedes the adjective:

Ich bin mir **dessen** bewußt.	Er ist **eines solchen Gedankens** nicht fähig.
I am aware of that.	He is not capable of such a thought.

For other adjectives which in older German governed the genitive exclusively, substitutes with the accusative or a preposition have developed. Of these the most frequently encountered are: **müde** (*tired of*), **satt** (*tired of, sick of*), **voll** or **voller** (*full of*), **wert** (*worth*).

(*a*) Both **müde** and **satt** are commonly used with the accusative as well as the genitive:

Ich bin **dieser ewigen Streitereien** (**diese ewigen Streitereien**) müde.
I am sick of this eternal quarrelling.

(*b*) Except for a few set phrases (such as: **der Mühe wert,** *worth the effort,* or **der Rede wert,** *worth talking about*), the accusative has replaced the genitive with **wert:**

Dieser Stoff ist **keinen Pfennig** wert.
This material isn't worth a penny.

(*c*) The preposition **von** may occur instead of the genitive with the adjective **voll:**

ein Buch voll (voller) **neuer Ideen** (OR: voll **von neuen Ideen**)
a book full of new ideas

A few adjectives governing the genitive, such as **ansichtig** and **gewahr** (*aware*), are found only as part of fixed verbal idioms:

Er wurde **einer dunklen Gestalt** in der Ecke gewahr (ansichtig).
He became aware (caught sight) of a dark figure in the corner.

Caution. Because adjectives with dependent genitives generally follow the genitive, the function of the genitive element may not always be immediately apparent, especially if the noun is separated from the adjective by modifiers of its own:

Dieses Verbrechens, das seine Karriere ruiniert hat, hat ihn keiner seiner Freunde für **fähig** gehalten.	None of his friends considered him capable of this crime which has ruined his career.

Genitive with *sein*

6. The genitive is used in combination with **sein** (usually also **werden** or **bleiben**) to form some very common idioms:

> Sie war gestern sehr schlechter (guter) Laune.
> She was in a very bad (good) mood yesterday.

> Ich bin derselben Meinung (Ansicht, Überzeugung).
> I am of the same opinion (view, conviction).

Genitive in adverbial uses

7. The genitive of words designating time units is commonly employed adverbially with the indefinite article to express unspecified time in the sense of English "one day" ("morning," "evening"), or "some day" ("morning," "evening"):

> **Eines Tages** wird er mich sicher besuchen.
> One day (some day) he will certainly visit me.

> **Eines Abends** werden Sie mich nicht zu Hause finden.
> One evening you will not find me at home.

Caution. The German for *one night* is **eines Nachts,** even though **Nacht** is feminine.

On the other hand, the genitive of time units with the DEFINITE ARTICLE indicates repeated or usual occurrence in time: **des Morgens,** *in the morning;* **des Abends,** *in the evening;* and similar expressions. Frequently, however, adverbs derived from genitives are found instead, such as **morgens** or **abends.**

8. The genitive of a noun preceded by an attributive adjective but without an article is often encountered as an adverbial expression of manner. Such adverbial genitives are generally rendered in English with prepositional phrases:

> **Schweren Herzens** kehrte er nach Hause zurück.
> He returned home with a heavy heart.

> Die Räuber töteten **kalten Blutes** den gefangenen Polizisten.
> The robbers killed the captured policeman in cold blood.

9. For the genitive after certain prepositions, see Chapter 11.

Special Points

1. The (appositive) genitive of names of cities, states, countries, and months, used in English to explain a preceding noun (such as: the City *of* New York, the State *of* New Jersey, the month *of* April), is not found in German. Instead, the name follows without any indication of case:

die Stadt Berlin	**das Land Hessen**	**die Republik Deutschland**
the City of Berlin	the State of Hesse	the Republic of Germany

im Monat Mai
in the month of May

2. Similarly, nouns designating a measure, number, or kind of something (such as: a pound *of* butter, a glass *of* water) are followed in German by qualifying nouns which show no sign of case:

ein halbes Pfund Butter	**zwei Tassen Kaffee**
half a pound of butter	two cups of coffee

zehn Meter Seide
ten meters of silk

If the modifying nouns are preceded by adjectives, however, they can appear either in the genitive or in the same case as the noun they modify; the latter is preferred in modern usage:

Ich möchte ein Glas $\begin{cases} \text{warmer Milch (GEN.)} \\ \text{warme Milch (ACC.)} \end{cases}$ haben.

I would like to have a glass of warm milk.

RECOGNITION EXERCISES

A. *Translate:*

1. Das Haus, das ich so bewundert habe, hat einen schönen Garten. 2. Das Haus, das ich so bewundert habe, hat ein Ingenieur gekauft. 3. Die Frau, von der wir gerade reden, hat ein reicher Kaufmann geheiratet. 4. Die Frau, von der wir gerade reden, hat ein schönes Haus. 5. Frau Schmidt ist unserer Tochter unbekannt. 6. Frau Schmidt ist unsere Tochter. 7. Er wurde nach langem Dienst aus dem Amt entlassen. 8. Er wurde nach langem Studium Professor an der Hochschule für Musik. 9. Der fette Junge wird von seinen Freunden „der Dicke" genannt. 10. Einer radikalen Lösung, die so viel Mühe kostet, bedarf dieses Problem nicht. 11. Keiner der Söhne wollte sich der alten Mutter annehmen. 12. Anstößiger Worte, die man in Gegenwart einer Dame nicht gebrauchen kann, bedient er sich nie. 13. Den alten Mann, der aussieht,

als könnte er keiner Fliege wehtun, hat man des Diebstahls angeklagt. 14. Unserer Nachbarn, die den Mann durch den Garten schleichen sahen, bemächtigte sich eine solche Angst, daß sie sofort nach der Polizei telephonierten. 15. Die Bauern sahen sich durch die lange Hitze aller Früchte ihrer schweren Arbeit beraubt. 16. Der Lehrer, der mich im Deutschen und Spanischen unterrichtet hat, erinnert sich meiner kaum noch. 17. Der Lehrer, die mich im Deutschen und Spanischen unterrichtet haben, erinnere ich mich immer noch. 18. Der Schüler, die die Prüfung nicht bestanden haben, schämten sich die Eltern sehr. 19. Der Schüler, der die Prüfung nicht bestanden hat, schämt sich sehr. 20. Der hübschen jungen Dame, die ich vor vielen Jahren im Hause meines Onkels kennengelernt habe, und die mich an dem Abend so nett angelächelt hat, erinnere ich mich heute immer noch.

B. *Translate:*

1. Der Fehler, den er in der mündlichen Prüfung gemacht hatte, hat uns sehr überrascht. 2. Der Fehler, die er in der mündlichen Prüfung gemacht hatte, war er sich gar nicht bewußt. 3. Eines Gedankens, der einen großen Eindruck machen könnte, ist er gar nicht fähig. 4. Seiner Hilfe, die er ihnen so oft angeboten hat, können sie ganz sicher sein. 5. Einer solchen Tat, der sich sogar ein ganz gemeiner Verbrecher schämen würde, ist er bestimmt nicht fähig. 6. Unserer Meinung nach ist er der großen Ehre, die ihm erwiesen worden ist, gar nicht würdig. 7. Der Wagen seiner Firma, der ihm zur Verfügung steht, fährt nicht sehr gut. 8. Der Wagen seiner Firma, die ihm zur Verfügung stehen, bedient er sich nur selten. 9. Wir sind der Ausreden, die er immer bereit hat, wenn wir ihn fragen, ob er mit seinem Teil der Arbeit fertig ist, nun endlich satt. 10. Ich werde sie nicht wieder einladen, denn ihrer Absagen, die ich immer erhalte, wenn ich sie anrufe, bin ich nun wirklich müde. 11. Die große Mühe, die wir uns damit gegeben haben, ist diese Aufgabe wahrscheinlich nicht wert. 12. Ein dünnes Buch voll neuer Ideen ist mehr wert als ein dicker Band voller alter abgestandener (**stale**) Gedanken. 13. Eines dunklen Gegenstandes, der aussah, als könnte er ein größeres Tier sein, wurde er eines Abends im Walde hinter seinem Hause gewahr. 14. Wir waren gestern, nachdem wir die unangenehme Nachricht bekommen hatten, sehr schlechter Laune. 15. Ich glaube, er ist, obwohl er es nie gestehen würde, auch unserer Ansicht. 16. Gesenkten Hauptes ging der alte Mann die Straße entlang. 17. Findet er des Abends seinen Freund nicht zu Hause, so geht er schweren Herzens in sein kleines Zimmer zurück.

ACTIVE EXERCISES

A. *Complete the following sentences by giving the correct German equivalent of the English words in parentheses:*

1. (The girl) geht noch nicht in die Schule. 2. Der Bruder (of the girl) geht schon in die Schule. 3. Herr Maier ist (his teacher). 4. Er ist (a very good teacher). 5. Fritz ist (the best student) in seiner Klasse. 6. Das Kind (of

this woman) ist ein kleiner Teufel. 7. Er sitzt allein in der Ecke (of the room) und raucht. 8. Das Haus (of my father) ist so alt, daß es kein Badezimmer hat. 9. Niemand nimmt sich (the old woman) an. 10. Er bedient sich oft (the strangest expressions). 11. Er hat mich (of all my money) beraubt. 12. Er schämt sich (of his mother). 13. Sie ist heute (in a good mood). 14. Wir sind alle (of his opinion). 15. (Some day) wird er sich einen neuen Wagen kaufen. 16. Sie wohnen mitten in der Stadt (of Paris). 17. Diese Blumen blühen nur im Monat (of May). 18. Bringen Sie uns bitte drei Tassen (of coffee). 19. Ich möchte zwei Flaschen (of milk) haben. 20. Die Dame möchte ein Pfund (of sweet butter) haben.

B. *Translate into German:*

1. The man with the gray hair (*use plural*) is our professor.
2. Our son wants to become a successful businessman.
3. My father's car, which is seven years old, does not run (**fahren**) very well.
4. Someone has stolen the old woman's pocketbook.
5. Anna's mother is my best friend's sister.
6. These people, who are now unemployed, really need our help.
7. On this holiday we remember (**gedenken**) our forefathers who came to America in the seventeenth century.
8. She took care of my sick father while I was in Germany last summer.
9. He still remembers the time when they were so happily living together in the same house.
10. My mother has accused this young man of a theft.
11. They robbed the old man of all his means.
12. She is ashamed of her father because he drinks too much.
13. I was not aware of this fact when he said that.
14. She is not at all capable of such a thought.
15. He is sick of her eternal complaints.
16. We can be absolutely sure of his help.
17. His essay is full of bad mistakes.
18. He is always in the best mood when I visit him.
19. One day you, too, will be of our opinion.
20. I would like a pound of coffee and a bottle of beer.

10

Uses of Dative and Accusative

A. The Dative

Dative of indirect object

1. The dative is primarily the case of the indirect object, which designates essentially the person (or thing) TO WHOM (or TO WHICH) something is given, sent, or said, or from whom (or which) something is taken:

Ich gebe **meinem Bruder** das Geld. Sie erzählte **mir** die Geschichte.
I give my brother the money. She told me the story.

Man hat **dem Kind** das Messer weggenommen.
They took the knife away from the child.

For the position of indirect objects in a sentence or clause, see Chapter 2.

Dative of reference

2. The dative often denotes a person for whom, or with reference to whom, something is done, takes place, or exists. Such datives are frequently rendered in English by a prepositional phrase with *for:*

Das Dienstmädchen machte **mir** die Tür auf.
The maid opened the door for me.

Das ist **meiner Frau** ein großes Vergnügen.
That is a great pleasure for my wife.

Sometimes, especially when the German verb is reflexive, the dative of reference is best left untranslated in English: for myself

Jetzt möchte ich **mir** die Stadt ansehen.
Now I would like to have a look at the city.

81

Dative of possession

3. Frequently the dative is used as a substitute for a possessive adjective or a possessive genitive to denote a person to whom something (material or immaterial) belongs:

> Er schüttelte **dem Jungen** die Hand (FOR: die Hand des Jungen).
> He shook the boy's hand.

> Er schüttelte **ihm** die Hand (FOR: seine Hand).
> He shook his hand.

Verbs with dative objects

4. Certain verbs have only dative objects:

Wir helfen **der Mutter** in der Küche.	Sie begegnete **ihm** gestern.
We help Mother in the kitchen.	She met him yesterday.
Ich dankte **ihm** für das Geschenk.	Dieses Buch gehört **mir.**
I thanked him for the present.	This book belongs to me.

Impersonal verb

Some verbs governing the dative may have the impersonal pronoun **es** or a noun designating a thing as the grammatical subject. (For a listing of such verbs, see Table C, at the end of this chapter.) In such instances, the dative element expresses the person involved in the action of the verb and will often have to be made the subject of the English translation:

> Es gelang **mir** nicht, den Mann einzuholen.
> **I** did not succeed in catching up with the man.

> **Mir** fehlte das Geld für einen neuen Anzug.
> **I** was lacking (did not have) the money for a new suit.

The more commonly occurring verbs taking dative objects are listed at the end of this chapter for reference (Table B).

Adjectives with the dative

5. A large number of adjectives govern the dative case. The dependent dative usually precedes the adjective:

Er ist **mir** böse.	Ich bin **Ihnen** sehr dankbar.
He is angry at me.	I am very grateful to you.
Seine Haltung ist **mir** unbegreiflich.	Sie sind **ihrem Ziel** nahe.
His attitude is incomprehensible to me.	They are near their goal.

A list of the more common adjectives with the dative will be found at the end of this chapter for reference (Table D).

Caution. Since a noun in the dative, in any of the functions discussed above, may appear in first position in a principal clause, its use often cannot be immediately determined, particularly if it is modified by a relative clause (and possibly some other elements). Compare the following sentences which all begin with the same element; note that the English translation should begin with the subject:

VERB WITH DATIVE OBJECT

Dem alten Mann, der seine Wohnung aufgeben muß, weil er nicht mehr für sich selber sorgen kann, wird der Staat jetzt helfen.

The state will now help the old man who has to give up his apartment because he can no longer take care of himself.

ADJECTIVE WITH DATIVE

Dem alten Mann, der seine Wohnung aufgeben muß, weil er nicht mehr für sich selber sorgen kann, sind die Verhältnisse unverständlich geworden.

Conditions have become incomprehensible to the old man who has to give up his apartment because he can no longer take care of himself.

INDIRECT OBJECT

Dem alten Mann, der seine Wohnung aufgeben muß, weil er nicht mehr für sich selber sorgen kann, werde ich einen netten Brief schreiben.

I'll write a nice letter to the old man who has to give up his apartment because he can no longer take care of himself.

POSSESSIVE DATIVE

Dem alten Mann, der seine Wohnung aufgeben muß, weil er nicht mehr für sich selber sorgen kann, liefen die Tränen über das Gesicht.

Tears streamed down the face of the old man who has to give up his apartment because he can no longer take care of himself.

It is obvious that one cannot make up one's mind about the function of a dative in first position until the end of the sentence has been reached.

6. For the prepositions requiring the dative, see Chapter 11, Section B.

B. The Accusative

Direct object

1. The accusative is primarily the case of the direct object:

> Ich schreibe meiner Mutter **einen Brief.**
> I am writing a letter to my mother.

For the position of direct objects in a clause or sentence, see Chapter 2.

Double accusative

2. A double accusative, in which both objects, in parallel construction, refer to the same person, occurs after verbs expressing the idea of "naming" such as: **heißen, nennen** (both: *to call*), **schelten, schimpfen** (both: *to call*, in a derogatory sense), **taufen** (*to christen*):

> Er nannte **ihn** gerne **seinen besten Schüler.**
> He liked to call him his best student.

A double accusative, in which both the object of the person and the object of the thing are in the accusative, is also used after **angehen** (*to concern*), **fragen** (*to ask*), **kosten** (*to cost*), and **lehren** (*to teach*):

> Er fragte **mich** dann **etwas sehr Peinliches.**
> He then asked me something very embarrassing.

Das geht **dich nichts** an.	Das kostete **ihn sein Leben.**
That is no concern of yours.	That cost him his life.

> Er lehrte **uns** damals **viele neue Ausdrücke.**
> He taught us many new expressions then.

Accusative in adverbial expressions

3. The accusative may be employed adverbially to express the following ideas:

(*a*) Definite time, i.e., the specific time at which something takes place:

Diesen Sommer fahre ich nach Hause.	**Vorigen Monat** war ich in Berlin.
This summer I'm going home.	Last month I was in Berlin.
Nächste Woche ist er nicht hier.	Sie geht **jeden Morgen** in die Stadt.
He won't be here next week.	She goes downtown every morning.

(*b*) Duration of time, i.e., the length of the time during which something takes place:

Er hat **die ganze Nacht** gearbeitet.	Ich werde noch **einen Tag** warten.
He worked all night (the whole night).	I'll wait another day.

> Ich kann nur **einen Augenblick** bleiben.
> I can stay only a moment.

> Er möchte **ein ganzes Jahr** bleiben.
> He would like to stay a whole year.

Adjectives with accusative

4. In addition to the adjectives used with either the genitive or the accusative (see Chapter 8), two common adjectives, **los** (*rid of*), and **gewohnt** or **gewöhnt** (*accustomed to, used to*), normally govern the accusative:

> Endlich bin ich **diese Verpflichtungen** los.
> I'm finally rid of these obligations.

> Er war **dieses Klima** nicht gewohnt.
> He wasn't used to this climate.

Accusative for measurements

5. Certain adjectives, such as: **alt** (*old*), **breit** (*wide*), **dick** (*thick*), **groß** (*large, high*), **hoch** (*high*), **lang** (*long*), and **tief** (*deep*) can be used with an accusative to denote measurement in time or space:

> Die kleine Brücke ist nur **einen Meter** breit.
> The little bridge is only a meter wide.

> Das Baby ist heute **einen Monat** alt.
> The baby is one month old today.

Accusative for weight and price

The same is true of the adjectives **schwer** (*heavy*) and **wert** (*worth*), indicating weight and price:

Der Stein ist **ein Pfund** schwer.
The rock weighs a pound.

Das Buch ist **keinen Dollar** wert.
The book isn't worth a dollar.

Accusative absolute

6. An accusative (accusative absolute) may be followed by an adjective, a prepositional phrase, or a past participle (all with or without modifiers) to form a phrase which describes a person mentioned in the principal clause. Such an accusative is best rendered in English as the object of the preposition *with:*

> **Den Mund** weit offen, starrte er mich an.
> He stared at me with his mouth wide open.

> **Den Hut** in der Hand, wartete er geduldig auf Antwort.
> With his hat in his hand he waited patiently for an answer.

> **Den Kopf** gesenkt, stand er eine ganze Stunde lang da.
> With his head bowed he stood there for a whole hour.

Caution. When the past participle in an accusative absolute construction is modified, it will stand last in the phrase, whereas in English it will precede its modifiers:

Den Rücken der alten Burg zugekehrt, blickte sie zu den Sternen auf.
With her back turned to the old castle, she looked up to the stars.

7. For the accusative after certain prepositions, see Chapter 12.

Special Points

Appositives

1. Words in apposition (i.e., placed after another word for explanation) are in the same case as the word they explain:

NOMINATIVE:

Herr Schmidt, unser Milchmann, ist gestern verunglückt.
Mr. Schmidt, our milk delivery man, had an accident yesterday.

DATIVE:

Herrn Schmidt, unserem Milchmann, habe ich ein Trinkgeld gegeben.
I gave a tip to Mr. Schmidt, our milk delivery man.

~~NOMINATIVE~~: Accusative

Hast du Herrn Schmidt, unseren Milchmann, gesehen?
Did you see Mr. Schmidt, our milk delivery man?

Words connected by *als*

2. Similarly, when **als** (meaning *as*) is used as a connective to equate two words, the one following it is in the same case as the word it explains:

NOMINATIVE:

Er kam *als* reicher Mann nach Hause zurück.
He came home (as) a rich man.

ACCUSATIVE:

Ich habe ihn nur *als* armen Studenten gekannt.
I only knew him as a poor student (i.e., when he was a poor student).

TABLE B
Common Verbs Taking Dative *

*antworten (auf), to answer   begegnen, to meet
*befehlen, to order, command   beistehen, to assist

* Verbs which take a dative object of person and an accusative object of thing are preceded by an asterisk.

TABLE B (*Continued*)

beiwohnen, to attend
danken, to thank
dienen, to serve
drohen, to threaten
entfliehen, to escape from, flee
entkommen, to escape
fluchen, to curse
folgen, to follow
gehorchen, to obey
gehören, to belong to
*glauben, to believe
gleichen, to resemble
gratulieren, to congratulate
helfen, to help

leicht (schwer) fallen, to be easy (hard) for
nahen (sich nahen, sich nähern), to approach
nützen, to be useful to
passen, to suit
*raten, to advise (*with accusative in meaning:* to guess)
schaden, to harm, damage
schmeicheln, to flatter
trauen, to trust (*with accusative in meaning:* to marry)
*vergeben, to forgive
widersprechen, to contradict

TABLE C
Impersonal Verbs with Dative of Person

einfallen, to occur to, remember
fehlen (an), to be lacking, be the matter
gefallen, to please

gelingen, to succeed
genügen, to satisfy
geschehen, to happen

TABLE D
Common Adjectives with Dative

ähnlich, similar, like
angenehm, pleasant, pleasing
bekannt, known
böse, angry (*also with* mit)
dankbar, grateful
ergeben, devoted
fremd, foreign
lieb, dear, pleasing
nahe, near
nützlich, useful (*also with* für)

gehorsam, obedient
geläufig, familiar
gelegen, opportune
geneigt, favorably disposed
gewachsen, up to
gleich, gleichgültig, indifferent
günstig, favorable (*also with* für)
treu, faithful
verhaßt, hateful
willkommen, welcome

RECOGNITION EXERCISES

A. *Translate:*

1. Was fehlt Ihnen? Haben Sie sich erkältet? 2. Mir fehlt die letzte Seite des Buches. 3. Dem Mann, der für seine wachsende Familie ein Haus kaufen möchte, fehlt es leider an Geld. 4. Genügt Ihnen das immer noch nicht? 5. Das hübsche Mädchen, dem ich gestern im Park begegnet bin, traf ich heute schon wieder vor dem Hotel. 6. Der Hund hat die alte Frau gehört.

7. Der Hund hat der alten Frau gehört. 8. Die Frage ist nicht, wem dieses Projekt nützt, sondern wem es vielleicht schaden könnte. 9. Ihr ist gerade eingefallen, wo sie diesen Jungen, der ihrem Bruder so ähnlich sieht, früher schon einmal gesehen hat. 10. Das Wetter war ihrem Unternehmen, das sie seit Wochen geplant hatten, nicht besonders günstig. 11. Mir ist der Vorschlag, der soeben gemacht worden ist, gar nicht lieb, aber ich schließe mich der Mehrheit an. 12. Dem Dichter, der jahrelang an einem Roman gearbeitet hat, ist es noch nicht gelungen, einen Verleger dafür zu finden. 13. Gelingt mir die Ausführung dieses Planes, dann dürfen Sie mir gratulieren. 14. Ich bin Ihnen für die Vorschläge, die Sie mir gemacht haben, wirklich sehr dankbar. 15. Der nächsten Versammlung, in der diese Fragen weiter diskutiert werden sollen, riet er mir beizuwohnen. 16. Deutsch ist mir sehr leicht gefallen. 17. Deutsch hat ihm sehr gefallen. 18. Der Mutter, die blonde Haare und blaue Augen hat, gleicht das kleine Mädchen mit seinen dunklen Haaren gar nicht. 19. Der Mutter, die den ganzen Tag mit ihren Nachbarinnen Karten spielt, ist die Bettzeit ihrer Kinder völlig gleichgültig. 20. Meinem Vater, der seine alten Freunde immer gerne bei sich sieht, wird Ihr Kommen ein Vergnügen sein. 21. Der Junge hat dem armen Mann, der ihn um etwas Geld angebettelt hatte, eine kleine Münze in den Hut gelegt. 22. Dem Mann, der durch seine Unvorsichtigkeit das Kind verletzt hatte, tat es leid, daß er ihm nicht helfen konnte.

B. *Translate:*

1. Dem kleinen Jungen, der fast immer allein spielen muß, weil die Nachbarn keine Kinder haben, hat die Mutter ein neues Spielzeug mitgebracht. 2. Dem kleinen Jungen, der fast immer allein spielen muß, weil die Nachbarn keine Kinder haben, legte die Tante mitleidig die Hand auf den Kopf. 3. Dem kleinen Jungen, der fast immer allein spielen muß, weil die Nachbarn keine Kinder haben, war der Besuch seines Vetters eine ganz besondere Freude. 4. Dem kleinen Jungen, der fast immer allein spielen muß, weil die Nachbarn keine Kinder haben, gefällt das Alleinsein eigentlich ganz gut. 5. Diesen Dummkopf, der mich ununterbrochen stört, kann ich nicht leiden. 6. Diesen Dummkopf, der mich immer nur gestört hat, bin ich endlich los. 7. Die schwere Arbeit, die man von ihm verlangte, war er nicht gewohnt. 8. Die schwere Arbeit, die man von ihm verlangte, hat ihn sehr ermüdet. 9. Die viele Mühe, die wir uns mit der Ausführung seines Planes gemacht haben, war die ganze Sache nicht wert. 10. Die viele Mühe, die uns die Ausführung seines Planes gekostet hat, bedauern wir nicht. 11. Als Studenten habe ich ihn nicht gekannt. 12. Als Student habe ich sie nicht gekannt. 13. Wir lernten einander erst als Kollegen bei der Versicherungsgesellschaft kennen. 14. Ich lernte sie kennen, als ich eines Abends bei Freunden zum Abendessen eingeladen war. 15. Wie geht es Ihnen? Ich habe Sie eine Ewigkeit nicht gesehen! 16. Tränen in den Augen bat er seinen Vater um Verzeihung. 17. Den Pfennig in der Hand ging der kleine Junge in den Laden, um sich ein paar Bonbons zu kaufen. 18. Die Augen zu Boden gesenkt, begann er leise aber sehr deutlich zu reden.

ACTIVE EXERCISES

A. *Give the correct German form of the words in parentheses:*

1. (Ich) genügte das Essen nicht. 2. Er schreibt (sein Vater) (ein Brief).
3. Er nennt (sein Sohn) (ein Dummkopf). 4. Vergib (deine Feinde). 5. Bist
du (diese Aufgabe) gewachsen? 6. Waren Sie (letzter Sommer) in Berlin?
7. Er gibt (sein Sohn) (ein Federhalter). 8. Danken Sie (Herr Schmidt)
dafür. 9. (Ein Tag) war (er) die richtige Antwort eingefallen. 10. (Der
Photograph) ist dieses Bild wirklich gut gelungen. 11. Er gleicht nicht so sehr
(sein Vater) wie (seine Mutter). 12. Er bringt (seine Freundin) (jeder Tag)
(eine Rose). 13. Ich bin (ein solcher Lärm) nicht gewohnt. 14. Glauben Sie
(ich), ich kann (Sie) nicht helfen. 15. (Wer) gehört dieses Buch? 16. (Wer)
sehe ich da mit einem Buch in der Hand? 17. (Jeder Sommer) treffe ich (sie)
in Paris. 18. Ich begegnete (sie) (ein Abend) in der Oper. 19. Das Wetter
ist (seine Experimente) nicht günstig. 20. Sie sind (wir) (jeder Tag) willkommen.

B. *Translate into German:*

1. One does not trust people who always flatter others.
2. Why do you call him a great man?
3. She served our family loyally for years.
4. They took the books away from the little boys.
5. We believed them the whole time.
6. I met him one evening in front of the movie theater (use **treffen** and
   begegnen).
7. My wife does not like (*use* **gefallen**) his new novel.
8. I am grateful to you that you told me the story.
9. What is the matter with your wife (*use* **fehlen**)?
10. It never occurred to her that he could be unfaithful (**untreu werden**) to
    her.
11. Can you open the door for me and help me with these suitcases?
12. One glass of wine will not harm anyone.
13. I am lacking one dollar; can you lend me one?
14. He did not succeed in following the instructions.
15. Are you angry with her or don't you trust her?
16. I resemble my mother and my sister resembles my father.
17. I advised her not to attend the lecture.
18. Don't thank me. I didn't help you.
19. I am satisfied if my book pleases only a few readers.
20. I knew her only as a little girl.

11

Prepositions with Genitive and Dative

Prepositions in general

German prepositions can be categorized according to the cases they govern and hence be divided into four groups: those which govern only the genitive, the dative, or the accusative, respectively, and those which may be followed by either the dative or the accusative. For active use of the language it is necessary to know exactly which prepositions are used with the various cases. From the point of view of reading, such knowledge is less vital. But whether the objective is either speaking or reading, it is very important to be thoroughly familiar with at least the basic meanings of the prepositions, because many of them have a considerable number of semantic possibilities. The following sentence will use an extreme case to illustrate the nature of the difficulties that might arise:

Nach dem Kriege fuhren sie **nach** New York, wo sie, den Berichten ihrer Freunde **nach,** wochenlang **nach** Arbeit suchten.	**After** the war they went **to** New York, where, **according to** the reports of their friends, they looked **for** work for weeks.

In addition to the "basic" meanings of the prepositions discussed in the various sections of this and the following chapters, however, there are idiomatic uses which will often require a translation deviating considerably from the "basic" meaning of a given preposition. Thus, for example, the four most common uses of **nach** are illustrated in the sentence above: *after, to, according to,* and *for,* but in the following idiomatic expression **nach is** the equivalent of *like* or *of* in English:

Es riecht hier **nach** Rosen.
It smells here of (like) roses.

Furthermore, even when a basic meaning of a preposition is involved, English idiom may demand a rendition which does not correspond to any one of the major translations found in ordinary grammar books. Thus, in the phrase **meiner Meinung nach, nach** is employed in the sense of *according to,* but English here prefers *in: in my opinion.* Once the basic meanings of the prepositions have been mastered, however, it is essentially a matter of becoming familiar with the idiomatic peculiarities —of both languages!—from experience. In many instances it will be possible to guess the proper English preposition because the rest of the German idiom will be fairly close to the English.

A. Prepositions with Genitive

The basic prepositions governing the genitive are listed below.

GERMAN	ENGLISH	EXAMPLES
anstatt (or: **statt**)	instead of	Er schrieb das **statt** einer Einleitung. He wrote that instead of (in place of) an introduction.
trotz	in spite of	Er kam **trotz** des schlechten Wetters. He came in spite of the bad weather.
während	during	Es regnete **während** der Nacht. It rained during the night.
wegen	because of on account of	**Wegen** seiner Krankheit kommt er nicht. He is not coming because of his illness.
um . . . willen	for the sake of	**Um** (des) Himmels **willen!** For Heaven's sake!

Note. (1) Although standard German prefers the genitive with **anstatt** (**statt**), **trotz, während,** and **wegen,** the dative is sometimes found not only in colloquial speech but also in the literary language. However, the set phrase **trotz allem,** *in spite of everything,* is always constructed with the dative.

(2) **um . . . willen** always frames its object.

(3) **wegen** frequently follows its object. In such instances, the function of the genitive may not be immediately apparent:

Der Nachricht über die Verhaftung der ihm persönlich bekannten Offiziere **wegen** war er sehr schlechter Laune.	He was in a very bad mood **because of the news** of the arrest of the officers he knew personally.

(4) Distinguish between the preposition **trotz** and the word **trotzdem,** which can be used as an adverb or a conjunction:

Trotz seiner Krankheit ging er an die Arbeit.
He went to work in spite of his illness.

Trotzdem er krank war, ging er an die Arbeit.
He went to work even though (in spite of the fact that) he was ill.

Trotzdem ging er an die Arbeit.
Nevertheless, he went to work.

The less common prepositions with the genitive (Table E) and with the dative (Table F) are found at the end of this chapter.

B. Prepositions with Dative

The most common prepositions taking a dative object are listed below.

aus

	(*motion from:* out of)	Er kommt gerade **aus** dem Haus. He is just coming out of the house.
from	(*origin*)	Sie ist **aus** Vermont. She is from Vermont.
out of (*motivation*)		Er tat es **aus** Liebe. He did it for (out of) love.
(made) of		Der Stuhl ist **aus** Holz. The chair is (made) of wood.

außer

except but	Alle **außer** ihm verstehen das. Everyone except him understands that.
besides in addition to	**Außer** dir kommt auch noch meine Tante. Besides you my aunt is also coming.
out of	Endlich ist sie **außer** Gefahr. Finally she is out of danger.
beyond	Das ist **außer** allem Zweifel. That is beyond all doubt.

bei

| near in the vicinity of | Godesberg **bei** Bonn. Godesberg near Bonn. | Wir wohnen **beim** Bahnhof. We live near the station. |

with, at	Er wohnt **bei** seiner Tante. Sie ist **beim** Friseur.
	He lives at (with) his aunt's. She is at the hairdresser's.
upon (*temporal*)	**Bei** seiner Ankunft . . .
	Upon his arrival . . .
while	Er erkältete sich **beim** Baden. While eating.
	He caught a cold while bathing. **Beim** Essen.

in	**Bei** solchen Krankheiten hilft nur eine Operation.
in the case (works) of	With (in the case of) such diseases only an operation will help.
with	**Bei** Schiller findet man das nicht.
	This is not found in Schiller's works.

considering	**Bei** der großen Entfernung kann er nicht früher hier sein.
in view of	Considering (in view of) the great distance he cannot be here earlier.

mit

with	Was soll ich **mit** dem Geld machen?
	What shall I do with the money?
by (means of) (*referring to travel*)	Er fährt **mit** der Bahn (dem Auto, dem Bus, etc.)
	He is travelling by train (car, bus, etc.)

nach

to	Sie fahren **nach** Berlin.
toward	They are going to Berlin.
in the direction of	Hier biegt die Straße **nach** Süden.
at	Here the street turns toward the South.
	Er blickte **nach** der Uhr.
	He looked at the clock.
after (*temporal*)	**Nach** zehn Jahren. **Nach** dem Essen.
	After ten years. After the meal.
according to	**Nach** Darwin. **Nach** dem Gesetz.
	According to Darwin. According to the law.
for (*in many verbal idioms*)	Er schickte **nach** dem Arzt. Er sehnt sich **nach** ihr.
	He sent for the doctor. He is longing for her.

Note. In the meaning of *according to*, **nach** may follow its object and make it difficult to recognize the function of the dative:

Den Berichten der Zeitungen über den Unfall **nach** war er der einzige Insasse außer dem Piloten.	According to the reports about the accident in the newspapers, he was the only occupant besides the pilot.

seit

since	Seit dem Unfall habe ich ihn nicht gesehen. I have not seen him since the accident.
for (*temporal*)	Er ist schon **seit** zehn Tagen hier. He has been here for ten days.

von

	(*place*)	Er reiste **von** Berlin nach Paris. He travelled from Berlin to Paris.
from	(*origin*)	Das Geld ist nicht **von** ihm. The money is not from him.
	(*time*)	Ich war **von** Montag bis Donnerstag bei ihm. I was with him from Monday to Thursday.

about (*i.e.*, concerning) of	Wir sprachen gerade **von** Ihnen. We were just talking about you. Ich habe nie **von** diesem Buch gehört. I have never heard of (about) this book.
by (*in passive constructions*)	Die Gedanken wurden dann **von** Freud weiterentwickelt. The ideas were then further developed by Freud.
of	Die Straßen **von** Paris. The streets of Paris. Drei **von** meinen Freunden. Three of my friends.

Note. **ab** or **an** may be used after the object of **von** to form the concept of *from . . . on:*

vom nächsten Sonntag **an** from next Sunday on	*von* jetzt **ab** from now on

Similarly, **aus** may be found after the object of **von,** but it is usually not translated:

Von meinem Fenster **aus** kann ich ihn sehen.
I can see him from my window.

zu

to	Er kommt **zu** mir. He is coming to me.	Ich gehe **zum** Bahnhof. I am going to the station.
at (*time*)	**Zu** Weihnachten At Christmas	**Zu** Anfang des Jahres At the beginning of the year
in, at (*place*)	Die Universität **zu** München. The University at (in) Munich.	Ich bin **zu** Hause. I am at home.

for (the purpose of, on occasion of; with meals)

Wir reisen nur **zum** Vernügen.
We are only travelling for pleasure.

Man braucht Wasser **zum** Kochen.
One needs water for cooking.

Das gebe ich ihr **zu** Weihnachten.
I'll give her that for Christmas.

Was gibt's **zum** Frühstück?
What's for breakfast?

TABLE E
Less Common but Important Prepositions with Genitive

angesichts, in view of
anhand, by means of
anläßlich, on the occasion of
anstelle, in place of
aufgrund, on the basis of
außerhalb, outside of
bezüglich, with reference to
diesseits, this side of
einschließlich, including
halber (*only following noun*), because of
hinsichtlich, as far as . . . is concerned
infolge, as a result of
inmitten, in the midst of
innerhalb, inside of, within
jenseits, on the other side of, beyond
kraft, because of, on the strength of
laut (*also with dative*), according to
mangels, for the lack of
mittels, vermittels, by means of
oberhalb, above
rücksichtlich, regarding
seitens, on the side of, by
unterhalb, below
unweit, not far from, near
vermöge, on the strength of
zeit, for the time of
°**zufolge** (*also, if following noun, with dative*), as a result of
zwecks, for the purpose of

TABLE F
Less Common but Important Prepositions with Dative

binnen (*also with genitive*), within
dank, thanks to
entgegen (*also following noun*), towards

° With genitive when object follows preposition, but with dative when object precedes preposition.

TABLE F (*Continued*)

gegenüber (*also following noun*), opposite, toward, with respect to

gemäß (*also following noun*), according to

mitsamt, samt, together with

nächst, next to

nahe (*also following noun*), near

nebst, together with

zuliebe (*following noun*), for the sake of, for

zuwider (*following noun*), against

RECOGNITION EXERCISES

A. *Translate:*

1. Statt seines Vaters hat er seiner Mutter die Geschichte erzählt. 2. Statt seinen Vater während der Ferien zu besuchen, ist er nach Mexiko gefahren. 3. Während er seine Ferien in New York verbrachte, blieb seine Frau mit den Kindern zu Hause. 4. Er ist trotz des heißen Wetters in die Stadt gefahren, um seinen Freund zu besuchen. 5. Trotzdem ist er heute hingefahren, denn er hat während der Woche keine Gelegenheit dazu. 6. Trotzdem er heute hingefahren ist, ist es ihm nicht gelungen, seinen Freund zu treffen. 7. Wir haben unserer Mutter wegen ihres schwachen Herzens die schlechte Nachricht noch nicht mitgeteilt. 8. Wir haben unserer Mutter wegen die Reise nicht gemacht. 9. Um meinem Vater einen Gefallen zu tun, hat meine Schwester die Großmutter besucht. 10. Um meines Vaters willen hat sie das getan. 11. Der Ankunft eines von ihnen seit Jahren ersehnten Kindes wegen geben sie heute eine große Gesellschaft. 12. Sie glaubt, er hat es aus Liebe getan. 13. Wir wissen aber, daß er es nur aus Versehen getan hat. 14. Der Tisch sieht aus, als wäre er aus Holz, aber er ist wirklich aus Metall. 15. Der Mann, der gerade aus dem Gebäude kommt, ist aus Texas. 16. Alle Studenten in dieser Klasse außer der hübschen Blondine aus Connecticut sind sehr tüchtig; sie versucht es mit ihrem Charm. 17. Außer dir glaubt niemand, daß wir schon außer Gefahr sind. 18. Es ist außer allem Zweifel, daß wir das Geld nicht bekommen. 19. In dem jenseits des Flusses gelegenen Häuschen wohnen außer meinem alten Onkel auch noch zwei Männer, die in der Fabrik arbeiten. 20. Wenn der Verbrecher immer noch innerhalb der Stadtgrenzen ist, wird ihn die Polizei sicher finden. 21. Ist er schon außerhalb der Stadt, so wird er wohl entkommen. 22. Infolge der Nachlässigkeit der Wache gelang es dem Gefangenen, mittels einer in einem Paket versteckten Säge aus dem Gefängnis zu entkommen.

B. *Translate:*

1. Bei solchen Experimenten muß man die Versuchsapparate sorgfältig vorbereiten. 2. Der Onkel, bei dem er während des Sommers wohnt, hat ein Häuschen in Pullach bei München. 3. Bei seiner Ankunft in Berlin war der Bahnhof der späten Stunde wegen fast leer. 4. Da sie heute morgen beim Arzt ist, kann sie uns bei der Arbeit nicht helfen. 5. Sie hat ihn beim Essen gestört, was schon ein Fehler ist. 6. Bei der großen Entfernung wird es ein Wunder

sein, wenn er vor Mitternacht ankommt. 7. Bei Chaucer findet man diese Erzählung nicht. 8. Was beschreibt er mit diesen Worten? 9. Mit anderen Worten, Sie wollen nicht bei uns bleiben. 10. Indem er nach seiner Uhr blickte, fragte er den Beamten, wann der nächste Zug nach Berlin abfahre. 11. Er erkundigte sich bei seiner Freundin nach ihrer Mutter, die krank gewesen war. 12. Nach Beethoven gab es jahrzehntelang keinen deutschen Komponisten, der so bedeutende Symphonien geschrieben hat. 13. Nach Beethoven hat Haydn, bei dem er Unterricht gehabt hatte, ihn nicht sehr viel gelehrt. 14. Wenn Sie nicht bald nach dem Feuer sehen, wird es ausgehen. 15. Den Berichten der Polizei über den Unfall nach war der Fahrer des einen Wagens ziemlich betrunken. 16. Obwohl er schon seit zehn Tagen hier ist, habe ich ihn seit seiner Ankunft noch nicht gesehen. 17. Sie war von Samstag bis Mittwoch bei ihrem Onkel in Godesberg bei Bonn. 18. Dann fuhr sie von Godesberg nach Bonn, wo sie vier von ihren Freunden besuchen wollte. 19. Das Buch von Thomas Mann, von dem wir gerade reden, ist ein Geschenk von ihrem Vater. 20. Von seinen sehr reichen Verwandten ist er nicht mehr abhängig. 21. Von seinen sehr reichen Verwandten hat er eben einen neuen Wagen bekommen. 22. Von seinen sehr reichen Verwandten sieht er nicht mehr viel. 23. Von seinen sehr reichen Verwandten ist er enterbt worden. 24. Zu dieser Jahreszeit reisen wir immer zum Vergnügen zu meiner Tante nach Paris. 25. Von unserem Haus aus, das gegenüber dem Bahnhof liegt, können wir die Züge sehr gut sehen. 26. Seine Haltung anderen Menschen gegenüber ist nicht ganz normal.

ACTIVE EXERCISES

A. *In the following exercise complete the German sentences by substituting German prepositions for the English prepositions in parentheses:*

1. Er schreibt jetzt einen Roman (instead of) einer Novelle. 2. (During) der Ferien fahren wir ein paar Mal nach New York. 3. Diese Handtasche ist (made of) Leder. 4. Wir sind (in spite of) seiner Hilfe nicht fertig geworden. 5. Er ist (from) Berlin. 6. Alle Studenten (except) Fritz sind hier. 7. (Because of) des schlechten Wetters gehen wir heute nicht spazieren. 8. Er wohnt diesen Sommer (with) seinem Onkel. 9. (Since) dem Ende des Semesters haben wir ihn nicht gesehen. 10. Wir fahren morgen früh (to) Paris. 11. Wollen Sie (with) uns fahren? 12. (According to) dem letzten Wetterbericht soll es morgen regnen. 13. Wir sind schon (for) zehn Tagen hier. 14. (After) dem Tanz gehen wir in ein kleines Café. 15. Wir sind (from) New York (to) Boston gefahren. 16. (Besides) dir wird nur Fritz kommen. 17. Wir haben gerade (about) Marie gesprochen. 18. (At) der Zeit wohnten wir immer noch in Berlin. 19. Dieses Bild ist (by) meiner kleinen Tochter gemalt. 20. Sie geht morgen (to) ihrer Großmutter.

B. *Translate into German:*

1. During his vacation he visited his girl friend instead of his aunt.
2. Because of his mother's illness he'll stay home tonight.

3. I saw my old friend as he was coming out of *(the)* church.
4. We came by (the) bus today because of the snow.
5. Everyone (**alle**) except me knows what happened yesterday.
6. In spite of the rain we are going downtown this afternoon.
7. My uncle, with whom I live during the winter, often goes to the movies with me.
8. After supper we are driving to New York (*in order*) to go to the theater.
9. She is coming to me because I can help her.
10. At that time I did not know why he was so nice to me.
11. According to the report I just heard she will not marry him.
12. Since his arrival he has scarcely gone out of the house.
13. I have been here for three days but I still have not heard a word from him,
14. We are going to school today even though it snowed hard (**heftig**) during the night.
15. From now on I'll do my assignments myself.
16. At this hour even (**auch**) the streets of New York are almost empty.
17. This story is by Kafka who is from Prague.
18. Because of his poor grades his father will not give him the money for his trip.
19. This elegent chair, (which is) made of steel, cost me 400 dollars.
20. She has never heard of a chair that costs so much.

Prepositions with Accusative and Dative or Accusative

A. Prepositions with Accusative

bis

The preposition **bis** is used alone only if its object is not preceded by an article:

until (time)	Ich warte **bis** morgen. Er bleibt **bis** Weihnachten.
	I'll wait til tomorrow. He'll stay until Christmas.
up to as far as (*place*)	Wir sind nur **bis** Rom gekommen.
	We got only as far as Rome.
by (*i.e.*, not later than)	**Bis** morgen wird er wieder hier sein.
	He'll be back here by tomorrow.

When its object is a noun which requires an article, **bis** is followed by another preposition which determines the case to be used:

> Er ist **bis an** die Grenze mitgefahren.
> He went along as far as the border.

> Er wartet immer **bis zum** letzten Augenblick.
> He always waits to the last moment.

durch

through	Er geht **durch** den Garten.
	He walks through the garden.
	Ich habe das **durch** ihn gehört.
	I heard that through him.
by (*in passive*)	Die Stadt wurde **durch** Bomben zerstört.
	The city was destroyed by bombs.

99

durch used in the TEMPORAL sense of *through* or *throughout* usually follows its object, in which case the stronger form **hindurch** can take its its place:

> Man hat die ganze Aufführung **hindurch** gelacht.
> They laughed through the whole performance.

für

für corresponds closely to English *for:*

> Er hat das **für** mich getan.
> He did that for me.

There are, however, a number of common verbal expressions using **für** in which the English equivalent of the preposition will not be *for,* such as **halten für** (*to consider, take to be*), **sich interessieren für** (*to be interested in*).

gegen

against	Ich bin **gegen** den Krieg. I am against the war.
toward (*attitude*)	Er war immer freundlich **gegen** mich. He was always polite toward me.
compared with	**Gegen** sein Haus ist meins nur eine Hütte. Compared with his house mine is only a hut.
about (*approximately*)	**Gegen** zwanzig Studenten haben gefehlt. About twenty students were absent. Er kommt **gegen** drei Uhr. He'll come about three o'clock.

ohne

ohne is generally the equivalent of English *without:*

> Er geht **ohne** mich.
> He is going without me.

um

around (*place*)	Sie saßen **um** den Tisch. They sat around the table.
around (*time: approximately*)	Sie eröffnet ihr Geschäft **um** den 1. Januar. She'll open her shop around January 1.

um - could mean "in order to"

at (*precise time*)	Ich gehe gewöhnlich **um** zehn Uhr zu Bett.
	I usually go to bed at ten o'clock.
by (*measure of difference*)	Die Temperatur fiel **um** zehn Grad.
	The temperature dropped (by) ten degrees.

In the first two meanings above, **um** may be reinforced by **herum** placed after the object:

Sie saßen **um** den Tisch **herum**.
Sie eröffnet ihr Geschäft **um** den 1. Januar **herum**.

wider

In most cases, **wider** (notice the spelling!) is interchangeable with the more colloquial **gegen,** but only in the sense of *against:*

Er hat das nur **wider** Willen getan.
He did that only against his will.

B. Prepositions with Dative or Accusative

The prepositions governing either the dative or the accusative are:

an, auf, hinter, in, neben, über, unter, vor, zwischen

When used in a context of spatial relations, i.e., to specify the relationship of things to one another, these prepositions govern the dative or the accusative according to the so-called rule of motion, the case depending on the type of action expressed by the verb. Two basic situations should be carefully distinguished:

1. IF THE VERB INDICATES MOTION TOWARD THE OBJECT OF THE PREPO-SITION (or toward a point or place in front of, behind, next to, above or below it), THE ACCUSATIVE IS USED:

| Max klettert **auf** *die* Bank. | Sie schiebt den Braten **in** *den* Ofen. |
| Max climbs up on the bench. | She pushes the roast into the oven. |

2. IF NO SUCH MOTION IS EXPRESSED, THE DATIVE IS USED:

Max sitzt **auf** *der* Bank.	Der Braten ist **im** Ofen.
Max is sitting on the bench.	The roast is in the oven.
Er marschierte **neben** *mir*.	Sie geht **im** Park spazieren.
He marched next to me.	She goes for a walk in the park.

Caution. These prepositions are frequently used in phrases or idioms to express ideas which do not indicate the relationship of things in space:

Sie wartet **auf** mich.	**Auf** diese Weise macht man keinen Fortschritt.
She is waiting for me.	In this way one doesn't make any progress.

In such instances the rule of motion does not apply, and the case (dative or accusative) in each situation must be learned from experience.

In the following listing of basic meanings, the uses with the rule of motion are given in tables, while other common meanings are discussed in the associated text.

an

	WITH ACCUSATIVE		WITH DATIVE
up to to	Er tritt **an** *das* Bett. He steps up to the bed.	at by alongside	Er steht **am** Bett. He stands at (by) the bed.
on (*but not:* on top of)	Er hängt das Bild **an** *die* Wand. He hangs the picture on the wall.	on (*but not:* on top of)	Das Bild hängt **an** der Wand. The picture hangs on the wall.

In a temporal sense, **an** is used with the dative and may correspond to English *in, at,* or *on:*

am Abend	am Mittag	am Samstag
in the evening	at noon	on Saturday

In a number of common idioms, however, **an** may correspond to English *in* or *of:* **denken an** (*to think of*), **glauben an** (*to believe in*), **ein Interesse haben an** (*to have an interest in*), **Mangel an** (*lack of*), **sterben an** (*to die of*), and others.

auf

	WITH ACCUSATIVE		WITH DATIVE
on (top of)	Er legt das Buch **auf** *den* Tisch. He puts the book on the table.	on (top of)	Das Buch liegt **auf** *dem* Tisch. The book is lying on the table.
to	Er geht **aufs** Land (**auf** *die* Post, *den* Bahnhof). He goes to the country (the post office, the station)	in at	Er ist **auf** *dem* Lande (*der* Post, *dem* Bahnhof) He is in the country (at the post office, at the station)

In addition, **auf** is used in time expressions with the accusative, usually translated by _for_ in the sense of _how long:_ *for a short time*

Er mietet das Zimmer **auf** _eine Woche_.   Sie ist nur **auf** _kurze Zeit_ da.
He is renting the room for a week.   She's there only for a short time.

The accusative object of **auf** may be followed by **zu,** expressing the idea of _toward:_

Er kommt **auf** mich **zu.** *toward*
He is coming toward me.

With a number of common verbal idioms **auf** will correspond to a variety of English prepositions: **achtgeben auf** (_to pay attention to_), **schauen** (OR **sehen**) **auf** (_to look at_), **sich verlassen auf** (_rely on_), **warten auf** (_to wait for_), and others.

hinter

	WITH ACCUSATIVE		WITH DATIVE
behind in back of	Er stellt die Lampe **hinter** _das_ Sofa. He places the lamp behind the couch.	behind in back of	Die Lampe steht **hinter** _dem_ Sofa. The lamp is standing behind the couch.

in

	WITH ACCUSATIVE		WITH DATIVE
in into	Er geht **ins** Haus. He goes into the house.	in	Er ist **im** Haus. He is in the house.
to	Ich gehe **in** _die_ Schule (Oper, **ins** Kino). I am going to school (the opera, the movies).	in, at	Ich war **in** _der_ Schule (Oper, **im** Kino). I was in school (in the opera, the movies).

neben

	WITH ACCUSATIVE		WITH DATIVE
next to alongside of	Sie stellt den Tisch **neben** _das_ Sofa. She places the table next to the couch.	next to alongside of	Der Tisch steht **neben** _dem_ Sofa. The table is standing next to the couch.

neben may be used with the dative in the sense of _in addition to:_

Neben *seinem* Gehalt hat er noch ein weiteres Einkommen.
In addition to his salary he has some further income.

über

	WITH ACCUSATIVE		WITH DATIVE
over above	Ich hänge das Bild **über** *den* Tisch. I am hanging the picture over the table.	over above	Das Bild hängt **über** *dem* Tisch. The picture is hang- ing over the table.
across (*from one side of some- thing to the other*)	Der Vogel fliegt **über** *den* See. The bird flies across the lake.	over above	Der Vogel fliegt **über** *dem* See. The bird is flying above the lake.

In addition, **über** has the following common meanings (with the accusative):

(*a*) *about, concerning,* or *on:*

> Er schreibt ein Buch **über** *den* Weltkrieg.
> He is writing a book on the World War.

(*b*) *more than:*

> Er bleibt **über** *eine* Woche.
> He stays more than a week.
>
> Ich habe **über** *eine* Mark bezahlt.
> I paid more than one mark.

(*c*) *via,* or *by way of:*

> Ich reise **über** *die* Schweiz nach England.
> I am travelling via Switzerland to England.

unter

	WITH ACCUSATIVE		WITH DATIVE
under	Der Hund legt sich **unter** *den* Tisch. The dog lies down under the table.	under	Der Hund liegt **unter** *dem* Tisch. The dog lies under the table.
among	Er geht **unter** *die* Armen. He is going among the poor.	among	Er wohnt **unter** *den* Armen. He is living among the poor.

vor

	WITH ACCUSATIVE		WITH DATIVE
before in front of	Er stellt die Milch- flaschen **vor** *die* Tür. He places the milk bottles in front of the door.	before in front of	Die Milchflaschen stehen **vor** *der* Tür. The milk bottles are standing in front of the door.

With the dative, **vor** has the following additional meanings:

(*a*) *before*, in a temporal sense:

> Das war noch **vor** *dem* Kriege.
> That was still before the war.

(*b*) *ago*, when the object of **vor** designates a unit of time:

> **Vor** zwei Jahr*en* war ich in Berlin.
> Two years ago I was in Berlin.

(*c*) *of, for* (or *with*), or *because of* when the object of **vor** indicates the cause of something:

> Sie weinte **vor** Freude.   Ich sterbe **vor** Lange(r)weile.
> She cried for (with) joy.   I am dying of boredom.

> Sie konnte **vor** Angst nicht schlafen.
> She couldn't sleep because she was afraid (because of fear).

zwischen

In the case of **zwischen,** the accusative is used when the verb expresses motion to a point between objects:

	WITH ACCUSATIVE		WITH DATIVE
between	Sie stellte die Lampe **zwischen** *das* Sofa und *den* Tisch. She placed the lamp between the couch and the table.	between	Die Lampe steht **zwischen** *dem* Sofa und *dem* Tisch. The lamp stands between the couch and the table.

RECOGNITION EXERCISES

A. *Translate:*

1. Sie kann nur bis morgen warten. 2. Wir wollten heute von Boston nach Philadelphia fahren, aber wir sind wegen des schlechten Wetters nur bis New York gekommen. 3. Bis morgen werden wir bestimmt bis Washington kommen.

4. Er schreibt eine Geschichte der deutschen Literatur von der Reformation bis zur Gegenwart. 5. Man muß erst durch einen kleinen Garten gehen, um an das Haus zu kommen. 6. Die Stadt Lissabon wurde im Jahre 1755 durch ein Erdbeben zerstört. 7. Das ganze Mittelalter hindurch glaubte man, daß die Erde flach sei. 8. Wer nicht für mich ist, der ist wider mich. 9. Wir halten diesen jungen Mann, der sich sehr für Musik interessiert, für äußerst begabt. 10. Es ist nicht leicht, gegen solche Leute freundlich zu sein. 11. Obwohl er ziemlich intelligent ist, ist er gegen seinen jüngeren Bruder ein Dummkopf. 12. Gegen fünfzig Leute waren erwartet, aber nur zwanzig sind erschienen. 13. Er sollte um zwei Uhr hier sein, aber er ist erst gegen vier angekommen. 14. Um seinen Vater, der ein bekannter Chirurg war, sammelten sich einige der besten Ärzte der Stadt. 15. Um seinen Vater, der ein bekannter Chirurg war, während der Ferien sehen zu können, mußte er nach New York fahren. 16. Um den 1. März herum soll er von seiner Reise nach Deutschland zurückkehren. 17. Um den Garten steht ein weißer Zaun. 18. Ihre Mannschaft hat uns um zehn Punkte geschlagen. 19. Ohne seine Frau, die ihm immer bei der Arbeit hilft, kann er keine Entscheidung treffen. 20. Ohne seine Frau, die ihm sonst immer bei der Arbeit geholfen hatte, überhaupt um Rat zu fragen, hat er selber die Entscheidung getroffen. 21. Seine Hilfe brauche ich nicht, ich bin schon zufrieden, wenn er nicht gegen mich arbeitet.

B. *Translate:*

1. Da er ganz aufgeregt am Fenster stand, trat auch ich ans Fenster, um zu sehen, was draußen los war. 2. Das Bild, das vor einer Stunde noch auf dem Tisch lag, hängt jetzt an der Wand. 3. Am Abend sitze ich gewöhnlich in meinem Zimmer und lese die Zeitung, aber gerade an dem Abend, da sie angekommen war, war ich ausgegangen. 4. Ich denke oft an sie, aber sie erinnert sich wohl nicht mehr an mich. 5. Ich habe überhaupt kein Interesse an seinem neuen Plan. 6. Der Arzt selbst ist gestern an Lungenentzündung gestorben. 7. Er kann diese Woche nicht für uns auf die Bank gehen, denn er ist gestern zu seiner Mutter aufs Land gefahren. 8. Auf dem Bahnhof wartet er jetzt auf seine Freundin, die auf dem Lande lebt, ihn aber auf ein paar Tage besuchen kommt. 9. Da wir nur auf kurze Zeit hier sind, hoffen wir wenigstens auf gutes Wetter. 10. Auf einen Mann, der so selten die Wahrheit sagt, kann man sich nicht verlassen. 11. Auf einen Mann, der immer zu spät kommt, werden wir nicht länger warten. 12. Auf Kinder, die auf der Straße spielen, muß man gut achtgeben. 13. Sie fahren jetzt auf Paris zu, werden aber erst morgen abend dort ankommen. 14. Die beiden Herren, die heute abend mit uns in die Oper gehen, wohnen in einem großen Haus in der Hauptstraße. 15. Den Tisch, der früher am Fenster stand, habe ich gestern neben das Sofa gestellt. 16. Neben seinem Beruf interessiert er sich auch noch sehr für Literatur. 17. Die Wildenten sind eben über die Felder und in den Wald geflogen. 18. Die Schwalben fliegen über den Feldern. 19. Er spricht schon über eine Stunde über sein neues Buch. 20. Wir sind eben über Paris geflogen. 21. Wir fliegen über Paris nach London. 22. Ich habe seine Uhr unter einem Haufen von Papieren auf seinem Schreibtisch gefunden. 23. Unter den Briefen auf

seinem Schreibtisch befindet sich auch einer von ihr. 24. Vor dem Krieg stand ein Denkmal auf dem Platz vor der Kirche. 25. Vor vielen Jahren, als ich noch in der Fabrik arbeitete, glaubte ich manchmal, ich würde vor Langerweile sterben.

ACTIVE EXERCISES

A. *In the following exercise complete the German sentences by substituting German prepositions for the English prepositions in parentheses:*

1. Er hat meine Aufgabe (for) mich getan. 2. (Without) seine Hilfe werde ich damit nie fertig. 3. (Since) seinem Tod haben wir seine Frau nicht mehr gesehen. 4. Das Buch liegt (on) dem Schreibtisch (next to) der Lampe. 5. (On) der Wand hängt ein Bild (of) meinem Vater. 6. Wir haben nur (as far as) Seite 70 gelesen. 7. Wir sind alle (against) seinen Plan. 8. Die Kinder liefen (in) dem Garten (around) einen großen Baum. 9. Der Dieb ist (through) *durch* das Fenster (into) das Haus gedrungen. 10. Ich stehe gewöhnlich (at) sieben Uhr auf. *um*

B. *Complete the following sentences by supplying the correct case of the words in parentheses, which are given in the nominative:*

1. Auf (der Boden) liegt ein Haufen Bücher. 2. Er stellt die Vase vor (die Lampe). 3. Ich habe den Spiegel in (mein Zimmer) an (die Wand) gehängt. 4. Sie tritt an (der Tisch), an (der) er sitzt. 5. Ich habe einen Brief von (meine Mutter) bekommen. 6. Durch (sein Vater) hat er die Stelle bekommen. 7. Er hat gerade ein Buch über (der Krieg) gelesen. 8. Die Lampe hängt über (der Tisch). 9. Neben (unser Haus) liegt ein kleiner Park mit (ein Kinderspielplatz). 10. Vor (der Krieg) *dem* war er ein berühmter Sänger.

C. *Translate into German:*

1. He did it for his sister, but not out of love. *aus Liebe*
2. She stepped up to the table around which we were sitting. *an dem Tisch – um den*
3. On the way to the university I always go through the little park behind the church. *zur Universität durch* *hinter der Kirche*
4. I shall wait for her only until tomorrow. *bis morgen*
5. They did it against our advice and without our help. *gegen ..... ohne*
6. The first semester begins about the middle of September. *etwa Mitte September*
7. In the evening I like to sit with my wife on the veranda. *auf der Veranda*
8. He lives in the country, but I prefer to live in the city where I can go to the theater. *auf dem Land ..... in der Stadt ..... ins Theater*
9. On that evening she was sitting in front of the house next to her husband. *vor dem Hause* *neben*
10. We shall see you in New York before the beginning of the semester. *vor dem Anfang des Semesters*
11. Two months ago I wrote a paper (die Arbeit) on Kafka. *Vor zwei Monaten* *über*
12. My younger brother is standing between my mother and my father.
13. Among the books on the table you'll find a play by Schiller. *Unter* *auf dem Tisch* *von Schiller*

14. If (**falls**) you are looking for the cat, you'll find her under the bed. *unter dem Bett*

15. We are travelling to Munich by way of Paris. *Nach München* *über Paris*

Um —16. In order to fly from New York to London one must fly across the ocean. *zu* *Von* *Nach* *über*

17. He was sitting on the table because there were not enough chairs in the room. *auf* *in*

18. The picture by Picasso is hanging on the wall over the sofa. *von* *an der* *über*

19. I met (**kennenlernen**) my wife at the theater through my best friend. *im*

20. On our walk we went only as far as the bridge. *durch*

Auf

nur bis (zur or an die) Brücke

13—

Personal and Interrogative Pronouns; *da-* and *wo-* Compounds

A. Personal Pronouns

Forms

1. The basic forms of the personal pronouns are:

SINGULAR

	FIRST	SECOND	THIRD				POLITE
NOM.	ich	du	er	sie	es		
GEN.	meiner	deiner	seiner	ihrer	seiner	(dessen)	
DAT.	mir	dir	ihm	ihr	ihm		
ACC.	mich	dich	ihn	sie	es		

PLURAL

	FIRST	SECOND	THIRD	POLITE
NOM.	wir	ihr	sie	Sie
GEN.	unser	euer	ihrer	Ihrer
DAT.	uns	euch	ihnen	Ihnen
ACC.	uns	euch	sie	Sie

Note. (1) The genitive of the personal pronoun is relatively rarely used, and then mainly with verbs and adjectives which govern the genitive; if the pronoun in the genitive refers to a thing, **dessen** is substituted:

> Ich schäme mich **seiner** (BUT: **dessen**). Wir sind **ihrer** sicher.
> I am ashamed of him (of it). We are sure of them.

(2) With the prepositions governing the genitive, the personal pronouns

are generally avoided, but **wegen** and **um . . . willen** combine with a modified form of the genitive pronouns: **meiner, deiner, seiner,** and **ihrer** change their final **r** to a **t,** while **unser** and **euer** add **–et;** the altered forms are connected with the prepositions as follows: **meinetwegen, deinetwegen, seinetwegen, ihretwegen, unseretwegen, euretwegen** (*for my sake, for your sake,* and so on). Likewise with **um . . . willen: um meinetwillen** (*for my sake*), and so forth.

Sie tut das **unseretwegen.**   Ich komme **ihretwillen.**

She is doing that for our sake.   I am coming for her sake.

Agreement

2. In German, personal pronouns AGREE IN GENDER AND NUMBER with the nouns to which they refer or which they replace. Their CASE IS DETERMINED BY THEIR FUNCTION in the clause in which they occur:

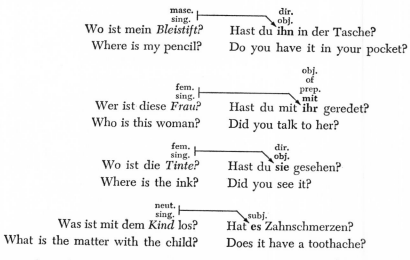

Wo ist mein *Bleistift?*   Hast du **ihn** in der Tasche?

Where is my pencil?   Do you have it in your pocket?

Wer ist diese *Frau?*   Hast du mit **ihr** geredet?

Who is this woman?   Did you talk to her?

Wo ist die *Tinte?*   Hast du **sie** gesehen?

Where is the ink?   Did you see it?

Was ist mit dem *Kind* los?   Hat **es** Zahnschmerzen?

What is the matter with the child?   Does it have a toothache?

Note.   The only exceptions to this rule are the nouns **das Mädchen** (*girl*) and **das Fräulein** (*miss*) where the natural gender (feminine) may be preferred over the grammatical (neuter):

Das Mädchen arbeitet in unserem Büro.   **Sie** ist recht hübsch.

The girl is working in our office.   She is quite pretty.

Function of *sie*

Caution.   Since the forms **sie** and **ihr** each have several functions, careful attention must be paid to the context in which they appear before the correct meaning can be determined.

(1) **sie** can be nominative or accusative, singular as well as plural. Thus, as a nominative **sie** can mean *she* (referring to a person), *it* (referring to a thing), or *they:*

> **Sie** geht nach Hause.   **Sie** gehen nach Hause.
> She goes home.   They go home.

> Ich habe eine Taschenlampe, aber **sie** brennt nicht.
> I have a flashlight but it doesn't work (burn).

As an accusative, **sie** can mean *her* (referring to a person), *it* (referring to a thing), or *them:*

> Das ist meine Freundin. Kennst du **sie?**
> That's my girl friend. Do you know her?

> Wo ist meine Uhr? Hast du **sie?**
> Where is my watch? Do you have it?

> Das sind meine Freunde. Kennst du **sie?**
> Those are my friends. Do you know them?

Function of *ihr*

(2) The situation with **ihr** is complicated by the fact that **ihr** can be a possessive adjective as well as a pronoun. Thus, **ihr** can mean *you, her,* or *it* as a pronoun, and *her, their,* or *its* as a possessive. As a pronoun, **ihr** may be:

(*a*) Nominative, the subject of a verb in the second person plural:

> **Ihr** versteht das nicht, Kinder.
> You don't understand that, children.

(*b*) Dative, meaning *her* or *it* according to whether the antecedent is a person or a thing:

> Ich gab **ihr** etwas Geld.
> I gave her some money.

> Ich habe meine Uhr fallen lassen, aber es hat **ihr** nicht geschadet.
> I dropped my watch but it did not damage it.

As a possessive adjective, the meaning of **ihr** depends on the antecedent:

> die Mutter und **ihre** Kinder   die Lehrer und **ihre** Studenten
> the mother and her children   the teachers and their students

> die Regierung und **ihre** Minister
> the government and its ministers

da-compounds

3. A pronoun is ordinarily the object of a preposition only if it refers to a person:

> Ich gehe zu meinem Lehrer und spreche *mit* **ihm.**
> I go to my teacher and talk with him.

If the reference is to a thing, **da** replaces the pronoun, forming a compound which consists of **da-** (**dar-**, if the preposition begins with a vowel) and the preposition:

Wo ist mein Buch? Was hast du **damit** getan? Die Zeitung liegt **darauf.**	Where is my book? What did you do with it? The newspaper is lying on top of it.

Caution. The prepositions with the genitive as well as the prepositions **außer, ohne, seit,** and **gegenüber** do not form **da**-compounds: **ohne es, außer ihm,** and so forth.

> Er geht nie *ohne* seinen Regenschirm aus. Er geht nie *ohne* **ihn** aus.
> He never goes out without his umbrella. He never goes out without it.

man

4. The impersonal pronoun **man** (*one, you, people*) has no genitive forms and borrows the dative and accusative from the pronoun **einer: einem, einen:**

Wenn man in einem fremden Land ist, muß man erwarten, daß die Leute **einen** nicht verstehen.	If you are in a foreign country you have to expect that the people do not understand you.

Note. Since **man** can only be a nominative form, the location of the subject of a clause in which **man** occurs is never a problem:

Dieses Bild, das sich jetzt nur ein Millionär leisten kann, hat **man** früher für wertlos gehalten.	People used to think that this picture, which now only a millionaire can afford, was worthless.

B. Relative Pronouns

The relative pronouns have been discussed in Chapter 4. At this point, the following additional observations have to be made:

wo-compounds (relative)

If a relative pronoun refers to an inanimate object and is preceded by a preposition, **wo–** MAY BE SUBSTITUTED for the pronoun to form a compound consisting of **wo-** (**wor-**, if the preposition begins with a vowel) and the preposition:

Kennst du das Buch, **worüber** (OR: **über das**) er spricht?
Do you know the book about which he is speaking?

Dies sind die Bücher, **womit** (OR: **mit denen**) wir dieses Jahr arbeiten.
These are the books with which we are working this year.

Caution. The prepositions with the genitive and the prepositions **außer, ohne, seit,** and **gegenüber** cannot form **wo**-compounds:

> Das sind Bedingungen, **ohne die** man nicht leben kann.
> Those are conditions without which one cannot live.

C. Interrogative Pronouns

1. The interrogative pronouns **wer?** (*who?* referring to people, singular or plural), and **was?** (*what?* referring to things, abstracts, or actions, in the singular or in the plural), are declined as follows:

NOM.	wer	was
GEN.	wessen	wessen
DAT.	wem	—
ACC.	wen	was

Both **wer** and **was** can be used in direct or in indirect questions:

DIRECT:

> **Wer** hat das gesagt?   **Wen** haben Sie gesehen?
> Who said that?   Whom did you see?

INDIRECT:

> Ich weiß nicht, **wer** das gesagt hat (**wen** Sie gesehen haben).
> I don't know who said that (whom you saw).

wo-compounds (interrogative)

2. If a form of the interrogative pronoun **was?** would be preceded by a preposition, a **wo**-compound (see Section B, above) MUST BE USED:

> **Womit** hast du das gemacht?
> With what did you do that?

Thus, in a question the **wo-** of a **wo**-compound is the equivalent of English *what*. The appropriate forms of **wer?**, on the other hand, are regularly used as objects of prepositions (since they refer to people, and not to things):

> *Mit* **wem** bist du fortgegangen?
> With whom did you leave?

wer and *was* with predicate nominative

3. If the nominative forms **wer?** or **was?** are used with the verb **sein** and a predicate nominative, the verb agrees in number with the predicate nominative:

> Wer **ist** *der Mann* da?
> Who is the man over there?

> Wer **sind** *die Männer* da?
> Who are the men over there?

welcher

4. The **der**-words **welcher, welche,** and **welches** (see Chapter 6, Section A, paragraph 2) can also be used as interrogative pronouns in the meaning of *which one* (of a given number of people or things):

> Ich habe zwei Brüder. **Welchen** meinen Sie?
> I have two brothers. Which one do you mean?

Special Points

Anticipatory *da*-compounds

1. If the object of a preposition is not a noun or a pronoun but rather an entire clause or an infinitive phrase, the preposition combines with **da-** (or **dar-**) to form a **da**-compound. This type of **da**-compound is most commonly found when the preposition is part of a verbal phrase, such as **denken an** (*to think of*), or **bestehen auf** (*to insist on*).

> Ich denke nicht **daran,** ihn zu besuchen.
> I wouldn't think of visiting him.

> Er besteht **darauf,** daß ich komme.
> He insists on my coming.

The **da-** in these compounds does not refer back to a noun, as it does when it serves as a substitute for a pronoun. Instead, it points ahead to a dependent clause or an infinitive phrase which is the real object of the preposition. Hence, these compounds are often called anticipatory **da**-compounds.

Translation of anticipatory *da*-compounds

2. Such da-compounds and their following clauses or infinitive phrases can usually be handled in English in one of the following ways:

(*a*) By translating the infinitive of an infinitive phrase or the verb of a daß-clause as a gerund when there is no English equivalent of the **da-** in the **da-**compound:

Ich könnte mich nie **daran** gewöhnen, nur einmal die Woche Fleisch zu essen.
I could never get used to *eating* meat only once a week.

Er hat mir **dafür** gedankt, daß ich ihm geholfen habe.
He thanked me for *helping* him.

Er wurde **dadurch** ein reicher Mann, daß er seine Kunden beschwindelte.
He became a rich man by *swindling* his customers.

(*b*) By translating the **da-** of the **da-**compound as *the fact* and rendering the following **daß-**clause as a *that-*clause in English:

Wir sprachen eben **darüber**, daß er nicht mitkommen will.
We were just talking about *the fact that* he does not want to come along.

Ich interessiere mich gar nicht **dafür**, daß er das Examen bestanden hat.
I am not at all interested in *the fact that* he passed the exam.

Note, however, that instead of using *the fact that* it is sometimes possible to ignore the **da-** and to use a gerund for the verb of the **daß-**clause, as in the first example: We were just talking about his not wanting to come along.

(*c*) By omitting the **da-**compound completely and translating the following **daß-**clause as a *that-*clause or an infinitive phrase as an infinitive phrase. This can only be done if the equivalent English verb in the introductory clause does not need an English preposition to complete the verbal idea:

Sie erinnerte mich **daran**, daß ich versprochen hatte, zu ihr zu kommen.
She reminded me that I had promised to come and see her.

Sie sehnen sich **danach**, eines Tages nach Deutschland zurückzukehren.
They are longing to go back to Germany some day.

(*d*) By translating only the preposition of the **da-**compound and then the following clause. This procedure can usually be followed when the dependent clause is the equivalent of an indirect question:

Ich habe lange **darüber** nachgedacht, was ich diesen Sommer tun soll.
I have thought for a long time about what I am to do this summer.

Ich interessiere mich gar nicht **dafür**, ob er kommt oder nicht.
I am not at all interested in whether he is coming or not.

Infinitive phrase or *daß*-clause?

3. For active use of such verbs with **da-**compounds, it should be observed that an infinitive phrase is called for if the performer of the action is the same as the subject of the introductory clause:

> Sie besteht **darauf,** ihn jeden Tag zu sehen.
>
> She insists on seeing him every day.

A **daß-**clause is used, on the other hand, if the performer of the action is not the same as the subject of the first clause:

> Sie besteht **darauf,** daß er sie jeden Tag besucht.
>
> She insists on his visiting her every day.

es anticipating the object

4. The pronoun **es** may be found as the object of some verbs when the actual object is an infinitive phrase or a **daß-**clause. Thus, the **es** anticipates the clause or phrase which follows. If an infinitive phrase is involved, there is no equivalent for **es:**

> Er liebt **es,** die ganze Nacht im Wirtshaus zu verbringen.
>
> He likes to spend the whole night at the inn.

If a **daß-**clause follows, **es** may be rendered by *the fact,* or it may be omitted and the verb translated by a gerund:

Seine Frau liebt **es** nicht, *daß* er den gazen Abend im Wirts-haus verbringt.	His wife doesn't like the fact that he spends (OR: his spending) the whole evening at the inn.

was . . . Gutes, was . . . alles

5. The interrogative **was** can be used with an adjective functioning as a noun. **was** is then always separated from the noun in question, but the two parts must be brought together in English:

> **Was** habt ihr heute *Gutes* zu essen gehabt?
>
> What good things did you have to eat today?

Especially common is the combination of **was** with **alles:**

> **Was** hast du heute *alles* getan?
>
> What are all the things you did today?
>
> (What all did you do today?)

Note also the idiomatic combination of **was** with **nicht alles:**

> **Was** du *nicht alles* sagst!
>
> You don't say!

RECOGNITION EXERCISES

A. *Translate:*

1. Viele haben ihr Leben für uns gegeben. Leider gedenken wir ihrer nur einmal im Jahr. 2. Auch wenn sie sich überhaupt nicht schämt, schämen wir uns ihrer doch um so mehr. 3. Ich habe es nicht seinetwegen, sondern ihretwegen getan. 4. Wenn er so etwas um unseretwillen getan hat, können wir seiner sicher sein. 5. Wo ist mein Freund? Haben Sie ihn gesehen? 6. Wo ist mein Photoapparat? Haben Sie ihn gefunden? 7. Wo ist meine Tinte? Hat jemand sie geborgt? 8. Wo ist meine Tante? Ist sie schon ausgegangen? 9. Gestern ist sie zu spät gekommen. 10. Gestern sind sie zu spät gekommen. 11. Gestern sind Sie zu spät gekommen. 12. Das ist das Bild von meiner Schwester. Kennen Sie sie? 13. Das ist das Bild von meinen Schwestern. Kennen Sie sie? 14. Das ist das Bild von meinen Schwestern. Kennen Sie es? 15. Ich habe eine Armbanduhr, aber sie geht nicht richtig. 16. Kinder, Tante Anna hat euch etwas mitgebracht. Habt ihr ihr dafür gedankt? 17. Ich kenne die Eltern schon, aber ihre Kinder kenne ich noch nicht. 18. Ich kenne die Mutter schon, aber ich habe ihre Kinder noch nie gesehen. 19. Wir haben eine nagelneue Schule, aber ihre Lehrer sind steinalt. 20. Mein Freund und ich studieren auf der Universität. Ich fahre jeden Morgen mit ihm in seinem Wagen dahin. 21. Das ist sein Wagen. Wir fahren damit zur Universität. 22. Ich arbeite mit meinem Kollegen an einem neuen Projekt. 23. Woran arbeiten Sie mit ihm? 24. Kennen Sie die kleine Kirche in der Ludwigstraße? Wir wohnen direkt daneben. 25. Ich bin mit seinem Plan zufrieden, aber mein Kollege ist dagegen. 26. Was hast du mit meinen Büchern gemacht? Ich habe nichts damit gemacht. 27. Die Leute, mit denen wir jetzt arbeiten, sind sehr nett. 28. Das ist eine Frage, worauf ich keine Antwort habe. 29. Das Buch, worüber er gesprochen hat, habe ich noch nicht gelesen. 30. Worüber wird er heute sprechen? 31. Über wen sprechen Sie jetzt? 32. Wessen Schwester ist sie? 33. Wem hat er das Buch gegeben? 34. Mit wem fährt er in die Berge? 35. Womit hat er die Schreibmaschine repariert?

B. *Translate:*

1. Ich habe nie daran gedacht, eine Reise nach Südamerika zu machen, nur meine Frau denkt manchmal daran. 2. Sie können sich darauf verlassen, daß er rechtzeitig kommt. 3. Ich bin nicht dafür verantwortlich, daß sie ihre Arbeiten nicht macht. 4. Mein Chef glaubt aber, daß ich doch dafür verantwortlich bin. 5. Der Lehrer besteht darauf, daß die Schüler ihre Hausaufgaben ohne die Hilfe ihrer Eltern machen. 6. Ich kann mich nicht daran gewöhnen, morgens meinen Regenschirm mitzunehmen. 7. Ein guter Chef besteht nicht darauf, alles selber zu machen. 8. Ich habe noch nicht darüber nachgedacht, ob ich dieses Problem überhaupt lösen kann. 9. Er interessiert sich gar nicht dafür, daß ich nächsten Sommer nach Deutschland fahre. 10. Sie interessiert sich nicht im geringsten dafür, was er von ihr hält. 11. Wir warten alle darauf, daß er einmal einen Fehler macht. 12. Er wartet nur darauf, eine passende

Gelegenheit für seine Bemerkung zu finden. 13. Ich sehne mich nach der Ruhe, die ich im Sommer auf dem Lande gehabt habe. 14. Sie sehnt sich danach, eines Tages ihr Heimatdorf wiedersehen zu können. 15. Das erinnert mich daran, daß ich vergessen habe, die Tür abzuschließen. 16. Was erinnert Sie daran? 17. Diese Entwicklung hat dazu geführt, daß wir die Politik der Regierung nicht mehr unterstützen können. 18. Worüber sprechen Sie? 19. Wir sprechen eben darüber, daß er sich in einer anderen Stadt eine bessere Stellung sucht. 20. Davon hatte ich nichts gehört. 21. Ich liebe es, einen ganzen Abend nur über Politik zu reden. 22. Meine Frau liebt es nicht, daß ich immer nur über Politik rede. 23. Was haben Sie heute Interessantes zu berichten? 24. Wir haben nichts Interessantes zu berichten. 25. Was hat sie heute alles in der Stadt gekauft? 26. Sie schätzt es nicht, daß ihr Mann jeden Abend vor dem Fernseher sitzt und sich nicht mit ihr unterhält.

ACTIVE EXERCISES

A. *Restate the following sentences, changing the personal pronouns to the plural:*
1. Ich weiß nicht, was ich tun soll. 2. Meine Mutter hat mir einen Kuchen mitgebracht. 3. Sie geht heute nicht ins Kino. 4. Du weißt nicht, was du sagst. 5. Der Polizist hat dich wohl nicht gehört? 6. Was hat mein Vater dir gegeben? 7. Der Briefträger hat ihm zwei Briefe gegeben. 8. Ich habe ihn heute nicht gesehen. 9. Geben Sie ihr die Bücher. 10. Kein Mensch kennt mich in dieser Stadt.

B. *Restate the following sentences, substituting the appropriate personal pronouns or da-compounds for the nouns and their modifiers:*
1. Ich kann dieses Buch nicht lesen. 2. Er hat einen neuen Roman gelesen. 3. Haben Sie diese Erzählung gelesen? 4. Ich fahre mit meiner Schwester. 5. Ich schreibe mit meiner Feder. 6. Er hat seinem Vater geholfen. 7. Er spricht gerade von seinem Bruder. 8. Sie spricht gerade von ihrem neuen Haus. 9. Meine Mutter kann heute nicht kommen. 10. Die Schreibmaschine muß repariert werden.

C. *Translate into German:*
1. I have a watch but I don't know what I have done with it.
2. My mother was ashamed of me because I did not help her.
3. The government and its officials do not pay any attention to (**hören auf**) the professors and their students.
4. Before dinner I was reading the newspaper, but now I can't find it.
5. She loves music, but I am not at all interested in it.
6. If she does not want to go with us, we shall go without her.
7. Who was the woman I saw with you yesterday?
8. Whom did you invite to the dance last evening?
9. I don't know whose pocketbook is lying on the sofa.

10. With whom are you going to the movies tomorrow?
11. What were you talking about when I arrived?
12. I don't know what he is waiting for.
13. I didn't intend to go home so early, but he insists on it.
14. They insist on visiting us once a week.
15. You can rely on his doing his assignments correctly.
16. I would like to forget what happened last summer, but she always reminds me of it.
17. She is already thinking of buying a more expensive car.
18. I hope we get the money. Without it we cannot take the trip.
19. Please bring me my pencil. It's on the table under the newspaper.
20. He would like to know on what she is working, but I don't know anything about it.

14

Demonstratives and Other Pronouns

A. Demonstratives

Demonstratives are words (used as adjectives or as pronouns) which either point out a person or a thing, or distinguish it from others: *That* line over there is the boundary. Not all applicants may go, only *those* who have tickets.

Definite article with demonstrative force

1. The forms of the definite article (see Chapter 6, Section A, paragraph 1) can be used demonstratively. In such instances, the form is stressed either by spacing or by italics and is to be translated as *that* (singular) or *those* (plural):

D a s Mädchen ist hübsch!   *Den* Mann kenne ich nicht!

That girl is pretty!   I don't know *that* man!

D i e Kinder, die nicht mitkommen wollen, dürfen zu Hause bleiben.

Those children who do not want to come along may stay home.

Demonstrative pronouns *der, die, das*

2. der, die, das, in addition to serving as articles and relative pronouns (see Chapter 4, paragraph 2), can be used as so-called demonstrative pronouns. They are then declined like the relative pronouns, except for slight deviations in the genitive plural:

NOM.	der	die	das	die
GEN.	dessen	deren	dessen	deren, derer
DAT.	dem	der	dem	denen
ACC.	den	die	den	die

Functions of demonstrative pronouns

3. These pronouns have three major functions:

(*a*) They are used as demonstratives, pointing out persons or things, and translated in English as *that, the one* (in the singular), and *those, the ones* (in the plural). They occur before genitives, prepositional phrases, and relative clauses:

BEFORE GENITIVES:

Seine Stimme habe ich nicht gehört, sondern **die** *seiner Frau.*

I didn't hear his voice but rather that of his wife (OR: his wife's).

BEFORE RELATIVE CLAUSES:

Ich kann nur **die** brauchen, *die richtig arbeiten wollen.*

I can use only those who really want to work.

BEFORE PREPOSITIONAL PHRASES:

„Welche Frau meinst du?" „**Die** *im roten Kleid.*"

"Which woman do you mean?" "The one with the red dress."

Note. (1) The genitive plural form **derer** may be encountered in all three demonstrative situations described above, but it is invariably used for persons when a relative clause follows:

Ich habe die Telephonnummer **derer,** *die mitarbeiten wollen.*

I have the phone number of those who wish to participate.

(2) The demonstrative adjectives **derjenige, diejenige, dasjenige** may be found as pronouns replacing **der, die, das**-forms in all three uses above, except that they carry unusual emphasis if they precede a prepositional phrase:

Seine Stimme habe ich nicht gehört, sondern **diejenige** seiner Frau.

Ich kann nur **diejenigen** brauchen, die richtig arbeiten wollen.

„Welche Frau meinst du?" „**Diejenige** im roten Kleid."

der for personal pronouns

(*b*) The demonstrative pronouns are used as emphatic replacements for the personal pronouns. English normally requires the personal pronoun in such cases:

Wer hat das gesagt? Otto? **Der** (FOR: Er) hat doch die komischsten Ideen!

Who said that? Otto? **He** really has the oddest ideas!

Kennst du Marie? **Die** (FOR: **Sie**) würde so etwas nicht tun.

Do you know Marie? **She** wouldn't do such a thing.

deren, dessen

Note. The genitive forms in this function are rarely used to refer to people, but they are fairly common if the antecedent is a thing or something indefinite:

Eine solche Auszeichnung bekommt nicht jeder. Man muß sich **deren** erst würdig zeigen.	Not everybody gets such a distinction. One first has to prove himself worthy of it.
Er war die ganze Woche nicht zu Hause, aber ich war mir **dessen** nicht bewußt.	He was not at home all week, but I wasn't aware of it.

Caution. Since commas are frequently used in German to separate two main clauses, one must be careful not to confuse a demonstrative substitute for a personal pronoun with a relative pronoun. Compare the following:

DEMONSTRATIVE:

Wir haben gute Kinder, **die** sind immer gehorsam.

We have good children. They are always obedient.

RELATIVE:

Wir haben gute Kinder, **die** immer gehorsam sind.

We have good children who are always obedient.

Note that in the relative clause the verb is at the end, while the clause beginning with the demonstrative pronoun has the verb in second position.

deren, dessen for possessive adjective

(c) The genitive forms **dessen** and **deren** are used as substitutes for the possessive adjectives **sein** (*his, its, one's*) and **ihr** (*her, their*), usually to avoid ambiguity. **sein** and **ihr** generally refer to the subject of the sentence, while **dessen** or **deren** refer to some other antecedent in the same or in a preceding clause. Compare the following two sentences:

Sie ging mit der alten Dame und **ihrer** Tochter.

She went with the old lady and her (own) daughter (REFERRING TO *she*)

Sie ging mit der alten Dame und **deren** Tochter.

She went with the old lady and her (i.e., the latter's, the old lady's) daughter.

das ist

4. Of special importance is the demonstrative construction **das ist** (*that is*). The form **das** here does not change to agree with the gender or number of the predicate nominative to which it points:

Das ist mein Freund.	**Das** ist meine Frau.	**Das** ist mein Buch.
That is my friend.	That is my wife.	That is my book.

If the predicate nominative is in the plural, the form of the verb **sein** must also be in the plural, but—unlike English—the demonstrative remains in the singular:

Das *sind* meine Bücher.	**Das** *sind* meine Freunde.
Those are my books.	Those are my friends.

Observe that **dies** (*this*, the contracted form of **dieses**) may be similarly used:

Dies *ist* meine Familie.	**Dies** *sind* meine Freunde.
This is my family.	These are my friends.

Demonstratives: *dieser and jener*

5. The demonstratives **dieser** (*this, these*) and **jener** (*that, those*) are used commonly when persons or things are being explicitly distinguished one from the other (for the declension, see Chapter 6, Section A, paragraph 2):

Diesen Jungen kenne ich, aber **jenes** Mädchen habe ich noch nie gesehen.
I know this boy but I have never seen that girl.

Diese Bücher habe ich schon gelesen, **jene** Zeitschriften aber nicht.
I have already read these books, but not those magazines.

If, however, a specific contrast between *this* and *that* is not implied, German prefers to use **dieser** instead of **jener,** even though the English equivalent is *that*. Thus, the **dieser** in the following sentence has two possible English versions:

Dieser Mann ärgert mich zu Tode!
This (or: that) man annoys me to death.

dieser, jener as pronouns

6. Like all the **der**-words (see Section B, below), **dieser** and **jener** can also function as pronouns. As such, they have the same forms as when used adjectivally (i.e. preceding nouns), and, of course, they must agree with their antecedents in gender and number. The English equivalents

of these pronouns are *this one* and *these* for **dieser** and *that one* and *those* for **jener**:

> Dieses Auto gehört mir, aber **jenes** (gehört) meinem Bruder.
> This car belongs to me, but that one belongs to my brother.

> Jene Linie dort is krumm, aber **diese** hier ist gerade.
> That line over there is crooked but this here is straight.

7. The pronouns **dieser** und **jener** are frequently equal to English *the latter* (**dieser**) and *the former* (**jener**):

Ohne es zu ahnen, frühstückten eines Morgens ein Advokat und seine neue Sekretärin zusammen im selben Restaurant. **Diese** saß vorne am Fenster, während **jener** sich im Hintergrund in der Nähe der Küchentür aufhielt.

Without knowing it, a lawyer and his new secretary were having breakfast one morning together in the same restaurant. The latter (OR: she) was sitting up front by the window, while the former (OR: he) was in the rear next to the kitchen door.

B. Some Other Pronouns

Other der-words as pronouns

1. In addition to **dieser** and **jener**, the remaining **der**-words **jeder, mancher, solcher,** and **welcher** can function as pronouns. The use of **welcher** was explained in Chapter 13, Section C, paragraph 4. The following points should be noted about the other **der**-words:

(*a*) **jeder,** as a pronoun, usually means *everyone* or *everybody*:

> **Jeder** mag kleine Kinder.
> Everybody likes little children.

Sometimes it may have the sense of *anybody* or *anyone:*

> **Jeder** könnte das sagen, aber nicht **jeder** würde es tun.
> Anybody could say that but not everybody would (do it).

alle, the irregular plural of **jeder,** is also used pronominally:

Wieviele Kinder gehen heute ins Kino? **Alle** (gehen).
How many children are going to the movies today? All (of them) are going.

The expression **ein jeder** is occasionally encountered as a substitute for **jeder:**

> **Ein jeder** kann das tun.
> Anybody can do that.

Observe, however, that in this construction **jeder** no longer has the endings of a **der**-word but acts like an adjective preceded by **ein** (see Chapter 7, Section A, paragraph 1*b*):

> Das kann man nicht **einem jed**en sagen.
> One can't say that to everyone.

(*b*) **mancher,** as a pronoun referring to people, can be translated as *many a man* (or *many a person*):

> Ich kenne **manchen,** der das auch gesagt haben könnte.
> I know many a person who could have said that also.

Instead of the pronoun form **mancher,** the phrase **manch einer** can be used. The first part of it is not declined, and **einer** has the ending of **ein** as a pronoun (see paragraph 2 below):

> **Mancher** (**Manch einer**) würde das nicht tun, ich aber doch.
> Many a man would not do it but I would.

For the plural forms, *some people* is the English equivalent:

> **Manche** mögen ihn, ich aber nicht.
> Some people like him but I don't.

The neuter singular forms of **mancher** as a pronoun are used to express the idea of *some things:*

> Wir haben dir **manches** zu erzählen.   In **manchem** hat sie recht.
> We have some things to tell you.   She is right in some things.

(*c*) **solcher,** in the singular, when referring to persons, is not used by itself as a pronoun. It must be preceded by **ein,** and it then functions like an adjective following an **ein**-word (like **ein jeder,** above). The meaning is *such a man* or *such a person:*

> **Ein solcher** würde nie den Mut dazu haben.
> Such a man would never have the courage for that.

As in the case of **mancher** and **manch einer,** the form **solch einer** (and the shorter and more colloquial **so einer**) will occur instead of the pronoun **ein solcher,** while again only **einer** is declined:

> **So einem** (**Solch einem**) gebe ich nichts.
> I won't give anything to such a person.

In the plural, however, the pronoun **solche** can stand by itself, meaning *such people, such things;* in English the noun referred to may have to be repeated:

Schmidts haben wirklich gute Freunde. **Solche** haben wir nicht!
The Schmidts really have good friends. We don't have such (friends).

Woher hast du die Blumen? Ich habe nie **solche** gesehen.
Where did you get the flowers? I have never seen such (flowers).

The neuter singular forms, on the other hand, are used without a preceding **ein** in the sense of *such a thing:*

> **Solches** (MORE COLLOQUIAL: **So etwas**) ist schwer zu verstehen.
> Such a thing is hard to understand.

ein-words as pronouns

2. The **ein**-words (**ein, kein,** and the possessive adjectives **mein, dein, sein, ihr, unser, euer, ihr,** and **Ihr**—see Chapter 6, Section A, paragraph 3) can be used as pronouns. THEY THEN HAVE THE SAME ENDINGS AS THE der-WORDS. Thus, the three forms which have no endings when used with nouns, have endings for the corresponding pronouns:

	M.	F.	N.	PL.
NOM.	keiner	keine	keines (keins)	keine
GEN.	keines	keiner	keines	keiner
DAT.	keinem	keiner	keinem	keinen
ACC.	keinen	keine	keines (keins)	keine

Note that the neuter nominative and accusative singular commonly drop the **e** of the ending **–es.**

einer, keiner

3. **ein** and **kein** as pronouns are the equivalent of English *one* and *none* (or: *not any*):

> Ich habe viele Bücher darüber gelesen, nicht nur **eins.**
> I have read many books about that, not only one.

> Er hat zwei Fische mitgebracht aber **keinen** selbst gefangen.
> He brought two fish along but did not catch any of them himself.

Note that **einer** and **keiner** can be used in the indefinite sense of *someone* and *no one:*

> **Einer** wird kommen, aber ich weiß noch nicht wer.
> Someone will come but I don't know yet who.

> **Keiner** kann eine solche Suppe essen!
> No one can eat such a soup.

meiner

4. As pronouns, the possessives have the following English equivalents:

mein—*mine;* **dein**—*yours;* **sein**—*his, its;* **ihr**—*hers, theirs;* **unser**—*ours;*
euer—*yours;* **Ihr**—*yours:*

> Meine Mutter ist schon zu Hause, aber **deine** ist noch in der Stadt.
> My mother is already at home but yours is still downtown.

> Hier ist mein Koffer, aber wo ist **deiner?**
> Here is my suitcase but where is yours?

> Dies ist sein Buch. Wo finde ich **ihrs?**
> This is his book. Where can I find hers?

Caution.   The possessive pronoun will be found without an ending if it is
a predicate nominative indicating the idea of ownership:

| Dieses Haus ist **mein.** | Dieser Platz ist **dein.** | Diese Flasche ist **sein.** |
| This house is mine. | This seat is yours. | This bottle is his. |

But if the subject of the sentence is **dies** or **das,** the possessive pronoun
as predicate nominative must have endings:

> Wessen Bücher liegen da auf dem   Whose books are lying there on the
>   Tisch? **Dies** ist mein*s* und **das**   table? This is mine and that is
>   ist sein*s*.   his.

Note.   (1) The idea of ownership, however, is more commonly expressed
with the verb **gehören** (*to belong to*):

> Dieses Buch gehört mir.
> This book is mine (belongs to me).

(2) If the predicate nominative expresses the idea of identity with the
subject (and NOT ownership), the possessive pronoun does have endings:

> Dein Wunsch ist auch **meiner.**
> Your wish is also mine.

der meine, der Meinige

5. In addition to the simple possessive pronouns **meiner, deiner,** etc.,
German has two further sets of possessive pronouns: **der meine, die
meine, das meine,** and (rather formal!) **der Meinige, die Meinige, das
Meinige.** The first element of both types is declined like the definite
article, while the second part has the endings of an adjective preceded
by the definite article (see Chapter 7, Section A, paragraph 1*a*). The
English equivalents are the same as for **meiner, meine, meins:**

> Wo ist Ihr Glas? **Das meine** (OR **Das**   Where is your glass? Mine is here and
>   Meinige, OR: **Meins**) ist hier und   his is on the table.
>   das seine (OR: das Seinige, OR
>   seins) steht auf dem Tisch.

Note. According to current usage the forms corresponding to **Meinige** are capitalized, while the other possessive pronouns are not. Uncapitalized forms of **Meinige,** however, will be encountered in older printing.

6. In the plural, both these sets of possessive pronouns can be used without antecedents in the special meaning of one's family, friends, or associates. In such instances, **meine** is also capitalized:

> Er schreibt **den Seinen** (OR: **den Seinigen**) einen Brief.
> He is writing a letter to his family.

RECOGNITION EXERCISES

A. *Translate:*

1. Ich bin abends meistens zu Hause, aber an dem [that] Abend mußte ich leider ausgehen. 2. D e n Film möchte ich nicht noch einmal sehen. 3. Nur d i e Leute, die vor sieben Uhr kommen, werden hereingelassen. 4. Der Wein ist ausgezeichnet! 5. Wir sprechen nicht von seinem Aufsatz, sondern von dem seines Kollegen. 6. Das Rezept meiner Mutter für saure Gurken ist gut, aber das meiner Frau ist noch besser. 7. Wir interessieren uns nicht nur für die Werke Johann Sebastian Bachs, sondern auch für die seines Sohnes C. P. E. Bach. 8. Kennen Sie diese Frauen? Die im roten Kleid ist meine Freundin, aber die mit den blonden Haaren habe ich noch nie gesehen. 9. Der Mann neben meinem Vater ist mein Onkel, aber der am Fenster ist mir unbekannt. 10. Alle Freunde kann ich diesmal nicht besuchen, nur die, die ich seit langem nicht gesehen habe. 11. Die Polizei verlangt nur von denen eine Aufenthalts-erlaubnis, die länger als drei Monate im Lande bleiben. 12. Wir haben schon die Namen derer, die uns helfen wollen. 13. Sie hat eine hübsche Figur, aber diejenige ihrer Schwester sollten Sie sehen! 14. Ich mag alle seine Töchter, aber die mit den blauen Augen gefällt mir am besten. 15. Wir wollen nicht alle seine Bücher kaufen, nur diejenigen, die wir brauchen können. 16. Ich kenne Anna, die würde so etwas nicht sagen. 17. Wir kennen Fritz, mit dem kann man nichts machen. 18. Meinen Sie Hans Schmidt? Ja, der ist ein guter Freund von mir. 19. Elisabeth ist eine tüchtige Frau. Auf die können Sie sich verlassen. 20. Man hat ihm eine große Ehre erwiesen. Meiner Meinung nach ist er deren nicht würdig. 21. Heute kommt er bestimmt rechtzeitig an, dessen können Sie sicher sein. 22. Wir haben faule Studenten, die machen ihre Auf-gaben immer schlecht. 23. Wir haben faule Studenten, die ihre Aufgaben immer schlecht machen. 24. Wir kennen solche Leute nur zu gut, die wollen einem nie helfen.

B. *Translate:*

1. Fritz ist mit seinem alten Lehrer und seiner Schwester in die Oper gegangen. 2. Er ist mit seinem alten Lehrer und dessen Schwester ins Theater gegangen. 3. Sie ist nicht nur von ihrer Familie, sondern auch von ihren

Freunden enttäuscht. 4. Sie ist nicht nur von ihrer Familie, sondern auch von deren Freunden enttäuscht. 5. Er mag die Frau, deren Tochter aber kann er nicht leiden. 6. Sie mag die Frau, deren Tochter jetzt mit ihrer eigenen Tochter spielt. 7. Dies ist meine Schwester, und das sind meine Brüder. 8. Dieser Wagen gehört meinem Vater, aber jener dort vor der Garage gehört meiner Schwester. 9. Obwohl er sehr nett zu mir ist, kann ich diesen Mann nicht ausstehen. 10. Jenes Radio muß repariert werden, aber dieses hier funktioniert tadellos. 11. Er hat zwei Söhne, Fritz und Richard. Dieser, der in München studiert hat und jetzt Arzt ist, wohnt in Berlin, während jener Rechtsanwalt in München ist. 12. Nicht jeder liest solche Geschichten gern. 13. Jeder, der sich nur ein wenig Mühe gibt, kann so etwas verstehen. 14. Alle außer ihm können das verstehen. 15. Ein jeder kann das lernen, aber nur wenige tun es. 16. Das kann man nicht einem jeden beibringen. 17. Wir kennen manchen, der das versucht hat, aber keinen, dem es gelungen ist. 18. Ich mag ihn gern, aber manchem gefällt er nicht. 19. Er weiß nicht sehr viel davon, aber in manchem hat er recht. 20. Wir haben Ihnen vieles zu erzählen, aber manches wird Ihnen nicht gefallen. 21. Ich habe zwei niedrige Stühle in meinem Zimmer. Würde Ihnen ein solcher helfen? 22. Leider kann man so einen nicht mehr kaufen. 23. Wir haben drei Kandidaten für diese Position, aber keiner ist wirklich ausgezeichnet. 24. Keiner kann dieses Gedicht verstehen. 25. Eines Tages wird einer kommen, der dieses Rätsel lösen kann. 26. Sein Paket ist schon angekommen. Ich erwarte das meine morgen. 27. Wir haben seine Bücher schon gefunden, aber keiner weiß, wo die Unsrigen sind. 28. Er ist bereit, den Seinen mit allen Mitteln zu helfen.

ACTIVE EXERCISES

A. *Complete the following sentences by supplying the correct German for the English in parentheses:*

1. (That) Junge ist intelligent! 2. (This) Mann kennen wir nicht. 3. (That) Frau ist aber reizend! 4. Kennen Sie (this) Frau? Welche? (The one) im blauen Kleid. 5. (Which) Mann ist Ihr Vater? (The one) im grünen Anzug. 6. Er mag nur (those), die ihn mögen. 7. Ich brauche die Adressen (of those), die mitkommen wollen. 8. Kennen Sie Hans Schultz? Nein, (him) kenne ich nicht. 9. Robert hat das gesagt? (He) ist wohl verrückt! 10. Ich bin (of it) sicher. 11. Wir kennen solche Leute, (they) wollen nie arbeiten. 12. Ich kenne Menschen, (who) nie arbeiten wollen. 13. Er ging mit seinem Freund und (his own) Bruder. 14. Sie ging mit ihrer Freundin und (the latter's) Bruder. 15. (That) ist mein Buch. 16. (Those) sind seine Sachen. 17. (This) ist meine Freundin. 18. (This) ist mein Mantel. Wo ist (his)? 19. (These) sind meine Bücher. (His) liegen auf dem Schreibtisch. 20. (This) Junge ist mein Bruder, aber (that one) kenne ich nicht. 21. (Everyone) mag dieses Kind. 22. Ich kenne (no one), der das kann. 23. Wir kennen (many a person), der das nicht kann. 24. (Someone) wird die Bücher mitbringen. 25. Mein Vater ist in seinem Büro. Wo ist (yours)?

B. *Translate into German:*

1. One does not meet such a person (*use pronoun!*) every day.
2. Here are my shoes, but I can't find hers.
3. No one knows where my book is. Can you lend me yours?
4. We don't know anyone who can help you.
5. Many a person (*use pronoun*) has tried to answer that question.
6. Everyone likes children who are polite.
7. Anyone can play this game, but not everyone can win.
8. She has two brothers, Robert, who lives in New York, and Richard, who works in Boston. The former is a doctor, the latter a well-known lawyer.
9. I have never seen that hat, but this coat belongs to me.
10. That child always disturbs me when I want to read.
11. I would like to buy this book, not that one.
12. This is my brother, and those are his friends.
13. The old woman met her daughter and her (the latter's) friend on the street.
14. They gave her a prize? She isn't worthy of it.
15. I did not read his essay (**die Arbeit**), only his sister's (*that of his sister*).
16. I know this woman, but who is the one with the blond hair?
17. Those who don't want to go along may stay here and wait for us.
18. *That* woman is very charming. I would like to know *her* better.
19. Give me the names of those who will be home this summer.
20. Did Marie say that? *She* is really not very intelligent!

PART III

Conjugation

15

Simple Tenses

German verbs fall into two main categories (i.e., conjugations): weak and strong. Weak verbs use the suffix –t to form the past tense and the past participle without changing their stem vowels, while strong verbs change their stem vowels in the past and in the past participle according to a fixed pattern of sound changes (**Ablaut**). The complete list of strong verbs (preceding the Vocabularies) will give their principal parts, and hence the vowel changes required. In addition, there is a small group of verbs which combine the two principles of verb formation: the irregular weak verbs (also precede Vocabularies).

Except for the weak verbs in **–ieren** (such as **stud–ieren, ras–ieren**), it is impossible to determine whether a verb is weak, strong, or irregular weak merely by examining the infinitive. Since there are many more weak than strong and irregular weak verbs, the best way of identifying weak verbs is by elimination, i.e., by being thoroughly familiar with the strong and irregular weak verbs. (In order to assure this familiarity, each set of exercises from now on will include a list of selected strong verbs for memorization.)

A. Present Tense

Formation

1. The endings for the present tense of weak, strong, and irregular weak verbs are attached to the stem of the verb (= infinitive less infinitive ending). They are:

(ich steh)–e	(wir steh)–en
(du steh)–st	(ihr steh)–t
(er steh)–t	(sie steh)–en

Since **haben, sein,** and **werden** show several irregularities, their present tense forms should be carefully committed to memory:

ich habe	wir haben	ich bin	wir sind	ich werde	wir werden
du hast	ihr habt	du bist	ihr seid	du wirst	ihr werdet
er hat	sie haben	er ist	sie sind	er wird	sie werden

Note also the irregular present tense form of **wissen** (*to know*) in the singular: **ich weiß, du weißt, er weiß.**

Forms of address

2. German has two forms for address, the familiar and the polite: **du** (singular) and **ihr** (plural) are used in familiar address, **Sie** (both singular and plural, always capitalized) in polite. In form, the polite **Sie** is the same as the third person plural.

The familiar forms are generally used where a personal or intimate relationship exists, i.e., in speaking to relatives, close friends, children, animals, and to God. Otherwise (and always, in case of doubt!) use **Sie.**

Hast **du** das Buch gelesen, Fritz?   Kennen **Sie** dieses Buch, Herr Mann?
Did you read the book, Fritz?   Do you know this book, Mr. Mann?

Herr, erbarme **dich** unser!   Mutter, was hast **du** mit dem Hemd gemacht?
Lord, have mercy on us.   Mother, what did you do with the shirt?

Stem changes in the present

3. Some STRONG VERBS CHANGE THEIR STEM VOWELS IN THE SECOND AND THIRD PERSON SINGULAR OF THE PRESENT TENSE:

(*a*) Most strong verbs with the stem vowel **a** or **au** change this stem vowel to **ä** or **äu:**

> **fallen** (*to fall*): ich falle, du fällst, er fällt
> **laufen** (*to run*): ich laufe, du läufst, er läuft

Similarly, the **o** is changed to **ö** in **stoßen** (to push):

> ich stoße, du stößt, er stößt

(*b*) Most strong verbs with the stem vowel **e** change this **e** to **i** or **ie** in the second and third person singular. Normally, long **ē** changes to **ie,** and short **ĕ** to **i,** but there are a few cases in which the vowel is long in the infinitive and short in the two present-tense forms involved:

LONG **ē** TO **ie:**

> **sehen** (*to see*): ich sehe, du siehst, er sieht

Similarly: **befehlen** (*to command*), **empfehlen** (*to recommend*), **geschehen** (*to happen*), and **lesen** (*to read*).

But:

> **geben** (*to give*): ich gebe, du gibst, er gibt
> **nehmen** (*to take*): ich nehme, du nimmst,* er nimmt *
> **treten** (*to step, kick*): ich trete, du trittst,* er tritt *
> **werden** (*to become*): ich werde, du wirst,* er wird

Short ĕ to i:

> **essen** (*to eat*): ich esse, du ißt, er ißt
> **sterben** (*to die*): ich sterbe, du stirbst, er stirbt

Caution. The common verbs **gehen** (*to go*), **genesen** (*to recover*), **heben** (*to lift, raise*), **stecken** (colloquially, in the sense of *to be*), and **stehen** (*to stand*) do not change the stem vowel in these forms; thus: **du gehst, er geht, . . .**

Insertion of –e–

4. An **e** is inserted between the stem of a verb and the endings **-st** and **-t,** if the stem ends in **d, t,** or a succession of consonants:

Weak verbs:

> **antworten:** du antwort–e–st, er antwort–e–t, ihr antwort–et
> **öffnen:** du öffn–e–st, er öffn–e–t, ihr öffn–e–t

Strong verbs:

> **finden:** du find–e–st, er find–e–t, ihr find–e–t

Caution. Some strong verbs, such as **halten** (*to hold*), **gelten** (*to be valid*), **raten** (*to guess, advise*), and **treten** (*to step*), which have stems ending in **t,** do not insert this **e** in the singular, only in the plural. They have no ending in the third person singular:

Singular:

> ich halt–e, du hält–st, er hält

Plural:

> wir halt–en, ihr halt–e–t, sie halt–en

Omission of s

5. The **s** in the ending of the second person singular is omitted if the stem ends in a sibilant (s-sound), except in the case of **sch:**

Weak verbs:

> **hassen** (*to hate*): du haß–t

Strong verbs:

> **stoßen** (*to push*): du stöß–t

* Note the irregularities in spelling.

but:

> löschen (*to extinguish*): du lösch–st

Thus, in these verbs the second and third persons singular are identical: **du haß–t, er haß–t; du stöß–t, er stöß–t.**

Verbs in –*el*, –*er*

6. Polysyllabic weak verbs which have the word accent on the first syllable and end in –**el** or –**er** drop the **e** of the ending –**en**:

> **wandern** (*to hike*): wir wander–n, sie wander–n
> **lächeln** (*to smile*): wir lächel–n, sie lächel–n

The strong verb **tun** (*to do*) also drops this **e**: **wir tun, sie tun.**

Uses of present tense

7. The present tense in German is essentially used as in English. Note, however, that German does not have (in any tense!) either a progressive or an emphatic form. Thus, depending on the context, **er kommt** may mean: *he comes, he is coming,* or *he does come:*

> Er **kommt** jeden Tag um ein Uhr.
> He **comes** everyday at one o'clock.

> **Kommt** er? Ja, er **kommt,** ich sehe ihn schon.
> **Is** he **coming?** Yes, he **is coming,** I (can) see him already.

> **Kommt** er oft? Nein, er **kommt** nicht oft, nur einmal die Woche.
> **Does** he **come** often? No, he **does** not **come** often, only once a week.

Present tense for future

8. The present tense is usually used to refer to the future if it is clear from the context that futurity is implied:

> Morgen **esse** ich in der Stadt.
> Tomorrow I shall eat (am eating, am going to eat) downtown.

It must be used, however, in the **wenn**-clause of a factual (real) condition (see Chapter 18, Section A) which refers to the future:

> Wenn Sie sein Gesicht **sehen,** werden Sie sich wundern.
> When (if) you see his face you'll be surprised.

Present for action begun in past

9. In German, the present tense is employed, usually together with the adverb **schon** (where English uses the present perfect), to indicate an action or a condition which began in the past but is still going on or existing in the present:

Ich **bin schon** seit zwei Monaten hier.

I have been here for two months.

Er **ist schon** ein ganzes Jahr in Europa.

He has been in Europe for a whole year.

Note that the time element can be expressed either as the object of the preposition **seit,** or in the accusative without a preposition. In a negative statement of this kind, on the other hand, German also uses the present perfect:

Er **ist** schon seit zwei Monaten nicht hier **gewesen.**

He hasn't been here for two months.

Historical present

10. In narration, the present tense is frequently found instead of the past to indicate the narrator's feeling of closeness to, or identification with, the events related, as if they were still very much present in his imagination. This is especially so when there is a sudden switch from the past tense to the present, as can be seen clearly in the following example from Stefan Zweig's "Der Amokläufer":

So **saß** ich damals . . . über einem Atlas und **träumte** mir Reisen aus. Da **klopft** es aufgeregt an die Tür, der Boy **steht** draußen.

So I was sitting there then . . . over an atlas, dreaming about trips, when there was an excited knocking at the door. My servant was standing outside.

B. Past Tense

Formation

1. The past tense of weak verbs is formed by first adding the suffix **t** to the stem, and then the endings:

(ich wohn)–t–e	(wir wohn)–t–en
(du wohn)–t–est	(ihr wohn)–t–et
(er wohn)–t–e	(sie wohn)–t–en

Caution. Note the different endings for the third person singular in the present and past tenses (present tense, **–t;** past tense, **–te**).

Formation of strong verbs

2. The past tense of strong verbs is formed by using the past stem and adding to it the following endings:

(ich sprach)–	(wir sprach)–en
(du sprach)–st	(ihr sprach)–t
(er sprach)–	(sie sprach)–en

Caution. Note that the forms for the first and third persons singular have no endings. The past stems, if not known, will have to be looked up in a dictionary or in the list of strong verbs in the Appendix.

haben, sein, werden

3. The past-tense forms of **haben, sein,** and **werden** are somewhat irregular:

ich hatte	ich war	ich wurde (ward)
du hattest	du warst	du wurdest (wardst)
er hatte	er war	er wurde (ward)
wir hatten	wir waren	wir wurden
ihr hattet	ihr wart	ihr wurdet
sie hatten	sie waren	sie wurden

The forms **ward, wardst,** and **ward** are old forms no longer used in colloquial German, but they will be found in writers with a conservative approach to style.

Irregular weak verbs

4. The irregular weak verbs **brennen** (*to burn*), **kennen** (*to know, be familiar with*), **nennen** (*to call*), **rennen** (*to run*), **senden** (*to send*), and **wenden** (*to turn*) form their past tense (and their past participle) like weak verbs, except that they also change their stem vowel to **a**:

brennen:	brannte (PAST PARTICIPLE: gebrannt)
senden:	sandte (PAST PARTICIPLE: gesandt)

The irregular weak verbs **bringen** (*to bring, take to*) and **denken** (*to think*) show, in addition to this vowel change, a change in consonant:

bringen:	brachte (PAST PARTICIPLE: gebracht)
denken:	dachte (PAST PARTICIPLE: gedacht)

Caution. senden and wenden also have regular weak forms for the past tense (and the past participle): **sendete, gesendet; wendete, gewendet.**

wissen and kennen

5. The verb **wissen** (*to know*) also acts like an irregular weak verb, but it changes its stem vowel to **u** in the past tense (and in the past participle):

wissen: wußte (PAST PARTICIPLE: gewußt)

Note that there are two verbs in German meaning *to know:* **wissen** and **kennen:**

(a) **kennen** is *to know* in the sense of *to be familiar* (or *acquainted*) *with;* it can only be followed by an object, NOT by a dependent clause:

> Ich **kenne** diese Leute nicht.
> I don't know these people.

(*b*) **wissen** is *to know* in the sense of *to be aware of* or *to have knowledge of;* it may take an object (usually a pronoun) or be followed by a dependent clause:

Ich **weiß** *das* nicht.	Wir **wissen** nicht, *wer er ist.*
I don't know that.	We don't know who he is.

Uses of past tense

6. The past tense is primarily used for narration and description in the past (as it is also in English). In German, however, it is predominantly literary in flavor:

Es **war** einmal mitten im Winter, und die Schneeflocken **fielen** wie Federn vom Himmel herab, da **saß** eine Königin an einem Fenster, das einen Rahmen von schwarzem Ebenholz **hatte**, und **nähte**. Und wie sie so **nähte** und nach dem Schnee **aufblickte, stach** sie sich mit der Nadel in den Finger, und es **fielen** drei Tropfen Blut in den Schnee.*	Once upon a time, in the middle of winter when the snow was falling like feathers from the sky, a queen was sitting and sewing at a window which had a frame of black ebony. And as she sewed and looked at the snow, she pricked her finger with a needle and three drops of blood fell into the snow.

German past for English past perfect

7. The past tense is ordinarily used (where English requires the past perfect) to denote an action or a state which was already in progress or in existence when another one occurred:

> Er **war** schon lange da, als wir ins Hotel kamen.
> He had been there a long time when we came into the hotel.

8. For a discussion of the use of the past tense in contrast to that of the present perfect, see the next chapter.

Special Points

Omission of ending —e

1. The verbal ending —e is frequently dropped in the present tense

---

* Grimm, *Fairy Tales:* the beginning of "Snow White."

(ich geh', wir stehn, sie sehn) and, in the case of weak verbs, also in the past. An apostrophe sometimes, especially in older editions of books, points out such an omission:

Was damals die Leute „Ut der Welt" erzählten, **sucht** ich mir fleißig zu merken, doch **wußt** ich leider zu wenig, um zu wissen, was wissenschaftlich bemerkenswert wäre.°	What the people at that time told about the world I tried to remember as best I could, but unfortunately I knew too little to know what was scientifically noteworthy.

False strong verb forms

2. Some weak verbs (especially **fragen**) will occasionally be found to have also strong forms: **er frägt** (for: **er fragt**), **er frug** (for: **er fragte**). These forms are incorrect, but they were (and still are) in wide use even with good writers (particularly in Northern Germany).

RECOGNITION EXERCISES

A. *Review the principal parts of strong verbs. Memorize carefully before doing any of the following exercises:*

INFINITIVE	THIRD PERSON SINGULAR PRESENT	PAST	PAST PARTICIPLE	ENGLISH
bleiben		blieb	(ist) geblieben	to remain
brechen	bricht	brach	gebrochen	to break
essen	ißt	aß	gegessen	to eat
gehen		ging	(ist) gegangen	to go
kommen		kam	(ist) gekommen	to come
lassen	läßt	ließ	gelassen	to leave, let
lesen	liest	las	gelesen	to read
liegen		lag	gelegen	to lie
rufen		rief	gerufen	to call
schweigen		schwieg	geschwiegen	to be silent
sitzen		saß	gesessen	to sit
sprechen	spricht	sprach	gesprochen	to speak
stehen		stand	gestanden	to stand
treten	tritt	trat	(ist) getreten	to step

B. *Translate, distinguishing carefully between past and present tenses:*

1. Sie singen, wenn sie einen Spaziergang machen. 2. Sie gingen im Walde spazieren. 3. Am Sonntag brachen wir früh auf. 4. Am Sonntag wachen wir

° Wilhelm Busch, from an autobiographical essay.

nicht so früh auf. 5. Sie bangen um ihr Leben. 6. Die Bettler sangen und standen da mit dem Hut in der Hand. 7. Sie passen nie auf, wenn ich etwas sage. 8. Sie saßen vor dem Hotel, als ich vorbeikam. 9. Wir schwiegen immer in seiner Gegenwart. 10. Wir wiegen immer zu viel, wenn wir zum Arzt gehen. 11. Wir sagen Ihnen die Wahrheit: sie lagen noch im Bett, als wir sie morgens um elf Uhr besuchten. 12. Wir warten auf euch. 13. Wir warteten auf euch. 14. Wartet ihr auf uns? 15. Wo wart ihr letzten Sommer? 16. Er liest die Zeitung im Wohnzimmer. 17. Ihr ließt die Zeitung im Wohnzimmer liegen. 18. Sie lasen die Bücher in der Bibliothek. 19. Sie lassen die Bücher in der Bibliothek. 20. Er antwortet uns nicht. 21. Er antwortete ihr nicht. 22. Warum antwortet ihr uns nicht? 23. Ihr antwortetet mir nicht, Kinder. 24. Sie bleiben oft stundenlang in ihrem Zimmer. 25. Sie blieben oft stundenlang in der Bibliothek. 26. Sie lieben es nicht, daß wir so oft ins Kino gehen. 27. Ihm fließen die Tränen über das Gesicht. 28. Sie ließen uns bald danach nach Hause gehen.

C. *Translate, paying careful attention to the English equivalent of the German present and past tenses:*

1. Ißt er oft im Restaurant? 2. Er ißt nur einmal die Woche im Restaurant. 3. Ich möchte ihn sprechen, aber wenn er jetzt ißt, rufe ich ihn später wieder an. 4. Nein, er ißt jetzt nicht. Er ißt erst um sieben Uhr. 5. Gehen Sie oft ins Kino? 6. Ich gehe ins Kino, sooft man einen guten Film gibt. 7. Gehen Sie heute abend ins Kino? 8. Ich gehe, wenn ich Zeit habe. 9. Seit wann sind Sie hier? 10. Ich bin schon eine ganze Woche hier. 11. Sind Sie schon einmal hier gewesen? 12. Ich bin schon einmal eine ganze Woche hier gewesen. 13. Er bleibt ein ganzes Jahr in Deutschland. 14. Er war ein ganzes Jahr in Deutschland. 15. Er ist schon ein ganzes Jahr in Deutschland. 16. Der Professor sprach eine ganze Stunde über Goethe. 17. Der Professor sprach schon eine ganze Stunde über Goethe, als ich in den Hörsaal trat. 18. Sie spielte eine Sonate von Mozart. 19. Als ich den Konzertsaal betrat, spielte sie eine Sonate von Mozart. 20. Als ich eintrat, spielte sie schon seit zehn Minuten eine Sonate von Mozart. 21. Mein Freund war noch im Wartesaal des Bahnhofs, als mein Zug ankam. 22. Er wartete schon seit drei Uhr, als der Zug ankam.

ACTIVE EXERCISES

A. *Change the following sentences to the past tense:*

1. Wir gehen einmal die Woche ins Kino. 2. Er bleibt nur eine Woche hier. 3. Sie lesen immer dieselbe Zeitung. 4. Ich kenne ihn nicht so gut. 5. Die Zeitung liegt auf dem Schreibtisch. 6. Sie schweigt immer in seiner Gegenwart. 7. Er bringt mich heute abend rechtzeitig nach Hause. 8. Manchmal erzählt er uns eine wirklich komische Geschichte. 9. Weil wir nicht viel Geld haben, essen wir heute zu Hause. 10. Er sagt mir selten, was er auf dem Herzen hat.

B. *Change the following sentences to the present tense:*

1. Er trat ganz leise ins Zimmer. 2. Sie ließen ihre Mäntel im Wohnzimmer.
3. Sie wartete vor dem Haus auf ihren Freund. 4. Was aßen Sie zum Frühstück? 5. Sie standen vor dem Laden und rauchten. 6. Er brach sein Versprechen und ging früh nach Hause. 7. Er sprach oft über dieses Thema.
8. Warum haßtest du ihn so? 9. Sie dachte oft an ihren Freund. 10. Er kam
selten rechtzeitig nach Hause.

C. *If the present tense is used, change it to the past. If the past tense is used,
change it to the present:*

1. Er saß allein in der Ecke. 2. Er steht vor der Tür. 3. Er sagte, daß er das
haßte. 4. Ich wurde damit nicht fertig. 5. Hast du genug Geld bei dir? 6. Er
ißt gern Leberwurst. 7. Ist er ein guter Lehrer? 8. Er rannte nach Hause.
9. Ihr bricht das Herz. 10. Er rief mich jede Woche an.

D. *Translate into German:*

1. He reads a German newspaper every day.
2. She will thank him tomorrow for the nice present.
3. She always thought of him when she heard that old song.
4. Do you go home every weekend?
5. No, I go only when I have no homework.
6. Formerly he rarely spoke about his childhood; now he speaks about it often.
7. First they ate and drank; then they sang all night.
8. I was reading an interesting book when you called (**anrufen**).
9. Where were you? We waited for you for an hour.
10. Where are you? We have been waiting for you for two hours.
11. Does he always eat so slowly? He's been eating since seven o'clock.
12. I don't know if he knows this girl, but I do know that he didn't know her
    last month.
13. She always brought the children candy when she visited us.
14. She was in New York for three weeks.
15. She had been in Berlin for ten days when I arrived.
16. They have been in Paris for two months.
17. I have never been in Paris in the spring.
18. When I am in Vienna I always go to the opera.
19. He was already sitting at a little table in the corner when we came
    (**treten**) into the restaurant.
20. When I ask him something he almost always remains (**is**) silent.

16

Compound Tenses; Participles; Imperative

A. Future Tense

Formation

1. The future tense is formed by combining the infinitive of a given verb with the forms of the present tense of **werden**. The infinitive goes to the end of a principal clause, but in a subordinate clause it is in penultimate position, followed by the finite verb:

PRINCIPAL CLAUSE:

> Es **wird** morgen *regnen.*
> It will rain tomorrow.

SUBORDINATE CLAUSE:

> Ich glaube, daß es morgen *regnen* **wird.**
> I believe that it will rain tomorrow.

Caution. In addition to its function as the auxiliary of the future, **werden** can be used as an independent verb (meaning *to become, to grow, to get*) and, in conjunction with a past participle, as the auxiliary of the passive voice (see Chapter 21). Since **werden** can thus be employed in three different ways, it is especially important to wait until the end of the clause before deciding which function is involved:

INDEPENDENT VERB:

> Dieses Lied **wird** überall, sogar in Europa, populär.
> This song is becoming popular everywhere, even in Europe.

Future:

> Dieses Lied **wird** überall, sogar in Europa, populär *bleiben.*
> This song will remain popular everywhere, even in Europe.

Passive:

> Dieses Lied **wird** überall, sogar in Europa, *gesungen.*
> This song is sung everywhere, even in Europe.

Uses

2. In general, the future is less frequently used in German than in English. If the reference to the future is obvious from the context, German prefers the simpler present tense (see previous chapter):

> Es **regnet** morgen (for: Es wird morgen regnen).

Future to express present probability

3. Often the future may express (strong) probability in the present, especially when it is combined with the adverb **schon** or **wohl.** In such cases, English uses the present tense together with the adverb *probably* or *undoubtedly:*

> Soll ich es ihm sagen? Nein, er **wird** es *schon* **wissen.**
> Shall I tell him? No, he undoubtedly knows it already.

Note, however, that future probability is expressed in the same way: the context should make it clear if the future is required in English:

> Er **wird** das *schon* eines Tages **verstehen.**
> One day he will probably understand (that).

B. Participles

Formation of present participle

1. The present participle is formed for all verbs alike by adding the ending **–end** (**–nd** in the case of verb stems ending in **–el** or **–er**) to the stem:

fragen: frag*end* **kommen:** komm*end* **wissen:** wiss*end* **wandern:** wander*nd*

Formation of past participle

2. To form the past participle, weak verbs add the suffix **–t** to the infinitive stem, while strong verbs have the ending **–en.** Both weak and strong verbs place the prefix **ge–** before the stem: **ge-frag-t, ge-sproch-en.**
The observation concerning the insertion of an **e** after certain stem

endings in the present tense (see Chapter 15, Section A, paragraph 4) also applies to the past participle of weak verbs: **ge-antwort-e-t, ge-öffn-e-t.**

Caution. The prefix **ge–** is omitted with verbs in **–ieren** (**studieren: studiert**) and those beginning with the inseparable prefixes **be–, emp–, ent–, er–, ge–, miß–, ver–,** and **zer–** (**beantworten: beantwortet; erfinden: erfunden**).

C. Perfect Tenses

Formation

1. The perfect tenses are formed by combining the past participle of a given verb with the present, past, or future forms, respectively, of the auxiliaries **haben** or **sein.**

RULE: ALL TRANSITIVE AND MANY INTRANSITIVE VERBS USE **haben,** but **sein** IS THE AUXILIARY OF INTRANSITIVE VERBS (weak, strong, or irregular weak) WHICH INDICATE EITHER:

    (*a*) A CHANGE OF POSITION OR LOCATION, like **reisen** (*to travel*), **gehen** (*to go*), **rennen** (*to run*), or

    (*b*) A CHANGE IN CONDITION, like **werden** (*to become*), **aufwachen** (*to wake up*), **sterben** (*to die*)

The two exceptions to this rule are the verbs **sein** and **bleiben** (*to remain*), which are always conjugated with **sein** in the perfect tenses.

2. A synopsis of the two verbs **fragen** (*to ask*) and **fahren** (*to travel*) will illustrate the use of **haben** and **sein** in the perfect tenses:

	fragen	**fahren**
PRESENT PERFECT:	ich habe gefragt	ich bin gefahren
PAST PERFECT:	ich hatte gefragt	ich war gefahren
FUTURE PERFECT:	ich werde gefragt haben	ich werde gefahren sein

Caution. Since **haben** and **sein** can be used both as independent verbs and as auxiliaries of the perfect tenses, it is often not possible to decide which function is involved in a main clause until the end of the clause has been reached:

haben

Wir **haben** zwei Flaschen Wein im Keller.
We have two bottles of wine in the cellar.

Wir **haben** ⸻⟶ *getrunken.*
       zwei Flaschen Wein im Keller
We drank two bottles of wine in the cellar.

sein

Er **ist** diesen Sommer in einem kleinen Dorf in Deutschland.
He is in a small village in Germany this summer.

Er ist ——————————————————————————————→ *erkrankt.*
        diesen Sommer in einem kleinen Dorf in Deutschland
He got sick in a small village in Germany this summer.

Uses of the present perfect

3. Except for actions begun in the past but still going on in the present (see Chapter 15, Section B, paragraph 7), literary German uses the present perfect for the same situations as English, i.e., when a past action is thought of as still having some connection with the present or is represented as being often repeated:

Er **hat** heute schon 20 Zigaretten **geraucht.**   Ich **habe** sie oft **gehört.**
He has already smoked 20 cigarettes today.   I have often heard her.

For English past tense

4. The present perfect is found in German in many instances, however, where English requires the past tense. Generally speaking, German uses the present perfect in informal, everyday conversation (where English uses the past) to express past events or actions:

Gestern abend **haben** wir in einem italienischen Restaurant *gegessen* und **sind** dann ins Kino *gegangen,* wo wir einen ausgezeichneten Film *gesehen* **haben.**

Last evening we ate in an Italian restaurant and then went to the movies, where we saw an excellent picture.

Literary usage

5. In literary German, where the past tense is normally used to narrate past events (see Chapter 15, Section B, paragraph 6), the present perfect may be found if the author does not look upon a statement as part of the chain of events he is narrating:

Bald danach fuhr er nach München, mietete sich ein kleines Zimmer und begann sofort, an seinem neuen Drama zu schreiben. Drei Monate später überreichte er dem Verleger das vollendete Werk, **das die Nachkriegsgeneration so stark beeinflußt hat.** Dann reiste er nach Italien, um sich am Meer auszuruhen.

Soon afterwards he went to Munich, rented a small room and began right away to work on his new play. Three months later he handed to his publisher the completed work, which had such a strong influence on the postwar generation. Then he went to Italy to rest up at the seashore.

6. Even in conversational German, however, the simple past tense is used to describe a past action or situation which was continuous in the past or lasted a considerable length of time:

> Er **spielte** den ganzen Abend Klavier.
> He played the piano all evening.

If such a past tense form denotes an action in progress at the time when another event takes place, English requires the past progressive:

> Während sie noch **tanzten,** bin ich nach Hause gegangen.
> I went home while they **were** still **dancing.**

Use of past perfect

7. The past perfect is used, as in English, to denote an action which was already completed when another occurred:

> Er hatte sein Haus schon **verkauft,** als ich ihn kennenlernte.
> He had already sold his house when I met him.

Use of future perfect

8. The future perfect is essentially used in German as it is in English; it is equally rare in both languages.

> Morgen um diese Zeit **werde** ich schon in Paris **angekommen sein.**
> By this time tomorrow I shall have arrived in Paris.

Note, however, that in German (contrary to English) the present perfect may be substituted for the future perfect if the idea of futurity is clear from the context:

> Morgen um diese Zeit **bin** ich schon in Paris **angekommen.**

To express past probability

9. The future perfect is perhaps most common in German when used to express past probability, usually in combination with the adverb **schon** or **wohl.** The English equivalent will be a past tense together with the adverb *probably* or *undoubtedly:*

> Er **wird** *wohl* gestern in Paris **angekommen sein.**
> He probably arrived in Paris yesterday.

D. Imperatives

1. The German imperative has separate forms for familiar and polite address which correspond to the use of familiar and polite forms in the conjugation of verbs (see previous chapter). In the singular, the familiar

imperative is normally formed by adding an **–e** to the present stem of the verb:

sagen: sage!   gehen: gehe!   reden: rede!

The plural of the familiar imperative is formed by adding a **–t** to the present stem. When the stem ends in **d, t,** or a succession of consonants, however, an **e** is inserted before the **–t**:

sagen: sagt!   gehen: geht!   reden: redet!   öffnen: öffnet!

The polite imperative is the same as the polite form of address (singular and plural), except that the pronoun **Sie** FOLLOWS the verb:

Sie sagen: sagen Sie!   Sie gehen: gehen Sie!   Sie reden: reden Sie!

Dropping of –e

2. In colloquial German, the familiar singular ending **–e** is commonly dropped, except for polysyllabic verbs which have the accent on the first syllable:

Frag mich was!
Ask me something.

But:

Antworte auf meine Frage!
Answer my question.

Strong verbs with vowel changes

3. Strong verbs which change the stem vowel from **e** to **i** or **ie** in the present tense (see Chapter 15, Section A, paragraph 3) have this change also in the SINGULAR OF THE FAMILIAR IMPERATIVE and OMIT THE ENDING **–e**:

sehen: sieh!   essen: iß!   nehmen: nimm!   treten: tritt!

Caution. Ordinarily the familiar imperative does not use pronoun forms, while the polite imperative requires the verb to be followed by the pronoun **Sie**. In the familiar imperative the pronoun is added only where the person addressed is to be singled out:

FAMILIAR:

Erzähl(e) mir die Geschichte noch einmal, Fritz!
Tell me the story again, Fritz.

But:

Erzähl(e) du mir die Geschichte noch einmal, Fritz!
(Why don't) You tell me the story again, Fritz.

Polite:

> Sagen Sie mir, was Sie davon halten, Herr Schmidt.
> Tell me what you think of it, Mr. Schmidt.

Infinitive and past participle as imperatives

4. Both the infinitive and the past participle may be used occasionally with imperative force and they are then usually more emphatic than the regular imperatives:

Bitte **einsteigen!**	Maul **gehalten!**
All aboard!	Shut up!

5. For the use of subjunctive forms as substitutes for the imperative, see Chapter 18, Section C, paragraph 1 *b*.

Special Points

Intransitive verbs used transitively

1. Some verbs which are used intransitively to express a change of location can also be used transitively with a different meaning:

> Er **ist** im Wagen seines Freundes nach Boston **gefahren.**
> He rode in his friend's car to Boston.

But:

> Er **hat** den Wagen seines Freundes nach Boston **gefahren.**
> He drove his friend's car to Boston.

Intransitive verbs with *sein* or *haben*

2. Certain intransitive verbs denoting motion may be conjugated with either the auxiliary **sein** or **haben. haben** is used when the verb expresses a motion which does not imply a change in location, i.e., going or coming from one place to another:

> Sie **haben** den ganzen Abend **getanzt.**
> They danced all evening.

But:

> Sie **sind** von einem Zimmer ins andere **getanzt.**
> They danced from one room to another.

> Er **hat** schon als Kind gerne **geschwommen.**
> Already as a child he liked to swim.

But:

> Er **ist** über den See **geschwommen.**
> He swam across the lake.

3. South German and particularly Austrian usage prefers the auxiliary **sein** with certain intransitive verbs which do not imply motion of any kind, such as **liegen, sitzen, stehen:**

Er **ist** (FOR: **hat**) an der Ecke **gestanden.**

He stood at the corner.

RECOGNITION EXERCISES

A. *Translate:*

1. Die Romane dieses Dichters werden jetzt auch in Amerika immer mehr beliebt. 2. Die Romane dieses Dichters werden jetzt auch in Amerika immer mehr gelesen. 3. Die Romane dieses Dichters werden bald auch in Amerika erscheinen. 4. Soll ich es ihm sagen? Nein, er wird es bald schon von seiner Mutter selbst erfahren. 5. Soll ich es ihr sagen? Nein, sie wird es schon wissen. 6. Ich habe zwei Dollar in meiner Tasche. 7. Ich habe zwei Dollar in meiner Tasche gefunden. 8. Er ist diese Woche in einem kleinen Hotel in den Bergen. 9. Er ist diese Woche in einem kleinen Hotel in den Bergen krank geworden. 10. Wir haben einen Wagen, der fünftausend Dollar gekostet hat. 11. Wir haben einen Wagen, der fünftausend Dollar kostet, nie gefahren. 12. Er ist schon ein ganzes Jahr in einem kleinen Dorf in den Alpen. 13. Vor dem Krieg ist sie ein ganzes Jahr in Paris gewesen. 14. Wann geht sie auf die Universität? Sie ist schon auf der Universität in München. 15. Sie ist schon auf der Universität in München einigen alten Freunden begegnet. 16. Die Lebensmittel werden jetzt auch bei uns teurer. 17. Lebensmittel werden jetzt auch in dem großen Warenhaus verkauft. 18. Er hatte damals ein kleines Haus auf dem Lande, wo wir viele schöne Sommer verbrachten. 19. Er hatte damals das kleine Haus auf dem Lande, wo wir so viele schöne Sommer verbrachten, noch nicht gekauft. 20. Sie spielten den ganzen Abend Karten. 21. Sie spielten Karten, als ich ins Zimmer trat. 22. Sie spielten schon seit zwei Stunden Karten, als ich ins Zimmer trat. 23. Während sie noch Karten spielten, verließ ich das Zimmer.

B. *Translate:*

1. Hoffentlich wird er bald den Scheck von seinem Vater erhalten. 2. Bis morgen wird er den Scheck von seinem Vater bestimmt erhalten haben. 3. Er wird wohl den Scheck von seinem Vater schon erhalten haben, denn er geht heute abend mit seiner Freundin aus. 4. Sie werden schon recht haben, er wird den Brief wohl gestern bekommen haben, während wir in der Stadt waren. 5. Bis nächste Woche werden wir in Berlin angekommen sein. 6. Vor einer Woche wird er schon in Berlin angekommen sein. 7. Gehen Sie heute abend in das kleine Café am Karlsplatz? 8. Gehen Sie heute abend in das kleine Café am Karlsplatz, dann treffe ich Sie dort um acht Uhr. 9. Gehen Sie heute abend in das kleine Café am Karlsplatz. Ich treffe Sie dort um acht Uhr. 10. Der erfolgreiche junge Mann ist in seinem eigenen Flugzeug von

New York nach Florida geflogen. 11. Der erfolgreiche junge Mann hat sein eigenes Flugzeug nach Florida geflogen. 12. Als Kinder haben wir oft in diesem kleinen See im Wald geschwommen. 13. Als Kinder sind wir oft über diesen kleinen See im Wald geschwommen. 14. Weil der Hund einfach nicht aufhören wollte zu bellen, ist der alte Mann schließlich wütend geworden und hat ihn getreten. 15. Weil der alte Mann das Bellen des Hundes einfach nicht mehr aushalten konnte, ist er schließlich ins Haus getreten.

C. *Review of strong verbs. Memorize carefully:*

INFINITIVE	PRESENT	PAST	PAST PARTICIPLE	INFINITIVE
fahren	fährt	fuhr	(ist) gefahren	to drive, travel
finden		fand	gefunden	to find
fliegen		flog	(ist) geflogen	to fly
geben	gibt	gab	gegeben	to give
halten	hält	hielt	gehalten	to hold
nehmen	nimmt	nahm	genommen	to take
schlafen	schläft	schlief	geschlafen	to sleep
schreiben		schrieb	geschrieben	to write
schwimmen		schwamm	(ist) geschwommen	to swim
sehen	sieht	sah	gesehen	to see
sterben	stirbt	starb	(ist) gestorben	to die
trinken		trank	getrunken	to drink

ACTIVE EXERCISES

A. *Change the following sentences to the future tense:*

1. Er kommt morgen nicht. 2. Ich schreibe ihm bald einen langen Brief. 3. Du gibst ihm das Paket. 4. Wir fahren am Dienstag nach Boston. 5. Sie trinkt nicht sehr viel. 6. Wir können das morgen nicht tun. 7. Da ich morgen in der Stadt bin, besuche ich ihn. 8. Obwohl er es tut, tut er es nicht gern. 9. Ihr seht mich nicht bald wieder. 10. Er kommt um sieben Uhr an.

B. *Change the following sentences to the present perfect:*

1. Sie kommt heute nicht, weil sie krank ist. 2. Er schläft sehr schnell ein. 3. Er schläft nicht lange. 4. Wir gehen heute in die Stadt. 5. Warum arbeitet er nicht? 6. Sie fahren oft nach New York. 7. Sie gibt ihm das Geld. 8. Was findet er im Wagen? 9. Du siehst heute gut aus. 10. Wo essen Sie heute abend?

C. *Change the following sentences to the past perfect tense:*

1. Er studierte Medizin. 2. Sie verstand uns nicht. 3. Sie erfuhren es nie. 4. Wir sagten das nicht. 5. Ich ging nicht ins Theater. 6. Sie tranken den Wein gern. 7. Als Kind fuhr er oft dahin. 8. Der Hund lag immer hinter dem Ofen. 9. Er kam diesmal zu spät an. 10. Das Feuer zerstörte den ganzen Ort.

D. *Translate into German:*

1. She will visit us if she has time.
2. I hope that he will write me soon.
3. He arrived after I had gone home.
4. Have you eaten often in this restaurant?
5. She has not yet told her sister that she is engaged.
6. We have been here for a week but we still have not seen our friends.
7. They were still talking about him when I left the room.
8. She had already fallen asleep when I knocked on the door.
9. Have you found the book you were looking for?
10. We have never flown from New York to Paris via London.
11. Fritz, give me the book which is lying on the table.
12. Children, take this money and buy me a pound of coffee.
13. We shall drive to New York tomorrow afternoon.
14. Read this article, Mr. Schmidt, and tell me what you think of it.
15. I have not (*yet*) driven my father's new car.
16. He has often driven in his friend's car to New York.
17. Barbara, look at me and tell me the truth.
18. The car has been in the garage (for) two days but no one has repaired it yet.
19. First they were drinking beer but now they are drinking wine.
20. Let's eat in the little restaurant where we got that good soup last week.

17

Subjunctive; Indirect Discourse

A. Formation

Tenses in the subjunctive

1. In contrast to the indicative, which has six tenses, the subjunctive functions with only four: the present, the past, the future, and the future perfect. There are, however, two complete sets of forms for each tense of the subjunctive. These two sets of forms can be designated subjunctive I and subjunctive II.

Endings

2. Both subjunctive I and subjunctive II operate with the same personal endings:

(ich) · · · –e	(wir) · · · –en
(du) · · · –est	(ihr) · · · –et
(er) · · · –e	(sie) · · · –en

Present subjunctive I

3. The present tense of subjunctive I is formed by adding the subjunctive endings to the present stem of the verb:

ich geb–e	ich hab–e	ich werd–e
du geb–est	du hab–est	du werd–est
er geb–e	er hab–e	er werd–e
wir geb–en	wir hab–en	wir werd–en
ihr geb–et	ihr hab–et	ihr werd–et
sie geb–en	sie hab–en	sie werd–en

The only irregularity in the formation of the present subjunctive I is the verb **sein:** it has no endings in the first and third person singular and may omit the **e** in the ending of the second person singular:

153

ich sei	wir seien
du sei(e)st	ihr seiet
er sei	sie seien

Other tenses of subjunctive I

4. The other tenses of subjunctive I are formed by combining the appropriate auxiliary verb in the present tense of subjunctive I with a past participle (for the past), an infinitive (for the future), and a perfect infinitive (for the future perfect):

PAST		FUTURE		FUTURE PERFECT	
ich habe		ich werde		ich werde	
du habest		du werdest		du werdest	
er habe	gegeben	er werde	geben	er werde	gegeben haben
wir haben		wir werden		wir werden	
ihr habet		ihr werdet		ihr werdet	
sie haben		sie werden		sie werden	

Caution. (1) Strong verbs which have vowel changes in the second and third person singular of the indicative (**ich nehme, du nimmst, er nimmt**) do not show any irregularities in the present of subjunctive I: **ich nehme, du nehmest, er nehme.**

(2) In contrast to the indicative, which has three tenses to express actions in the past (the simple past, the present perfect, and the past perfect), there is only one past tense in the subjunctive: a compound tense made up of an auxiliary (present subjunctive of **sein** or **haben**) and a past participle.

Present subjunctive II

5. The present tense of subjunctive II is formed by adding the subjunctive endings to the past stem of a verb. In addition, the stem vowels of strong verbs (where possible), as well as those of the auxiliaries **sein, haben,** and **werden,** have an umlaut:

THE WEAK VERB		THE STRONG VERB	
ich wohnt–e	wir wohnt–en	ich gäb–e	wir gäb–en
du wohnt–est	ihr wohnt–et	du gäb–est	ihr gäb–et
er wohnt–e	sie wohnt–en	er gäb–e	sie gäb–en

THE AUXILIARIES		
ich wär–e	ich hätt–e	ich würd–e
du wär–est	du hätt–est	du würd–est
er wär–e	er hätt–e	er würd–e
wir wär–en	wir hätt–en	wir würd–en
ihr wär–et	ihr hätt–et	ihr würd–et
sie wär–en	sie hätt–en	sie würd–en

Note that the present subjunctive II of weak verbs has the same forms as the past indicative.

Caution. (1) A few other verbs take an umlaut in the present subjunctive II:

(*a*) The modal auxiliaries that have an umlaut in the infinitive (**dürfen, können, mögen,** and **müssen**): **ich dürfte, ich könnte, ich möchte, ich müßte.**

(*b*) The irregular weak verbs **bringen, denken,** and **wissen: ich brächte, ich dächte, ich wüßte,** while **brennen, kennen, nennen,** and **rennen** change their stem vowel to **e: ich brennte, ich kennte, ich nennte, ich rennte.** The other two irregular weak verbs (**senden** and **wenden**) use the forms **ich sendete, ich wendete.**

(2) Some strong verbs have older subjunctive II forms in addition to those derived from the past stem as described above: **ich stände** *or* **ich stünde, ich hälfe** *or* **ich hülfe, ich begänne** *or* **ich begönne.** For a complete listing of such variant forms see the verb chart preceding the vocabularies. Note also that a few verbs, such as **sterben, verderben, werben,** and **werfen** have only the older subjunctive II forms: **ich stürbe, ich verdürbe, ich würbe, ich würfe.**

Other tenses of subjunctive II

6. The remaining tenses of subjunctive II are formed with the help of the present subjunctive II of the necessary auxiliary verbs in the same way as the corresponding subjunctive I forms:

PAST		FUTURE		FUTURE PERFECT	
ich hätte		ich würde		ich würde	
du hättest		du würdest		du würdest	
er hätte	gegeben	er würde	geben	er würde	gegeben haben
wir hätten		wir würden		wir würden	
ihr hättet		ihr würdet		ihr würdet	
sie hätten		sie würden		sie würden	

B. Use in Indirect Discourse

Definition

1. In indirect discourse someone reports a statement or question indirectly in a subordinate clause rather than in a direct quotation:

DIRECT:

Ich sagte: „Sie hat das Buch."
I said: "She has the book."

INDIRECT:

> Ich sagte, daß sie das Buch habe.
> I said that she had the book.

DIRECT:

> Er fragte: „Warum gehst du schon nach Hause?"
> He asked: "Why are you going home already?"

INDIRECT:

> Er fragte, warum ich schon nach Hause gehe.
> He asked why I was going home already.

Indicative and subjunctive in indirect discourse

2. The indicative is used frequently in indirect discourse, especially in colloquial speech:

> Ich höre, daß er eben angekommen **ist**.
> I hear that he has just arrived.

> Sie hat gesagt, daß er morgen **kommt**.
> She said that he's coming tomorrow.

In written or formal German, however, the subjunctive (either I or II) still is ordinarily found in the subordinate clause of an indirect statement or question. Theoretically, the forms of subjunctive I and subjunctive II are interchangeable; the forms of subjunctive I, however, are felt to be more formal than those of subjunctive II and are therefore encountered more often in literary usage:

> Er sagte, daß die Kinder krank **seien** (OR: **wären**).
> He said that the children were sick.
> Er fragte, wieviel Geld sie **habe** (OR: **hätte**).
> He asked how much money she had.

But if a subjunctive I or II is identical with the form of the corresponding tense in the indicative, the alternate form must be used:

Er berichtete, daß seine Freunde kein Geld mehr **hätten** (NOT: **haben**).
He reported that his friends had no more money.

Omission of *daß*

3. The conjunction **daß** of the subordinate clause in an indirect statement may be omitted, but, if it is, the clause will have normal, not transposed word order:

> Er berichtete, **seine Freunde hätten** kein Geld mehr.

Indirect question

It should also be remembered that the interrogative of a direct question acts as a subordinating conjunction in the indirect question (see Chapter 3, Special Point 1.)

DIRECT:

Er fragte: „**Wann** geht er ins Kino?"
He asked: "When is he going to the movies?"

INDIRECT:

Er fragte, **wann** er ins Kino gehe.
He asked when he was going to the movies.

If the direct question had no interrogative, the subordinate clause with the indirect question is introduced by the conjunction **ob,** meaning *if* or *whether:*

DIRECT:

Er fragte: „„Kommt sie?"
He asked: "Is she coming?"

INDIRECT:

Er fragte, **ob** sie komme.
He asked if she was coming.

Tenses in indirect discourse

4. The tense of the subjunctive used in indirect discourse is normally the same as the tense of the indicative in the direct statement upon which the indirect is based, except that the three past tenses of the indicative (simple past, present perfect, past perfect) all correspond to the one past tense of the subjunctive:

DIRECT	INDIRECT
Er sagte:	Er sagte,
„Sie kommt." (*present*)	sie komme (käme). (*present*)
„Sie kam." (*past*) „Sie ist gekommen." (*pres. perf.*) „Sie war gekommen." (*past perf.*)	sie sei (wäre) gekommen. (*past*)
„Sie wird kommen." (*future*)	sie werde (würde) kommen. (*fut.*)
„Sie wird gekommen sein." (*fut. perf.*)	sie werde (würde) gekommen sein. (*fut. perf.*)

Handling of German tenses in translation

5. In English, the tense of the verb in an indirect statement depends not only on the original tense of the verb in the direct statement, but also ON THE TENSE OF THE INTRODUCTORY VERB OF SAYING. Thus, if the

introductory verb is in the present, the present subjunctive (I or II) of the German indirect statement is translated as a present tense in English:

> Er sagt, daß er heute komme.
>
> He **says** that he **is coming** today.

But if the introductory verb is in the past tense, the same German present subjunctive is rendered as a past tense in English:

> Er sagte, daß er heute komme.
>
> He **said** that he **was coming** today.

Similarly, after an introductory verb in the present the German past subjunctive (I or II) is translated as either an English past or a present perfect:

> Er sagt, daß er die Aufgabe gemacht hätte.
>
> He **says** that he **did** (OR: **has done**) the lesson.

When the introductory verb is in the past, however, the German past subjunctive is translated as an English past perfect:

> Er sagte, daß er die Aufgabe gemacht hätte.
>
> He **said** that he **had done** the lesson.

A German future subjunctive (I or II) is translated as an English future after an introductory verb in the present, but as a conditional (*would* plus infinitive) after an introductory verb in the past:

> Er sagt, er werde morgen kommen.
>
> He **says** he **will come** tomorrow.

But:

> Er sagte, er werde morgen kommen.
>
> He **said** that he **would come** tomorrow.

Indirect commands

6. In reporting commands indirectly, German usually uses a **daß**-clause in which the finite verb is the present subjunctive (I or II) of **sollen** combined with the infinitive of the verb which was in the imperative in the original command:

DIRECT:

> Er sagte zu mir: „**Gib** mir das Geld!"
>
> He said to me: "Give me the money."

INDIRECT:

> Er sagte mir, daß ich ihm das Geld **geben** *sollte* (*solle*).
>
> He told me that I should give him the money.

Note how **sagen zu** is used when a direct statement follows, while the **zu** is omitted before the dative when an indirect statement follows.

use of *mögen*

7. Occasionally, the present subjunctive of **mögen** may be encountered in indirect commands:

> Er teilte seinem Partner mit, er **möge** ihn vor dem Hotel treffen.
> He informed his partner that he should meet him in front of the hotel.

This use of **mögen** rather than **sollen** indicates that the original imperative was more in the nature of a request than a command. Note that in English *should* translates **sollen** as well as **mögen**.

Caution. English can employ an infinitive construction to express an indirect command:

> Er sagte mir, daß ich nach Hause gehen solle.
> He said that I should go home.

OR:

> He told me to go home.

German has no equivalent for this construction.

Special Points

Extended reports in indirect discourse

1. Indirect discourse in German is not necessarily confined to a single statement in a subordinate clause introduced by a verb of saying or reporting. The report may go on in successive sentences or even paragraphs in which the subjunctive is used. As long as the subjunctive continues, the reader assumes that what he is reading is still the indirect report. When the indicative is resumed, it is clear that the indirect statement has been completed:

Hans **sagte,** daß er gestern in die Stadt gefahren *sei* und seinen Onkel besucht *habe*. Nach dem Mittagessen *seien* er und der Onkel ins Kino gegangen. Dort *wären* sie einem alten Freund des Onkels begegnet, der sie zum Abendessen eingeladen *hätte*. Um neun Uhr *sei* er dann nach Hause zurückgekehrt. Hans **war** im Begriff weiterzuerzählen, als Fritz ihn **unterbrach**. . . .

Hans said that he had gone to the city yesterday and visited his uncle. After lunch he and his uncle had gone to the movies. There (he continued) they had met an old friend of his uncle's who had invited them to dinner. At nine o'clock he had then returned home. Hans was about to continue his story when Fritz interrupted him. . . .

Observe that in translating such extended indirect discourse it is often helpful in English to insert from time to time such phrases as *he continued* or *he went on to say* to remind the reader that the indirect discourse is still in progress. In German, such reminders are unnecessary.

Omission of introductory verb of saying

2. Very frequently indirect discourse in German is encountered without any introductory verb of saying or reporting. The use of the subjunctive is quite sufficient to convey the idea that an indirect statement is beginning. In English an introductory verb MUST BE INSERTED:

Das Dienstmädchen des Richters . . . erscheint, bestellt dem Herrn einen Gruß von der gnädigen Frau, und Onkel Vittorio *wäre* gekommen und *wollte* zum Essen dableiben, und der Herr Richter *möchte* doch sehen, daß er recht frühzeitig fertig *würde.**	The judge's maid . . . appeared, conveyed to her master a greeting from his wife, **and said** that Uncle Vittorio had arrived and wanted to stay for dinner. **She also said that** the judge should see to it that he finished quite early.

RECOGNITION EXERCISES

A. *Translate:*

1. Er sagt, daß sie rechtzeitig kommen werde, aber ich glaube ihm nicht.
2. Er sagte, daß sie rechtzeitig kommen werde, aber ich glaube ihm nicht.
3. Sie sagt, daß sie kein Geld dafür hätte. 4. Sie sagte, daß sie kein Geld dafür hätte. 5. Er sagt, daß er bald käme. 6. Er sagte, daß er bald käme. 7. Die Zeitung berichtet, daß die Polizei den Verbrecher endlich gefangen habe. 8. Die Zeitung berichtete, daß die Polizei den Verbrecher endlich gefangen habe. 9. Sie teilen uns mit, daß er schon einmal hier gewesen sei. 10. Sie teilten uns mit, daß er schon einmal hier gewesen sei. 11. Am ersten Schultag fragte die Lehrerin das kleine Mädchen mit den roten Haaren, die in der ersten Reihe saß, wie sie heiße, wie alt sie sei, wo sie wohne und ob sie Geschwister habe. 12. Das Mädchen stand auf und sagte, ihr Name sei Barbara Schmidt und sie wohne in der Ludwigstraße. 13. Sie sei acht Jahre alt und habe eine jüngere Schwester, die noch in den Kindergarten gehe. 14. Dann setzte sie sich wieder und die Lehrerin wandte sich an den nächsten Schüler. 15. Frau Graf trat in die Metzgerei und wünschte Herrn Weißwurst einen guten Morgen. Sie brauche heute etwas besonders Gutes, da sie Besuch erwarte, und ob Herr Weißwurst ihr vielleicht ein gutes Roastbeef zurücklegen könne. 16. Sie werde dann später wiederkommen und das Fleisch abholen. 17. Herr Weißwurst lächelte und sagte, er habe gerade das richtige Stück für sie, sie solle nur um zwei Uhr wieder vorbeikommen. 18. Sie könne

---

* Paul Ernst, „Der Hecht."

es dann gleich mitnehmen. Frau Graf dankte und verließ das Geschäft.
19. Der Mann schrieb, daß ich ihn um fünf Uhr in der Bar treffen solle.
20. Sagen Sie der alten Dame, die mich sprechen will, sie möge sich ins
Wartezimmer setzen und auf mich warten. Sie brauche bestimmt nicht länger
als zehn Minuten zu warten.

B. *Translate:*

1. Till Eulenspiegel, ein bekannter Spitzbube des 15. Jahrhunderts, kam
eines Tages in eine Stadt und erklärte, er könne alle Krankheiten heilen. 2. Als
der Arzt des Krankenhauses davon hörte, ließ er ihn sofort zu sich kommen
und fragte ihn, ob das, was er da behaupte, auch wahr wäre. 3. Eulenspiegel
versicherte ihm, er hätte die Wahrheit gesprochen, und verlangte von dem
Arzt, er sollte ihm 200 Gulden geben, wenn es ihm gelänge, alle Patienten des
Krankenhauses zu heilen. 4. Er brauche ihm aber gar nichts zu bezahlen, wenn
auch nur ein einziger Patient im Krankenhaus bliebe. 5. Da der Arzt mit
diesem Vorschlag einverstanden war, ging Eulenspiegel zu den Kranken und
flüsterte jedem einzelnen ins Ohr, er müsse den Kränksten von ihnen, der
nicht mehr laufen könne, zu Pulver verbrennen, um daraus eine Arznei zu
machen, mit denen er die anderen kurieren werde. 6. Wenn er am nächsten
Morgen mit dem Arzt hereinkäme, solle jeder um sein Leben laufen. 7. Niemand solle vergessen, daß der Schwächste, der nicht mehr laufen könne,
sterben müsse. 8. Als Eulenspiegel am nächsten Tag kam und verkündete, daß
jeder, der nicht krank sei und gehen könne, das Krankenhaus verlassen solle,
da rannten sie alle, so schnell sie konnten, da keiner der letzte sein wollte.
9. Der Arzt war hocherfreut und gab Eulenspiegel das Geld. Dieser bedankte
sich und bedauerte, daß er nun gleich weiterreisen müsse. 10. Als die Kranken
am nächsten Tag ins Krankenhaus zurückkamen, erzählten sie dem Arzt, wie
der Spitzbube ihn betrogen hätte. 11. Man sagt, der Arzt sei wütend geworden
und habe verlangt, die Polizei solle den Spitzbuben sofort verhaften, aber
leider war Eulenspiegel schon über die Grenze geflohen.

C. *Strong verbs.* *Memorize:*

INFINITIVE	PRESENT	PAST	PAST PARTICIPLE	INFINITIVE
beginnen		begann	begonnen	to begin
betrügen		betrog	betrogen	to deceive
einladen	lädt ein	lud ein	eingeladen	to invite
fangen	fängt	fing	gefangen	to catch
gelingen		gelang	(ist) gelungen	to succeed
heißen		hieß	geheißen	to be called
helfen	hilft	half	geholfen	to help
laufen	läuft	lief	(ist) gelaufen	to run
scheinen		schien	geschienen	to seem; shine
treffen	trifft	traf	getroffen	to hit; meet
tun		tat	getan	to do
vergessen	vergißt	vergaß	vergessen	to forget

ACTIVE EXERCISES

A. *Change the following direct statements into indirect discourse:*

1. Er sagte: „Ich komme morgen um zehn Uhr." 2. Sie sagte: „Mein Freund erwartet mich übermorgen." 3. Wir antworteten: „Wir haben diesen Film gestern gesehen." 4. Ich erklärte: „Ich war vorgestern krank." 5. Sie sagten: „Wir hatten das Haus schon verlassen, als er ankam." 6. Meine Schwester antwortete: „Ich werde ihm nie wieder etwas geben." 7. Seine Frau klagte: „Ich kann meinen Mann nicht verstehen." 8. Ich sagte: „Ich muß jetzt meine Aufgabe für morgen machen." 9. Er behauptete: „Ich weiß die Antwort auf diese Frage nicht." 10. Sie sagte: „Ich bin gestern ins Kino gegangen, aber der Film hat mir gar nicht gefallen."

B. *Change the following direct questions and commands into indirect questions and commands:*

1. Er fragte mich: „Wann gehen Sie wieder in die Stadt?" 2. Er sagte zu mir: „Setzen Sie sich und warten Sie auf mich." 3. Sie fragten uns: „Warum haben Sie das Bier nicht getrunken?" 4. Er sagte zu ihr: „Gib mir meinen Ring zurück." 5. Wir fragten sie: „Haben Sie seinen ersten Roman schon gelesen?" 6. Sie sagten zu uns: „Kommen Sie morgen nach der Klasse zu uns." 7. Sie fragte das kleine Mädchen: „Wie alt bist du?" 8. Ich sagte zu den Kindern: „Nehmt dieses Geld und kauft euch etwas Eis." 9. Sie fragten mich: „Wo sind Sie gestern um diese Zeit gewesen?" 10. Ich fragte ihn: „Werden Sie diesen Sommer nach Paris fahren?"

C. *Translate into German:*

1. My father said he would give me the money tomorrow.
2. The pretty little girl with the blue eyes asked me if I had seen her mother.
3. My younger sister said she was coming today, but she has not arrived yet.
4. The teacher said that I should do my assignments more carefully.
5. He says that he was there yesterday, but I did not see him.
6. They said that they hadn't seen him either.
7. His mother told him to come home on time.
8. My professor asked me when I was going to hand in my paper (**die Arbeit**).
9. The newspaper reported last night that the police had caught the criminal, but they did not say what his name was (*what he was called*).
10. We did not believe that he would treat us so badly.
11. He called me up and told me to wait for him in front of the library.
12. He explained how he had solved the problem so quickly.
13. He explained to her what he had done, but she told (**sagen**) him to explain it again because she hadn't understood it.
14. She claims that he promised to buy her a fur coat.
15. He told me he earned two hundred dollars a week.
16. My friend told me where he had gotten that excellent wine, but I can't remember (**it**).

17. When I asked him whether he knew my sister he replied that he had never met her.
18. The doctor told me not to smoke so much.
19. The salesman said that the package would arrive on Monday.
20. He claims that his girl friend smokes cigars.

18

Conditions; Other Uses of the Subjunctive

A. Conditions

Definition

1. A conditional sentence consists of a subordinate clause introduced by the conjunction *if* (**wenn**) and a principal clause which tells what will take place if the condition stated in the *if*-clause is fulfilled. The dependent clause (the *if*-clause) may either follow or precede the principal clause:

Wir kommen mit, wenn es nicht regnet.

OR: Wenn es nicht regnet, kommen wir mit.

We'll come along if it does not rain.

Use of indicative

2. Conditional sentences use either the indicative or the subjunctive. The indicative is used if it is possible for the condition to be fulfilled:

Wenn ich Zeit **habe, gehe** ich ins Theater.

If I have time I'll go to the theater.

Use of subjunctive

There are, on the other hand, two types of conditions which employ the subjunctive: contrary-to-fact conditions and suppositions. In a contrary-to-fact condition the implication is that the condition will not or cannot be fulfilled:

Wenn ich Zeit **hätte, ginge** ich ins Theater.

If I had time I would go to the theater.

In such a statement it is implied that the speaker does not have the time and hence cannot go to the theater.

Subjunctive II in contrary-to-fact conditions

3. In contrary-to-fact conditions ONLY SUBJUNCTIVE II FORMS ARE POSSIBLE. If the sentence refers to the present (or the future), the present subjunctive II is used in both clauses:

> Wenn ich Geld **hätte,** kaufte ich mir ein Haus.
> If I had money I'd buy a house.

But instead of the present subjunctive II, the future subjunctive II may also be used, but ONLY IN THE PRINCIPAL CLAUSE:

Wenn ich Geld **hätte,**
> ⌠**kaufte** ich mir ein Haus.
> ⎨   OR:
> ⌡**würde** ich mir ein Haus **kaufen.**

If the sentence refers to a past time of action, the past subjunctive II is used in both clauses; however, in the principal clause the future perfect subjunctive II may be substituted for that of the past:

Wenn ich Geld **gehabt hätte,**
> ⌠**hätte** ich mir ein Haus **gekauft.**
> ⎨   OR:
> ⌡**würde** ich mir ein Haus **gekauft haben.**

If I had had the money I would have bought a house.

Suppositions

4. In a condition which contains a supposition, the speaker supposes what would happen if a certain condition were fulfilled without implying that it cannot or will not be fulfilled:

Wenn mein Vater mir das Geld **gäbe,**
> ⌠**kaufte** ich mir ein Haus.
> ⎨   OR:
> ⌡**würde** ich mir ein Haus **kaufen.**

In such suppositional conditions subjunctive II forms are used in exactly the same way as in contrary-to-fact conditions. In the if-clause, however, the present subjunctive II of sollen with a dependent infinitive often occurs instead of the present subjunctive II of the verb in question:

Wenn mein Vater mir das Geld geben **sollte,** würde ich mir ein Haus kaufen.

If my father were to (OR: should) give me the money I would buy myself a house.

Caution. Both clauses of a contrary-to-fact condition do not have to be in the same tense. The *if*-clause can refer to the past, for instance, and the principal clause to the present:

Wenn ich gestern nicht so viel ge- trunken hätte, hätte ich heute keine Kopfschmerzen.	If I had not drunk so much yesterday I would not have a headache today.

Omission of wenn

5. It should be remembered that in German the conjunction **wenn** may be omitted (see Chapter 3, paragraph 4b), in which case the verb begins the clause and the principal clause ordinarily is introduced by **dann** or **so**:

Hätte ich das Geld, **dann** (OR: **so**) würde ich mir ein Haus kaufen.	**Sollte** mir **mein Vater** das Geld geben, **so** (OR: **dann**) würde ich mir ein Haus kaufen.

If the principal clause precedes the dependent clause, the omission of **wenn** is rare and usually requires the addition of **nur**:

	Ich hätte gewartet, wenn ich das gewußt hätte.
OR:	Ich hätte gewartet, hätte ich das **nur** gewußt.
	I would have waited if I had known that.

wenn-clauses to express wishes

6. The **wenn**-clause of a contrary-to-fact condition is often used alone (i.e., without a concluding principal clause) to express either a wish which cannot be fulfilled (present subjunctive II) or regret about something in the past which could not be fulfilled (past subjunctive II). Usually **nur** or **doch** (or both) are added in such exclamations:

Wenn ich das **doch** (OR: **nur, doch nur**) hätte!
If I only had that!

Wenn ich das **doch** (OR: **nur, doch nur**) gehabt hätte!
If I only had had that!

B. als ob-Constructions

1. The subjunctive is usually employed in subordinate clauses introduced by **als ob** (OR: **als wenn**), meaning *as if*. Although subjunctive II is more commonly found in such constructions, more and more authors seem to be using subjunctive I forms or even the indicative:

Er tut, **als ob** er mich nicht **verstünde** (OR: **verstehe, versteht**).
He acts as if he doesn't understand me.

Sie sah aus, **als ob** sie überhaupt nicht **geschlafen hätte** (**habe, hat**).
She looked as if she hadn't slept at all.

Note that the **als ob**-construction is particularly common after such verbs and verbal phrases as: (**so**) **tun, als ob** (**wenn**) (*to act as if*); **mir** (**dir, ihm,** etc.) **ist** (**war,** etc.), **als ob** (*it seems, seemed,* etc. *to me, you,* etc., *as if*); **scheinen, als ob** (*to seem*); **zumute sein, als ob** (*to feel*).

Omission of *ob, wenn*

2. The **ob** (or **wenn**) in the **als ob**-construction is frequently omitted, in which case the verb immediately follows the **als** instead of coming at the end of the clause:

> Sie sah aus, **als** hätte sie überhaupt nicht geschlafen.

Thus, WHENEVER ALS BEGINS A CLAUSE AND A VERB (usually in the subjunctive) FOLLOWS IT, **als** must be translated by *as if.*

C. Other Uses of Subjunctive

Present subjunctive I

1. The present subjunctive I is used:

(*a*) in wishes that something may happen or be done. In English, *may* will frequently render the German adequately:

Gott **segne** dich, mein Kind.
(May) God bless you, my child.

Es **lebe** der König!
Long live the king (i.e., may the king live long!)

(*b*) in certain types of suggestions, commands and requests. The first person plural with the verb in first position is the equivalent of English *let us . . .*

| **Gehen** wir! | **Essen** wir jetzt! | **Seien** wir froh darüber! |
| Let's go. | Let's eat now. | Let us be happy about it. |

Note that except for **sein** these subjunctives are identical in form with the present indicative.

The third person singular is frequently found instead of the imperative in instructions, directions, recipes, suggestions, etc. It can be translated by an English imperative when the subject of the subjunctive is **man:**

Man nehme zwei Eier . . .
Take two eggs . . .

Man lese diesen Paragraphen zweimal.
Read this paragraph twice.

If the subject of the subjunctive form of the verb is something other than **man,** the English translation can begin with "let," followed by the noun and verb in question:

Der Leser stelle sich vor, daß . . .
Let the reader (the reader should) imagine that . . .

Der erste Satz diene als Beispiel.
Let the first sentence (the first sentence may) serve as an example.

sei, seien with past participle

Often the third person singular or plural of **sein** (= **sein** or **seien**) is used in a similar way in conjunction with the past participle of another verb. Here, too, English can begin with *let* followed by the noun (or pronoun) and a *be* plus the past participle:

Es **sei** an dieser Stelle noch hinzugefügt, daß . . .
Let it be (it might, should be) added at this point that . . .

Die folgenden Tatsachen **seien** hier noch erwähnt.
Let the following facts (the following facts might, should) also be mentioned.

Present subjunctive II

2. The present subjunctive II is used:

(*a*) to express a wish, usually after **wünschen** or a similar verb of wishing. In this construction, the verbs in both clauses are in the subjunctive:

> Ich **wünschte,** ich **wäre** jetzt in Bermuda.
> I wish I were in Bermuda now.
>
> Ich **wollte,** er **ginge** endlich nach Hause.
> I wish he would finally go home.

(*b*) to express possibility, particularly in constructions using the modal auxiliaries **dürfen** and **können** (see Chapter 19, Section B, for **dürfen** and **können**):

Das **dürfte** wahr sein.   Das **könnte** stimmen.
That might possibly be true.   That might (could) possibly be true.

Special Points

Omission of wenn-clause

1. Frequently the concluding clause (the principal clause) of a contrary-to-fact condition will be found without an *if*-clause. The idea of the *if*-clause is then usually understood from the context:

Er **würde** bestimmt einen guten Leh-   He would definitely make a good
rer **abgeben.**   teacher (UNDERSTOOD: if he were
                                          to become one).

| Schade, daß Fritz nicht hier war. Er hätte das besser gemacht. | It's too bad Fritz wasn't here. He would have done it better (i.e., if he had been here to do it). |

Substitutes for *wenn*-clauses

2. Similarly, the idea of an *if*-clause of a contrary-to-fact situation can be expressed in some other way so that only the concluding clause (in the subjunctive) occurs:

Ohne mich **wäre** er längst verhungert.
Without me he would have starved long ago.

Here the phrase **ohne mich** has the force of **wenn ich nicht gewesen wäre** (*if it hadn't been for me*).

Es freut mich, daß er es getan hat, *sonst* **hätte** ich es tun müssen.
I am glad that he did it. Otherwise, I would have had to do it.

In this example the **sonst** is used instead of **wenn er es nicht getan hätte** (*if he hadn't done it*).

RECOGNITION EXERCISES

A. *Translate*:

1. Wenn ich mit meiner Arbeit fertig bin, gehe ich heute abend ins Kino. 2. Ich ginge heute abend ins Kino, wenn ich mit meiner Arbeit fertig wäre. 3. Wenn ich meine Aufgabe am Nachmittag gemacht hätte, wäre ich abends auch ins Kino gegangen. 4. Wenn ich meine Aufgabe vor dem Abendessen gemacht hätte, ginge ich jetzt mit meiner Freundin ins Kino. 5. Haben Sie morgen Zeit, zu mir zu kommen, um Ihre Reisepläne mit mir zu besprechen? 6. Haben Sie morgen Zeit, zu mir zu kommen, um Ihre Reisepläne mit mir zu besprechen, so finden Sie mich nachmittags von zwei bis fünf zu Hause. 7. Schade, daß Sie morgen arbeiten müssen. Hätten Sie morgen Zeit, zu mir zu kommen, so könnten wir dann Ihre Reisepläne besprechen. Jetzt werden wir bis nächsten Montag warten müssen. 8. Ist der Mann von der Gasgesellschaft, der gestern kommen wollte, auch heute nicht gekommen? 9. Ist der Mann von der Gasgesellschaft, der gestern schon kommen wollte, auch heute nicht gekommen, dann werde ich noch einmal anrufen. 10. Wäre der Mann von der Gasgesellschaft, der schon gestern kommen wollte, auch heute nicht gekommen, dann hätte ich noch einmal angerufen. 11. Wenn er uns heute besuchte, so würden wir uns sehr freuen. 12. Wenn er heute kommen sollte, so könnte er meine Schwester, die gerade bei uns zu Besuch ist, auch kennenlernen. 13. Hätte er die Wahrheit gewußt, so würde er bestimmt nicht sofort zur Polizei gelaufen sein. 14. Er würde sich geschämt haben, wenn er

gewußt hätte, daß ich wußte, was er da gestern getan hat. 15. Hätte er das nur nicht getan! 16. Wenn sie mich doch nur einmal nett ansähe! 17. Käme er doch nur diesmal rechtzeitig an! 18. Wenn er nur mehr gearbeitet hätte! 19. Wenn sie mich nur nicht immer behandelte, als wäre ich Luft!

B. *Translate:*

1. Er benimmt sich, als hätte ich ein Verbrechen begangen. 2. Sie lebt, als gäbe es kein Morgen. 3. Als ich ins Zimmer eintrat, sah sie mich an, als hätte sie ein Gespenst gesehen. 4. Wenn er es auch versucht hätte, seinen Plan auszuführen, wäre es ihm doch nicht gelungen. 5. Hätte er auch nicht bis zum letzten Augenblick gewartet, so hätte er es doch falsch gemacht. 6. Wären wir auch früher angekommen, wie geplant, so hätten wir ihn doch nicht mehr angetroffen, denn er ist schon letzte Woche abgereist. 7. Es lebe die Republik! 8. Gott gebe uns unser tägliches Brot. 9. Essen wir heute um fünf Uhr, damit wir früher ins Kino gehen können? 10. Essen wir heute um fünf Uhr, damit wir früher ins Kino gehen können. 11. Essen wir heute um fünf Uhr, so können wir früher ins Kino gehen. 12. Sind wir mit seinem Vorschlag zufrieden? 13. Seien wir mit seinem Vorschlag zufrieden! 14. Rezept für weichgekochte Eier: Man lege die Eier für ein bis zwei Minuten vorsichtig in kochendes Wasser und serviere sie dann sofort in Eierbechern. 15. Man lese den folgenden Paragraphen und beantworte dann die folgenden Fragen. 16. Der Leser schließe aber aus dem eben Gesagten nicht, daß das Problem endgültig gelöst worden ist. 17. Der Leser stelle sich vor, was geschähe, wenn jeder täte, als gäbe es für ihn kein Gesetz. 18. Das folgende Beispiel veranschauliche das eben entwickelte Prinzip. 19. Es sei hier erwähnt, daß nicht alle von uns durchgeführten Experimente diese Theorie bestätigen. 20. Die betreffende Stelle sei hier zitiert. 21. Nur die wichtigsten Verse seien hier angeführt. 22. Von den vielen Beispielen für dieses Phänomen seien hier nur zwei genannt. 23. Er wünschte, er wäre jetzt irgendwo anders, nur nicht hier. 24. Ich wollte, sie ließe mich endlich in Ruhe. 25. Schade, daß er nicht kommen konnte, er hätte sich bestimmt gut amüsiert. 26. Ich wünschte, Fritz wäre jetzt hier. Er würde das alles bestimmt viel besser erklären als ich. 27. Ohne seine Hilfe wäre ich wohl nie damit fertig geworden. 28. Glücklicherweise haben sie meine Fehler überhört, sonst hätten sie mich sicher ausgelacht.

C. *Strong verbs. Memorize:*

INFINITIVE	PRESENT	PAST	PAST PARTICIPLE	INFINITIVE
befehlen	befiehlt	befahl	befohlen	to command, order
bieten		bot	geboten	to offer
fallen	fällt	fiel	(ist) gefallen	to fall
fliehen		floh	(ist) geflohen	to flee
geschehen	geschieht	geschah	(ist) geschehen	to happen
leihen		lieh	geliehen	to lend
lügen		log	gelogen	to tell a lie
schließen		schloß	geschlossen	to close; conclude
schneiden		schnitt	geschnitten	to cut

INFINITIVE	PRESENT	PAST	PAST PARTICIPLE	INFINITIVE
singen		sang	gesungen	to sing
verstehen		verstand	verstanden	to understand
ziehen		zog	(ist) gezogen	to move; (*with* **haben**) to pull

ACTIVE EXERCISES

A. *Change the following conditional sentences in the indicative to contrary-to-fact conditions:*

1. Wenn ich Lust habe, singe ich. 2. Wenn er genug Geld hat, kommt er. 3. Wenn sie hungrig ist, wird sie essen. 4. Wenn er sie liebt, wird er sie auch heiraten. 5. Wenn er die Antwort weiß, wird er nicht schweigen. 6. Wenn du befiehlst, kann ich kommen. 7. Wenn sie arbeiten können, werden sie es tun. 8. Wenn Sie mitkommen, werde ich mich freuen. 9. Wenn du vorsichtig bist, schneidest du dich nicht. 10. Wenn ich das Auto habe, werde ich sie abholen.

B. *Change the following contrary-to-fact conditions in present time to contrary-to-fact conditions in past time:*

1. Wenn er einen neuen Anzug hätte, zöge er ihn an. 2. Wenn ich Zeit hätte, schnitte ich mir die Bilder aus. 3. Wenn sie das wüßte, würde sie wütend. 4. Wenn wir hungrig wären, gingen wir in ein Restaurant. 5. Wenn sie Lust hätten, würden sie ins Kino gehen. 6. Wenn wir das Buch hätten, würden wir es lesen. 7. Hätte ich eine nette Freundin, so bliebe ich hier. 8. Wenn er das Geld hätte, liehe er es Ihnen bestimmt. 9. Wenn er unschuldig wäre, würde er nicht fliehen.

C. *Translate into German:*

1. We'll stay home tonight if it snows.
2. If he had enough money he would buy himself a new car.
3. If I see her tomorrow I'll invite her for supper.
4. If she had known that she would not have said she would come.
5. If you had come yesterday I would have offered you a glass of wine.
6. What would she have done if I hadn't been there?
7. He could help the old woman if he had more time.
8. She acts as if she were sick.
9. My friend looked as if he hadn't eaten all week.
10. It often seems to me as if no one understands me.
11. He would not have lied if he had not been afraid.
12. If I only knew when he is coming!
13. If she were only here with me!
14. If he had only written me earlier!
15. If my father's letter had only arrived yesterday!

16. If I hadn't eaten so much yesterday I wouldn't be sick now.
17. Would you believe me if I told you the truth?
18. I wouldn't be here now if I hadn't done my assignment this afternoon.
19. Without my support he would never have become a doctor.
20. I wish Marie were here. She would know the answer to this question.

19

Modal Auxiliaries

A. Conjugation and Use of Modal Auxiliaries

Formation of present tense

1. The forms of the present tense of the modal auxiliaries are irregular in the singular:

	dürfen	können	mögen	müssen	sollen	wollen
	to be permitted to	*to be able to*	*to like to*	*to have to*	*to be to*	*to want to*
ich	darf	kann	mag	muß	soll	will
du	darfst	kannst	magst	mußt	sollst	willst
er	darf	kann	mag	muß	soll	will
wir	dürfen	können	mögen	müssen	sollen	wollen
ihr	dürft	könnt	mögt	müßt	sollt	wollt
sie	dürfen	können	mögen	müssen	sollen	wollen

2. Modal auxiliaries form their past tense and past participle like weak verbs except that those with umlaut in the infinitive drop the umlaut; note also that **mögen** changes its **g** to **ch:**

PAST TENSE:

ich: durfte   konnte   mochte   mußte   sollte   wollte

PAST PARTICIPLE:

gedurft   gekonnt   gemocht   gemußt   gesollt   gewollt

Used with dependent infinitive

3. An infinitive dependent on a modal auxiliary is not preceded by **zu:**

Ich **kann** heute nicht *kommen.*   Er **muß** jetzt nach Hause *gehen.*
I cannot come today.   He must go home now.

Omission of dependent infinitive

4. A dependent infinitive denoting motion toward a goal is often omitted if the idea of motion is clear from the context:

Ich **will** *nach Boston.*   Er **muß** jetzt *nach Hause.*

I want to go to Boston.   He has to go home now.

Similarly, the infinitive **tun** or **machen** (*to do*) need not be expressed:

Wir **dürfen** das nicht.

We must not do that.

Ihre Kinder **dürfen** alles, was sie **wollen.**

Their children may do everything they want to (do).

The dependent infinitive is also generally omitted (as it is in English) when what it expresses is clearly understood from a preceding statement:

Kann er uns sagen, wo sie ist? Ja, er **kann,** aber er **will** nicht.

Can he tell us where she is? Yes, he can, but he doesn't want to.

es as object

When the omitted infinitive is a transitive verb, the pronoun **es,** which is not translated in English, may be found as an object:

Darf sie keinen Wein trinken? Nein, sie darf *es* nicht.

Isn't she allowed to drink wine? No, she may not.

Formation of perfect tenses

5. The perfect tenses of the modals are formed with the auxiliary **haben.** The regular past participle of a modal auxiliary, however, can only be used when there is no dependent infinitive:

PRESENT PERFECT   PAST PERFECT

Er **hat** nach Hause **gemußt.**   Das **hatten** wir nicht **gedurft.**

He had to go home.   We had not been permitted to do that.

FUTURE PERFECT

Er **wird** das nicht **gekonnt haben.**

He will not have been able to do it.

"Double infinitive"

6. When a dependent infinitive is used in conjunction with a modal in a perfect tense, a form identical with the infinitive is used instead of the regular past participle of the modal; the resulting construction is often called the "double infinitive":

PRESENT PERFECT	PAST PERFECT
Er hat nach Hause *gehen müssen.*	Das hatten wir nicht *tun dürfen.*
He had to go home.	We had not been permitted to do that.

FUTURE PERFECT
Er wird es nicht *haben tun können.*
He will not have been able to do it.

Note that in the future perfect the infinitive of the auxiliary (**haben**) precedes the "double infinitive."

"Double infinitive" in future tense

7. A similar "double infinitive" also appears in the future tense of the modals:

Er wird bald *gehen müssen.*	Sie werden es nicht *tun können.*
He will have to go soon.	They will not be able to do it.

Position of auxiliary in subordinate clauses

8. Contrary to the rule of transposed word order (see Chapter 3, paragraph 1), the finite verb (the auxiliary **haben** or **werden**) usually comes before the "double infinitive" in subordinate clauses:

Ich höre, daß er gestern **hat** *abreisen müssen.*
I hear that he had to leave yesterday.

Ich glaube, daß er mehr **wird** *arbeiten müssen.*
I think that he will have to work harder.

Occasionally, the finite verb may even be encountered before an object or an adverbial element:

Ich höre, daß er **hat** nach Hause *gehen müssen.*
I hear that he had to go home.

B. Meanings of Modal Auxiliaries

One of the major problems in mastering the modal auxiliaries is the fact that they all have more than one meaning. How a modal is used in German can often be determined only on the basis of the context. But before any decisions can be made, the reader must be fully aware of the various possibilities discussed below:

dürfen

1. dürfen has two major meanings:

(*a*) *to be allowed to, to be permitted to, may:*

> **Darf** ich das tun?
> Am I allowed to do that?

OR:

> May I do that?

> Ja, du **darfst** das tun.
> Yes, you may do that.

In the present tense the negative of this usage (**nicht dürfen,** *not to be allowed to*) may also be translated in English by *must not:*

> Die Kinder **dürfen nicht** auf der Straße spielen.
> The children must not play on the street.

Note that in requests the present subjunctive II form of **dürfen** can also be used; it is more formal or polite than the indicative:

> **Darf** ich (OR: **dürfte** ich) Sie um das Salz bitten?
> May (OR: might) I please have the salt?

(*b*) *may* or *might* to express possibility, ordinarily in the present tense of subjunctive II:

> Das **dürfte** (OR: darf) stimmen.
> That may be correct.

Caution. Since the modal auxiliaries in English do not have forms for all the tenses, difficulties sometimes arise in finding a proper English equivalent for a German modal. Thus, since *may* has no past tense in English, a translation of the past tense of **dürfen** has to use one of the other possibilities suggested above:

Meine Tochter **darf** heute ins Kino.	Gestern **durfte** sie ins Kino.
My daughter may go to the movies today.	Yesterday she was allowed to go to the movies.

können

2. können has three major meanings:

(*a*) *to be able to, can:*

Ich **kann** das tun.	Er **konnte** mich nicht finden.
I can (am able to) do that.	He could not (was not able to) find me.

When **können** is used to express a mastery of a subject, it stands without a dependent infinitive and is the equivalent of English *to know:*

> Ich **kann** Deutsch.   Er **kann** seine Geographie.
> I know German.   He knows his geography.

(*b*) *can, may* (in the sense of *to be permitted to*); in this meaning, **können** is synonymous with the first meaning of **dürfen**:

> **Kann** (OR: **darf**) ich jetzt kommen?
> Can (OR: may) I come now?

(*c*) *can, may* (to express possibility, in which case **können** means the same as the present subjunctive II of **dürfen** as discussed above):

> Das **kann** (OR: **dürfte**) wahr sein.
> That can (may) be true.

To express a possibility in the past, the perfect infinitive is often used with the present tense of **können** (or, for that matter, with the present subjunctive II of **dürfen**):

> Er **kann** (OR: **dürfte**) es schon getan haben.
> He can (may) have done it already.

Caution. (1) Since English has only two forms corresponding to the simple tenses of **können,** namely *can* and *could,* the translation *to be able to* must be used for the compound tenses:

> Er **konnte** es nicht lesen.
> He could not read it.

But:

> Er **hatte** es nicht lesen **können.**
> He had not been able to read it.

(2) The present subjunctive II form **könnte** is generally the equivalent of English *could* and may be encountered in all of the three major uses of **können** listed above:

Ich **könnte** das tun.	**Könnte** ich heute kommen?	Das **könnte** wahr sein.
I could do that.	Could I come today?	That could be true.

Thus, English *could* translates not only the past tense but also the present subjunctive II form of **können.**

mögen

3. **mögen** has two major meanings:

(*a*) *to like to, to care to, to wish to:*

> Ich **mag** das nicht noch einmal hören.
> I don't care to hear that again.

mögen can be used with a direct object (and without a dependent infinitive) in the sense of *to like:*

Ich **mag** das nicht.   **Mögen** Sie warme Milch?
I don't like that.   Do you like warm milk?

The present subjunctive II of **mögen** in this meaning is usually rendered in English by *would like* (*to*):

Er **möchte** nach Hause gehen.   Ich **möchte** ein Glas Wasser.
He would like to go home.   I would like a glass of water.

(*b*) *may* (expressing possibility). This usage is synonymous with that of **können** and also with that of the present subjunctive II of **dürfen** to express possibility:

Das **mag** wahr sein. Das **dürfte** wahr sein. Das **kann** (könnte) wahr sein.
That may be true (i.e., it is possible that it is true).

Caution. In this meaning, the simple past tense of **mögen** occurs fairly often. Since English has no past equivalent of *may*, the translation can use either the past tense of the verb dependent on **mögen** in conjunction with *perhaps*, or *may have* with the past participle of the verb in question:

Das **mochte** wahr sein.
Perhaps that was true.
OR: That may have been true.

The idea of *may have* can also be expressed with either the present or past tense of **mögen** combined with the perfect infinitive:

Das **mag** (**mochte**) wahr *gewesen sein.*
That may have been true.

For **mögen** in the sense of *should* in indirect commands, see Chapter 17, Section B, paragraph 7.

müssen

4. müssen has two major meanings:

(*a*) *to have to, must* (in the sense of *to have to*):

Ich **muß** das tun.   Wir **müssen** jetzt nach Hause.
I must (have to) do that.   We must (have to) go home now.

Caution. (1) *must* can be used in English only to translate the present tense of **müssen**. For all other tenses, the forms of *to have to* must be employed:

Ich **mußte** das tun.   Er **wird** das eines Tages tun **müssen.**
I had to do that.   He will have to do that some day.

(2) Remember that English *must not* means *not allowed to* and is the equivalent of **nicht dürfen** in German (see above, under **dürfen**). Thus, for **nicht müssen,** forms of *to have to* must be used in English:

Ich muß es nicht tun.

I don't have to do it.

(*b*) *must have,* or *undoubtedly* used with a perfect infinitive, to express strong probability. This construction parallels English usage with *must* and a perfect infinitive:

Er muß das *getan haben.*

He must have done it.

OR: He has undoubtedly done it.

sollen

5. **sollen** has three major meanings:

(*a*) *to be to, to be supposed to* (in the sense of *to be expected to*). In this meaning, **sollen** generally presents the idea that a wish, command, or order has been expressed by someone other than the subject of **sollen:**

Fritz, deine Mutter ruft. Du **sollst** sofort nach Hause kommen.
Fritz, your mother is calling. You are (supposed) to come home immediately.

Gestern **sollte** ich meine Großmutter besuchen.
I was (supposed) to visit my grandmother yesterday.

Note that in this usage the present subjunctive II occurs in the sense of *should* or *ought to:*

Du **solltest** jetzt deine Hausarbeit machen.

You should (ought to) do your homework now.

(*b*) *to be (going) to, will* (in the sense of *to be destined by circumstances or fate to*):

Er weiß es noch nicht, aber er **soll** sie nie wiedersehen.
He doesn't know it yet but he will never (is never going to) see her again.

Although this usage is rare in the present, it is quite common in the past tense, where it is the equivalent of English *was to* or *would:*

Nach dem Tode seines Vaters sorgte er für seine Mutter, die er aber auch bald verlieren **sollte.**   After his father's death he took care of his mother whom, however, he was soon to lose also.

Caution. Since the past indicative and the present subjunctive II forms of **sollen** are identical, great care must be taken to distinguish between them on the basis of the context in which they appear. In general, if the time context is present or future, the subjunctive (in the meaning of *should* or *ought to*) is involved:

> Sie **sollten** morgen Ihre kranke Schwester besuchen.
>
> You should (ought to) visit your sick sister tomorrow.

In a past situation it is fairly safe to assume that *was to* can be used in English:

> Sie **sollten** gestern Ihre kranke Schwester besuchen.
>
> You were to visit your sick sister yesterday.

(*c*) *to be supposed to* (in the sense of *to be said to*, expressing hearsay):

> Er **soll** sehr krank sein.
>
> He is said (supposed) to be very sick.

OR:

> They say he is very sick.

If the hearsay refers to the past, **sollen** is generally used with a perfect infinitive:

> Er **soll** sehr krank *gewesen sein.*
>
> He is said to have been very sick.

Occasionally, however, the past tense of **sollen** may be found with the simple infinitive:

> Er **sollte** sehr krank *sein.*
>
> He was said to be very sick.

wollen

6. **wollen** has two major meanings:

(*a*) *to want to, to intend to, to wish to:*

Ich **will** das tun.	Sie **wollen** nicht mitkommen.
I want to do that.	They do not wish to come along.

Caution. German sometimes uses **wollen** in this meaning with a subject which is not a living being and which in English would not be thought of as being able to want something. In such instances, English cannot employ the translation suggested above, so that other equivalents must be found:

> Solche *Pflanzen* **wollen** jeden Tag begossen werden.
>
> Such plants require watering (LITERALLY: want to be watered) every day.

Noch eine andere *Tatsache* **will** berücksichtigt werden.
One further fact demands consideration (LITERALLY: wants to be considered).

(b) to claim:

> Er **will** etwas ganz Besonderes sein.
> He claims to be something quite special.

When a claim is made with reference to past time, the perfect infinitive is used:

Er **will** das getan haben.   Sie **will** schon einmal hier gewesen sein.
He claims to have done it.   She claims to have been here before.

C. Other Verbs Having Dependent Infinitives Without *zu*

1. There are a number of otherwise regular independent verbs which at times function like modal auxiliaries in that they have dependent infinitives without **zu** and use the "double infinitive" construction (instead of their normal past participle and a dependent infinitive).

lassen

2. The most important verb of this type is **lassen** which, as an independent verb, means *to leave:*

> Er **hat** seinen Mantel zu Hause **gelassen.**
> He left his coat at home.

With a dependent infinitive, **lassen** can express the following ideas:

(a) to have something done (in contrast to doing it oneself)

> Ich **lasse** mir die Haare *waschen.*
> I am having my hair washed.

> Ich **habe** mir die Haare *waschen lassen.*
> I had my hair washed.

Caution. This use of **lassen** is found in a number of common idioms where the English equivalent does not seem to indicate the idea of *having something done.* If the reader encounters such expressions with which he is unfamiliar, he will often find it easy to arrive at the correct meaning if he keeps this meaning of **lassen** in mind:

> Er **ließ** den Arzt *holen.*
> He sent for the doctor (i.e., he had the doctor fetched).

> Ich **lasse** mich *scheiden.*
> I am getting a divorce (i.e., I am having myself separated).

(b) to allow or *let somebody do something* or *to let something be done:*

> Ich **lasse** ihn noch eine Stunde *schlafen.*
> I'll let him sleep for another hour.

(c) to cause someone to do something or *something to be done:*

> Seine Bemerkung **ließ** mich weiter über diese Frage *nachdenken.*
> His remark caused me to think this question over further.

(d) can be . . . (with **lassen** used reflexively: **sich lassen**):

> Das **läßt sich** nicht mehr *feststellen.*
> That can no longer be determined.

> Das **hat sich** leider nicht *beweisen* **lassen.**
> Unfortunately, that could not be proved.

fühlen and similar verbs

3. Of the verbs which may take a dependent infinitive without **zu** only **lassen** consistently uses the "double infinitive" construction for the perfect tenses. Other verbs which will usually be found with the "double infinitive" but often also with the regular past participle (in combination with the dependent infinitive) are: **fühlen** (*to feel*), **helfen** (*to help*), **hören** (*to hear*), **lehren** (*to teach*), **lernen** (*to learn*), and **sehen** (*to see*):

Ich **sehe** ihn kommen.	Ich habe ihn kommen **sehen** (OR: **gesehen**).
I see him coming.	I saw him come.
Ich **helfe** ihm arbeiten.	Ich habe ihm arbeiten **helfen** (OR: **geholfen**).
I am helping him work.	I helped him work.
Ich **lerne** Deutsch lesen.	Ich habe Deutsch lesen **lernen** (OR: **gelernt**).
I am learning to read German.	I learned to read German.

Special Points

The past subjunctive II of the modal auxiliaries **können** and **sollen** are frequently used to express the ideas of *could have* and *should have,* respectively:

Sie **hätten** gehen **können.**	Er **hätte** zu Hause bleiben **sollen.**
They could have gone.	He should have stayed home.

Of less common occurrence are the same subjunctive forms of the other modals. Note the meanings in each case:

dürfen

> Ich **hätte** ins Kino gehen **dürfen,** wenn ich fertig gewesen wäre.
> I would have been allowed to go to the movies if I had been ready.

mögen

> Ich **hätte** ins Kino gehen **mögen,** aber niemand wollte mitkommen.
> I would have liked to go to the movies but nobody wanted to come along.

müssen

> Ich **hätte** sofort weggehen **müssen,** wenn er wirklich gekommen wäre.
> I would have had to leave immediately if he had really come.

wollen

> **Hätten** Sie das Buch lesen **wollen,** wenn Sie gewußt hätten, wie schlecht es ist?
> Would you have wanted to read the book if you had known how bad it is?

RECOGNITION EXERCISES

A. *Translate:*

1. Er wird diesen deutschen Satz, den ich nicht übersetzen kann, bestimmt übersetzen können, denn er kann viel besser Deutsch als ich. 2. Wir glaubten, daß sie dieses Rätsel lösen könnte, aber sie konnte es nicht. 3. Die Antwort auf die Frage, die er gestellt hat, habe ich noch nicht finden können. 4. Ich habe dem alten Mann, der so Schreckliches erlebt haben soll, ein wenig helfen wollen, aber ich habe es nicht gekonnt. 5. Wir wußten nicht, warum er es nicht hatte tun können. 6. Was er gesagt hat, kann wahr sein, aber es muß es nicht sein. 7. Kann ich heute abend um acht Uhr zu Ihnen kommen? 8. Er kann das Referat, das er für heute schreiben sollte, schon fertig haben, aber es läßt sich nicht genau feststellen. 9. Die Kinder dürfen heute nachmittag ins Kino, aber sie können trotzdem nicht hingehen, weil die Großmutter kommt. 10. Als Kinder durften wir alles tun, was wir wollten—und das soll nun schlecht für uns gewesen sein! 11. Darf ich Sie um eine Zigarette bitten? 12. Das dürfte richtig sein, aber wir können uns nicht darauf verlassen. 13. Kleine Kinder, die sich wie wilde Tiere benehmen, dürfen nicht im Wohnzimmer spielen. 14. Die kleinen Kinder meiner Schwester müssen noch nicht zur Schule. 15. Fritz, mußt du schon so früh nach Hause? 16. Mußtest du wirklich schon so früh zu Hause sein, Barbara? 17. Der Kleine mußte seine Aufgabe machen, ehe er mit den anderen Kindern spielen durfte. 18. Er muß schon nach New York gefahren sein, sonst wäre er heute zu uns gekommen. 19. Sie muß ihre Arbeit schon geschrieben haben, denn sie ist ausgegangen. 20. Wenn er die Aufgabe, die eigentlich heute hätte fertig sein sollen, jetzt nicht machen will, wird er sie ohne mich machen müssen. 21. Haben Sie es ihm schon gesagt? Ja, obgleich ich es nicht gewollt habe, habe ich es doch gemußt. 22. Er

könnte der alten Dame helfen, aber er will es einfach nicht. 23. Sie will eine
Nichte des letzten deutschen Kaisers sein. 24. Er will das Buch, das wir für
nächsten Montag lesen sollen, schon gelesen haben. 25. Eine solche Frage will
sofort beantwortet sein. 26. Die Rose ist eine zarte Blume und will sorgfältig
gepflegt werden.

B. *Translate:*

1. Ich mag diesen Film, den die Zeitungen so gelobt haben, nicht noch
einmal sehen. 2. Den Mann, der an der Ecke Zeitungen verkauft, mag sie
nicht. 3. Er mag warmes Bier nicht. 4. „Ich möchte etwas zu trinken haben."
„Möchten Sie ein kaltes Bier?" 5. Was er uns erzählt hat, mag stimmen, aber
beweisen kann er es nicht. 6. Das mochte der Fall sein, aber er wußte es nicht
genau. 7. Er mag gestern hier gewesen sein, aber ich habe ihn nicht gesehen.
8. Ich sollte jetzt meinen kranken Onkel besuchen, aber ich möchte lieber ins
Kino gehen. 9. Ich sollte gestern meinen kranken Onkel besuchen, aber ich
konnte nicht. 10. Herr Schmidt, Ihre Frau hat eben angerufen. Sie sollen
auf dem Nachhauseweg eine Flasche Milch besorgen. 11. Er sollte für seine
jüngere Schwester sorgen, aber er kümmert sich gar nicht um sie. 12. Als er
zwanzig Jahre alt war, verließ er seine Heimatstadt, die er nie wiedersehen
sollte. 13. Er soll eine kleine Tochter aus erster Ehe haben, aber niemand hat
sie je gesehen. 14. Der Vater meines Freundes soll 1929 sein ganzes Vermögen
verloren haben. 15. Vor dem Krieg soll er sehr arm gewesen sein. 16. Sie
könnte es tun, wenn sie wollte. 17. Sie hätte es bestimmt tun können, wenn sie
es wirklich hätte tun wollen. 18. Wenn der Chef es verlangte, müßte ich es
tun, auch wenn ich es nicht wollte. 19. Wenn sie es von mir verlangt hätte,
hätte ich es tun müssen. 20. Ich hätte gestern nicht ausgehen sollen, denn ich
wußte, daß meine Mutter mich anrufen würde. 21. Sie hätten die alte Dame
nicht so kränken sollen, Herr Schmidt. 22. Er hätte den Wagen selbst reparieren können, wenn er die richtigen Werkzeuge gehabt hätte. 23. Sie
werden den Wagen heute kaum benutzen können, denn wir müssen ihn erst
reparieren lassen. 24. Da er selbst nicht genug Deutsch konnte, ließ er den
gestern aus Deutschland gekommenen Brief von seiner in München geborenen
Sekretärin übersetzen. 25. Leider hat er den Hut, den er gewöhnlich trägt, aus
Versehen im Büro gelassen. 26. Er hat sich endlich von dem besten Schneider
der Stadt eine neue Jacke machen lassen. 27. Den Hund, der vor der Tür
bellte, ließ das Mädchen endlich herein. 28. Ihre Argumente ließen ihn die
ganze Sache noch einmal durchdenken. 29. Das mag wohl sein, aber es läßt
sich nicht beweisen. 30. Die Folgen seiner Tat ließen sich leicht voraussehen.
31. Er wird wohl immer noch zu Hause sein, denn wir haben ihn vor zehn
Minuten nach Hause kommen sehen.

C. *Strong verbs. Memorize:*

INFINITIVE	PRESENT	PAST	PAST PARTICIPLE	INFINITIVE
beißen		biß	gebissen	to bite
beweisen		bewies	bewiesen	to prove

MODAL AUXILIARIES

INFINITIVE	PRESENT	PAST	PAST PARTICIPLE	INFINITIVE
bitten		bat	gebeten	to ask (a favor)
genießen		genoß	genossen	to enjoy
gewinnen		gewann	gewonnen	to win
springen		sprang	(ist) gesprungen	to jump
stehlen	stiehlt	stahl	gestohlen	to steal
tragen	trägt	trug	getragen	to wear; carry
vermeiden		vermied	vermieden	to avoid
waschen	wäscht	wusch	gewaschen	to wash
werfen	wirft	warf	geworfen	to throw
zwingen		zwang	gezwungen	to force

Wed

ACTIVE EXERCISES

A. *Change the following sentences to the past tense:*
1. Niemand kann diese schreckliche Suppe essen. 2. Wir dürfen im Schlaf-zimmer nicht rauchen. 3. Ich mag diese Frau nicht darum bitten. 4. Sie kön-nen diese Schwierigkeiten leicht vermeiden. 5. Willst du ihn wirklich zwingen? 6. Sie soll ihre kranke Tante besuchen. 7. Sie müssen den Ball so werfen, daß man ihn fangen kann. 8. Wir wollen ihn so bald wie möglich sprechen. 9. Das mag wohl sein. 10. Sie will sich die Hände waschen.

Wel

B. *Change the following sentences to the present perfect:*
1. Ich kann diese Frage nicht beantworten. 2. Sie muß nach Hause. 3. Die Kinder dürfen draußen spielen. 4. Er läßt seine Mutter oft allein im Haus. 5. Sie läßt sich heute die Haare waschen. 6. Wir müssen zum Arzt gehen. 7. Er mag hübsche Mädchen immer gern. 8. Ich will den frechen Menschen hinauswerfen. 9. Wir mögen seine Bilder nicht. 10. Meine Mutter läßt mich am Sonntag immer lange schlafen.

C. *Translate:*
1. May I please have the newspaper if you have finished with it?
2. If he cannot come today we shall have to invite him another time.
3. He said that he had not been able to avoid these difficulties.
4. Fritz, you must not throw rocks (*translate:* with rocks).
5. He really shouldn't drink so much if he has to work tomorrow.
6. He was supposed to take (**bringen**) me home, but I didn't want to wait for him.
7. He is supposed to be an excellent tennis player, but we have never seen him play.
8. If I have time this afternoon I shall have my hair cut.
9. I would like to buy myself a new hat if I could find the time for it.
10. She could not have avoided this mistake even if she had wanted to.

11. They have not been able to force him to move out.
12. You should have washed your red dress yesterday so that you could wear it today.

13. Somebody may have stolen his watch because he can't find it.
14. The dog surely would have bitten him if he had not been able to run so fast.
15. He met (**kennenlernen**) the girl, who was later to become his wife, in 1935.
16. Let's ask him about the movie. He must have seen it already.
17. They are said to have made a lot of money during the war.
18. He claims to have won that money, but he probably stole it.
19. She would have had to eat her spinach if her mother had been there.
20. You may go to bed now if you want to.

20

Reflexive and Impersonal Verbs

A. Reflexive Verbs

Definition

1. A reflexive verb is one in which the person or thing represented by an object pronoun is identical with the subject, i.e. "refers back" to it: **Ich wasche mich,** *I wash myself*—the persons washing and washed are the same.

A number of German verbs can be used only reflexively (**sich erkälten,** *to catch cold;* **sich schämen,** *to be ashamed*), but many other ordinary verbs can be made reflexive by combining them with reflexive pronouns. In many cases this involves a more or less radical change in meaning:

> **schlagen,** to beat, to hit: *sich* **schlagen,** to fight, to duel
> **treffen,** to hit (a target):   *sich* **treffen,** to meet

Note that the English equivalent of many German reflexive verbs is not reflexive.

Reflexive pronouns

2. Reflexive pronouns exist in only two cases, the dative and the accusative. The third person singular and plural, dative and accusative, have a form which is only used as a reflexive pronoun: **sich.** For all other persons the corresponding forms of the personal pronoun serve also as reflexives. Thus, the reflexive pronouns are:

	SINGULAR					PLURAL			POLITE
Dative	mir	dir	sich	sich	sich	uns	euch	sich	sich
Accusative	mich	dich	sich	sich	sich	uns	euch	sich	sich

Conjugation

3. A reflexive verb is conjugated by placing the appropriate reflexive pronoun for each person AFTER the finite verb:

187

sich setzen, to sit down

ich setze mich	wir setzen uns
du setzt dich	ihr setzt euch
er setzt sich	sie setzen sich

Position of subject in inverted word order

The situation changes, however, when a principal clause does not have normal word order (subject first). In inverted word order (subject NOT first) the relative position of subject, verb, and reflexive is as follows:

(*a*) Personal pronoun subjects precede the reflexives:

> Früher **ärgerte** *er* **sich** immer sehr darüber.
> He always used to get very annoyed about that.

(*b*) Demonstrative pronoun subjects follow the reflexives:

> Früher **ärgerte sich** *der* sehr darüber.
> **He** used to get very annoyed about that.

(*c*) Noun subjects may precede or follow the reflexives:

> Früher **ärgerte sich** *mein Vater* immer sehr darüber.
OR: > Früher **ärgerte** *mein Vater* **sich** immer sehr darüber.
> My father always used to get very annoyed about that.

In dependent clauses the relative position of noun or pronoun subjects and reflexives is the same, but the finite verb is at the end of the clause:

Ich glaube,
> daß *er* **sich** früher immer sehr darüber ärgerte.
> daß **sich** *der* früher immer sehr darüber ärgerte.
> daß **sich** *mein Vater* (*mein Vater* **sich**) früher immer sehr darüber ärgerte.

Caution. In a long dependent clause the reflexive pronoun can be separated by a considerable distance from the verb with which it is used:

Wir stellten bald fest, daß **sich** die Richtigkeit der von ihm aufgestellten Theorie über die Entstehung dieser Wortklasse, die wir hier vor uns haben, nicht leicht beweisen **läßt.**	We soon found out that the correctness of the theory propounded by him about the origin of this class of words with which we are dealing cannot easily be proved.

It is, therefore, particularly important that the reader keep the reflexive pronoun in mind until he has come to the finite verb at the end of the clause.

Reflexive pronoun in the dative

4. While most reflexive verbs use the reflexive pronoun in the accusative, verbs that take a dative object (Chapter 10, Section A, paragraph 4, and Table B) use the reflexive pronoun also in the dative:

ich helfe **mir**	wir helfen **uns**
du hilfst **dir**	ihr helft **euch**
er hilft **sich**	sie helfen **sich**

In addition, the reflexive pronoun will be in the dative if it is the indirect object, in which case the verb will also have a direct object in the accusative:

> Ich möchte **mir** gerne *einen neuen Wagen* kaufen.
> I would like to buy (myself) a new car.

Frequently, the English equivalent does not require the idea of the dative reflexive in German:

> Er nimmt **sich** *einen Apfel.*
> He takes an apple.

A reflexive pronoun in the dative is also commonly used instead of a possessive adjective when the object of the verb is a part of the body or an article of clothing belonging to the person represented by the subject:

Er wäscht **sich** gerade die Hände.	Ich putze **mir** die Schuhe.
He is just washing *his* hands.	I am polishing *my* shoes.

Reflexive verbs as passive substitutes

5. Reflexive verbs are frequently used as substitutes for the passive and can then be translated conveniently in English with the passive:

> Hier **zeigte es sich** wieder, daß . . .
> Here it was shown again that . . .

> In unserer Sammlung **findet sich** keine solche Fassung.
> No such version is found in our collection.

einander

6. Reflexive verbs can be used, particularly in the plural, to express a reciprocal action. In such cases the invariable **einander** can be substituted for the reflexive pronoun:

> Die beiden liebten **sich** (OR: **einander**) herzlich.
> The two loved each other tenderly.

B. Impersonal Verbs

Definition

1. Impersonal verbs are those which are used only in the third person singular in each tense, with the subject **es.** An example is **regnen,** *to rain:*

es regnet	es hat geregnet
es regnete	es hatte geregnet
es wird regnen	es wird geregnet haben

Phenomena of nature

2. The most obvious group of impersonal verbs pertains to phenomena of nature, especially the weather, such as: **blitzen,** *to lighten;* **dämmern,** *to dawn;* **donnern,** *to thunder;* **frieren,** *to freeze;* **hageln,** *to hail;* **rauschen,** *to rustle;* **schneien,** *to snow;* **stürmen,** *to storm;* **tauen,** *to thaw.*

Es blitzt.	Es schneite die ganze Nacht.
It is lightning.	It snowed all night.

Note that such verbs also have the impersonal *it* as subject in the English equivalents.

Other impersonal verbs

3. Unlike the verbs pertaining to the weather, however, most impersonal constructions in German DO involve a person who is included in the statement in either the accusative or the dative case. Since the English equivalents of these verbs are not impersonal, the dative or accusative element of the German clause becomes the subject of the English expression:

Es tut **mir** leid.	Es freut **mich,** daß Sie mitkommen wollen.
I am sorry.	I am pleased that you want to come along.
Es gelang **ihr** nicht.	Es ärgert **ihn,** daß sie nichts sagt.
She did not succeed.	He is annoyed that she doesn't say anything.
Es fehlt **ihm** an Bargeld.	Es ist **mir** übel geworden.
He is lacking cash.	I got sick.

Some of these impersonal verbs expressing mental, emotional, or physical states may be encountered with the dative or accusative noun (or pronoun) in first position, in which case the **es** is omitted:

Mich freut, daß Sie mitkommen wollen.
I am glad that you want to come along.

Ihn ärgert, daß sie nichts sagt.
He is annoyed that she doesn't say anything.

Mir ist übel geworden.
I got sick.

es gibt

4. Of special importance is the impersonal construction **es gibt** (*there is, there are*), **es gab, es wird geben, es hat gegeben, es hatte gegeben, es wird gegeben haben**. Note that it always takes the direct object:

Es gibt dieses Jahr keine Erdbeeren.   **Hat es** etwas Neues **gegeben?**
There are no strawberries this year.   Was there anything new?

es gibt is also used in speaking of food which is (or was) being served:

Was **gibt es** heute zu essen?
What is there to eat today?

Note also the expression: **Was gibts?** *What's up?*

Special Points

selbst, selber

1. Do not confuse the words **selbst** or **selber** (*myself, yourself, himself,* etc.), which are used after nouns or pronouns for emphasis, with the reflexive pronouns. In English, these emphatic words have the same forms as the reflexives:

He did it *himself:* {Er **selbst** (**selber**) hat es getan.
                     {Er hat es **selbst** (**selber**) getan.

But:

He washed *himself:*   Er hat **sich** gewaschen.

Note that **selbst** (but NOT **selber**) means *even* when it precedes a word:

Selbst *ich* weiß das.   Das hat er **selbst** *seiner Frau* nicht gesagt.
Even I know that.   He did not tell that even to his wife.

Selbst *wenn* ich das wüßte, sagte ich es nicht.
Even if I knew it I would not say it.

sich in infinitive and other constructions

2. In infinitive constructions, the reflexive pronoun **sich** may not refer to the subject of the principal clause but to a person who is implied or

understood and represented in the principal clause by some other part of speech than the subject:

> Er riet *den Student̲e̲n̲,* s̲i̲c̲h̲ für das Examen gut vorzubereiten.

He advised the students to prepare themselves well for the examination.

A similar usage may occur in a modified adjective construction:

> Er kannte den **s̲i̲c̲h̲** vorstellenden *Kandi̲d̲a̲t̲e̲n̲* nicht.

He did not know the candidate who presented himself.

RECOGNITION EXERCISES

A. *Translate:*

1. Dieses Bild mit den alten Häusern erinnert mich an die Straße, in der ich als Kind gewohnt habe. 2. Meine Mutter erzählt mir oft von der Straße, in der ich als Kind gewohnt habe, aber ich kann mich nicht mehr daran erinnern. 3. Ein besseres Beispiel für dieses Phänomen kann ich mir nicht denken. 4. Ich denke, es gibt kein besseres Beispiel für dieses Phänomen. 5. Er interessiert sich sehr für moderne Malerei, aber mich interessiert die gar nicht. 6. Sie können sich darauf verlassen, daß meine Eltern das Haus um Punkt 10 Uhr verlassen. 7. Ich kann mir gar nicht vorstellen, warum er mir seine Freundin nicht vorgestellt hat. 8. Vor dem Beginn der Vorstellung, die uns alle sehr unterhalten hat, unterhielten wir uns mit unseren Freunden. 9. Im Laufe des 15. und 16. Jahrhunderts entwickelte sich eine neue Auffassung des Menschen. 10. Im Laufe der Zeit entwickelte er ein neues Modell für seine Maschine. 11. Als er sah, was das kleine Paket enthielt, das ich ihm nur zum Spaß gegeben hatte, konnte er sich des Lachens nicht enthalten. 12. Nachdem sie die Weinflasche auf den Tisch gesetzt hatte, setzte sie sich an den Tisch. 13. Sie tun alles mögliche, um mich zu ärgern, aber über solche Kleinigkeiten ärgere ich mich nie. 14. Wer sich einbildet, er sei besser als die anderen, ist sehr eingebildet. 15. Wenn er sich neulich auch erkältet hat, hat er sich doch so schnell erholt, daß er schon wieder zur Schule geht. 16. Er verheiratete seine ältere Tochter an einen erfolgreichen Arzt, während sich seine jüngere Tochter mit einem armen Schullehrer verheiratet hat. 17. Er hat mir seine Unterstützung versprochen, aber davon verspreche ich mir nicht viel. 18. Der Kleine wäscht sich jeden Tag selbst, aber er vergißt dann oft, sich auch die Ohren zu waschen. 19. Weil sich dieser Satz nicht leicht verstehen läßt, läßt ihn sich der Student noch einmal erklären.

B. *Translate:*

1. Wo finden wir den Aufsatz über Goethe, den Sie uns empfohlen haben? 2. Der Aufsatz findet sich in einer kleinen Sammlung von Artikeln, die wir leider in unserer Bibliothek nicht haben. 3. Es empfiehlt sich aber, ihn zu lesen, bevor Sie sich an Ihre Seminararbeit machen. 4. Auch in seiner Antwort auf die zweite Frage zeigt sich seine mangelhafte Vorbereitung. 5. Es freut

mich, daß es Ihnen gut geht. Mir geht es schlecht, wie immer. 6. Ich freue mich nicht auf den Winter, denn mich friert dann die ganze Zeit. 7. Meinem Vater tut es leid, daß er Ihnen nicht helfen kann. 8. Mir wurde fast übel, als ich hörte, wie er von der Polizei behandelt worden ist. 9. Den Wissenschaftlern, die sich seit Jahren mit diesem Problem beschäftigen, wird es hoffentlich bald gelingen, eine Antwort auf diese Frage zu finden. 10. Heute hören wir einen Vortrag von dem Professor, dem es gelungen ist, ein Vakzin gegen die Masern zu entwickeln. 11. Den Leuten, die sich am meisten für Musik interessieren, fehlt es oft an Mitteln, sich Konzertkarten zu verschaffen. 12. Wenn er sich auch für sein Thema sehr begeistert, ist es ihm doch nicht gelungen, auch seine Zuhörer dafür zu begeistern. 13. Ich wundere mich gar nicht darüber, daß er es nicht selbst tun konnte. 14. So etwas sagt sich leicht, aber es läßt sich oft nicht leicht durchführen. 15. Wenn der Professor das Problem nicht selbst lösen kann, sollte er es auch nicht von seinen Studenten verlangen. 16. Warum sollten wir uns Sorgen darüber machen, wenn selbst der Professor das nicht erklären kann? 17. Selbst wenn der Professor uns dieses Problem nicht lösen kann, werden wir uns doch weiter um eine Lösung bemühen. 18. Der Offizier befahl den Soldaten, sich sofort in die Baracke zu begeben. 19. Der Professor erklärte den sich auf das Schlußexamen vorbereitenden Studenten, was von ihnen verlangt wurde. 20. Die ersten Paragraphen des Artikels beziehen sich auf einen vor zwei Jahren in derselben Zeitschrift erschienenen Aufsatz.

C. *Strong verbs. Memorize:*

INFINITIVE	PRESENT	PAST	PAST PARTICIPLE	INFINITIVE
sich benehmen	benimmt (sich)	benahm sich	sich benommen	to behave
sich beziehen		bezog sich	sich bezogen	to refer
gleichen		glich	geglichen	to resemble
graben	gräbt	grub	gegraben	to dig
leiden		litt	gelitten	to suffer
riechen		roch	gerochen	to smell
schleichen		schlich	(ist) geschlichen	to sneak
schreien		schrie	geschrien	to yell, scream
streiten		stritt	gestritten	to fight, quarrel
(sich) verbergen	verbirgt (sich)	verbarg (sich)	(sich) verborgen	to hide
verlassen	verläßt	verließ	verlassen	to leave
verlieren		verlor	verloren	to lose

ACTIVE EXERCISES

A. *Complete the following sentences by supplying the correct German for the English words in parentheses:*

1. Der Dieb verbarg (himself) im Keller. 2. Er (himself) hat dieses Bild gemalt. 3. Sie kauft (herself) ein neues Kleid. 4. Sie hat das (herself) ge-

macht. 5. Sie kennt (herself) nur zu gut. 6. Das kleine Mädchen kann (herself) schon selbst anziehen. 7. Die Kinder graben (for themselves) einen Tunnel im Garten. 8. Ich lasse (for myself) ein kleines Haus bauen. 9. Sie haben (each other) nie aus den Augen verloren. 10. Wenn ihm niemand hilft, wird er (himself) selber helfen müssen. 11. Sieh (yourself), wie dich die anderen sehen. 12. Warum benimmt sie (herself) immer so schlecht in Gesellschaft? 13. (Even) mein Vater kann das nicht. 14. Haben Sie das Kleid (yourself) genäht, Frau Schmidt? 15. Die beiden Mädchen glichen (one another), als wären sie Zwillinge.

B. *Change the following sentences which are in the plural to the singular, and those which are in the singular to the plural:*

1. Wir können uns das ganz gut denken. 2. Ich kann mich nicht darauf verlassen. 3. Sie läßt sich die Haare schneiden. 4. Ich kann mir so etwas einfach nicht vorstellen. 5. Wir werden uns bestimmt gut amüsieren. 6. Du erkältest dich, wenn du bei diesem Wetter ausgehst. 7. Bilde dir nicht ein, du könntest das besser machen. 8. Sie ärgern sich sehr darüber. 9. Er entschuldigt sich nie, wenn er sich schlecht benimmt. 10. Ich schlich mich ins Wohnzimmer.

C. *Translate:*

1. You simply cannot imagine how badly he behaved yesterday.
2. They are hiding behind the wall in the garden.
3. This poem is not found in any anthology I have.
4. If we could only see ourselves as others see us.
5. He is always annoyed at the high prices in that store.
6. It is thundering and lightning, but I don't think it will rain.
7. I am freezing. If you don't close the window I'll catch cold.
8. She is sorry that you did not have a good time.
9. That is a question to which there is no answer.
10. Fritz, if you don't hurry, we'll be late (**zu spät**) again.
11. She refused to concern herself (*occupy herself*) with that question.
12. My father and my uncle always quarrelled when they saw each other.
13. I am looking for a secretary I can rely on.
14. The child would not have screamed if it had not been afraid.
15. If you aren't willing (**bereit**) to help yourself, then I won't help you either.
16. The little boy is finally having his hair cut this afternoon.
17. He will make every effort (**sich sehr bemühen**) to prepare (*himself*) for the examination, even if he doesn't have much time.
18. He has suffered so much himself that he can understand what I have suffered.
19. His remark refers to the problem in the second chapter.
20. The flowers which smell so good are (*use* **sich befinden**) in the garden in front of the house.

21

Passive and Passive Substitutes

A. The Passive

Active and passive

1. To distinguish the passive voice from the active voice it is necessary to realize that in the active the action of the verb is performed by the subject:

Der Polizist verhaftet den Dieb.

The policeman arrests the thief.

In the passive, however, the subject is the recipient of the action:

Der Dieb wird von dem Polizisten verhaftet.

The thief is being arrested by the policeman.

Formation of tenses

2. The auxiliary for the passive in German is **werden** (while English uses *to be*). The various tenses are formed by combining the appropriate tense forms of **werden** with the past participle of the main verb: **ich werde gefragt,** *I am* (being) *asked;* **ich wurde gefragt,** *I was* (being) *asked,* and so on.

In the perfect tenses of the passive, the past participle of **werden** is **worden** (and NOT **geworden**) which is placed AFTER the past participle of the main verb:

Ich bin *gefragt* **worden.**   I have been asked.

Since **werden** is conjugated with **sein** in the perfect tenses, the finite verb of a perfect tense in the passive is also **sein: ich bin gefragt worden,** *I have been asked.*

werden / future passive to Become (handwritten annotation)

Synopsis

3. Compare the various German tense forms in the passive with their corresponding English forms in the following synopsis:

PRESENT:	Ich werde gefragt.	I am (being) asked.
PAST:	Ich wurde gefragt.	I was (being) asked.
FUTURE:	Ich werde gefragt werden.	I shall be asked.
PRESENT PERFECT:	Ich bin gefragt worden.	I have been (was) asked.
PAST PERFECT:	Ich war gefragt worden.	I had been asked.
FUTURE PERFECT:	Ich werde gefragt worden sein.	I shall have been asked.

Caution. (1) Do not confuse the present tense of the passive, made up of the present tense of **werden** and the past participle of a main verb, with the future tense of the active voice in which the present tense of **werden** is combined with an infinitive:

FUTURE ACTIVE:	Ich **werde** *fragen*.	I shall ask.
PRESENT PASSIVE:	Ich **werde** *gefragt*.	I am (being) asked.

(2) Some strong verbs with inseparable prefixes have the same form for the infinitive and the past particple (as: **empfangen, empfing, empfangen,** *to receive*). With such verbs the present passive and the future active look exactly alike. Observe in the following examples that a decision as to which form is involved can be made only on the basis of the other elements in the sentence:

PRESENT PASSIVE:

Ich **werde** bestimmt nicht vom Direktor selbst *empfangen*.
I shall certainly not be received by the director himself.

FUTURE ACTIVE:

Ich **werde** bestimmt nichts vom Direktor selbst *empfangen*.
I shall certainly not receive anything from the director himself.

Agent of the passive action

4. The performer (agent) of the action in a passive statement is ordinarily expressed in German as the object of the preposition **von** (English *by*):

Die Stadt wurde von *den Rebellen* zerstört.
The city was destroyed by the rebels.

Instrument of passive action

5. The means by which an action is performed (instrument) is usually indicated as the object of the preposition **durch** (English *through, by*):

Die Stadt wurde **durch** *Bomben* zerstört.
The city was destroyed by bombs.

6. If a clear distinction between agent and instrument cannot be made, either preposition (**von** or **durch**) may be used:

Das Theater wird **von der** (**durch die**) *Regierung* unterstützt.
The theater is (being) supported by the government.

"Apparent passive"

our

7. It is necessary to distinguish between the passive, in which **werden** is used as an auxiliary and combined with a past participle, and the so-called "apparent passive," a construction which consists of the verb **sein** also combined with a past participle, and which resembles in form the English passive:

PASSIVE:

Die Tür **wird** jetzt **geschlossen.**
The door is being closed now.

APPARENT PASSIVE:

Die Tür **ist** jetzt **geschlossen.**
The door is closed now.

Note in the above examples that the passive statement describes the ACTION of the window being closed, while in the "apparent passive" the past participle functions merely as a predicate adjective describing the CONDITION or the STATE of the window which resulted from some previous action.

Caution. In general, German distinguishes rather carefully between these two constructions. There is, however, a tendency in colloquial German and in some dialects to substitute the "apparent passive" for the true passive with the result that occasionally the "apparent passive" is encountered in literature where a real passive would be expected.

Verbs with dative used in passive

8. Verbs which govern the dative in the active have no grammatical subject when they are used in the passive. The noun (or pronoun) in the dative is used in place of a subject (as the recipient of the action of the verb):

ACTIVE:

Man dankte **mir** dafür.
They (one) thanked me for it.

Das hat **ihm** sehr geholfen.
That helped him very much.

PASSIVE:

Mir wurde dafür gedankt.
I was thanked for it.

Ihm ist damit sehr geholfen worden.
He was very much helped by that.

Note that these datives in German passive constructions are translated in English as if they were nominatives. However, the impersonal pronoun **es** can be added in first position in such passive constructions, in which case the dative element follows the finite verb:

Es wurde **mir** dafür gedankt.   *Es* ist **ihm** sehr damit geholfen worden.

This **es**, which is not the grammatical subject, does not change the meaning in any way.

"Impersonal passive"

9. There is another type of passive construction without a grammatical subject (the so-called impersonal passive) which indicates only an activity without naming a recipient of the action:

Am Sonntag **wird** hier nicht **gearbeitet.**

Since English has no parallel construction without a subject, the impersonal passive can be translated in a variety of other ways. Thus, the above example can be rendered as follows:

No work is done here on Sunday.
There is no work done here on Sunday.
Nobody works here on Sunday.
People don't work here on Sunday.

The impersonal pronoun **es** may also introduce an impersonal passive construction as long as no other element begins the clause:

Es wird hier am Sonntag nicht gearbeitet.

But:

Hier wird am Sonntag nicht gearbeitet.

Passive infinitive

10. The passive infinitive of a verb is made up of the past participle and the infinitive of the auxiliary of the passive (**werden** in German, *to be* in English), as in **getan werden,** (*to*) *be done;* **gelesen werden,** (*to*) *be read,* and other verbal expressions.

The passive infinitive is used mainly in conjunction with modal auxiliaries:

Das *kann* (*konnte*) nicht **geduldet werden.**
That cannot (could not) be tolerated.

Er *muß* (*mußte*) unbedingt **bestraft werden.**
He absolutely must (had to) be punished.

Although theoretically any tense of the modal could be used in these constructions, in actual practice only the simple tenses (present and past) are commonly found.

Caution. The modal auxiliaries may also be encountered in combination with the passive infinitive in impersonal passive constructions without a subject:

Hier *kann* von einer eigentlichen Entdeckung nicht **gesprochen werden.**

Such a construction is perhaps best rendered by using the impersonal pronoun *one* (or *we*) as the subject of an English active sentence:

Here we cannot speak of a real discovery.

B. Passive Substitutes

There are a number of commonly occurring substitutes for the passive in German:

man with an active verb

1. When the specific agent of an action is not mentioned, German frequently prefers an active construction with the impersonal subject **man,** where English may use the passive:

Man tut das hier nicht.	Wie **nennt man** das?
That is not done here.	What is that called?
(One doesn't do that here.)	

läßt sich with active infinitive

2. The idea of the modal auxiliary **kann** (*can*) in conjunction with a passive infinitive (such as: **kann getan werden,** *can be done*) is often expressed in German more idiomatically by **läßt sich** (past: **ließ sich**) in combination with an active infinitive:

Das **läßt sich** (**ließ sich**) nicht *beweisen.* ⎱ FOR: ⎰ Das **kann** (**konnte**) nicht
That cannot (could not) be proved. ⎰ ⎱ *bewiesen werden.*

sein and active infinitive with *zu*

3. The same idea can also be stated in German with the verb **sein** and an active infinitive with **zu:**

$$\left.\begin{array}{l}\textbf{Das ist nicht zu beweisen.} \\ \text{That cannot be proved.}\end{array}\right\} \text{ FOR: } \left\{\begin{array}{l}\textbf{Das läßt sich nicht beweisen.} \\ \textbf{Das kann nicht bewiesen werden.} \\ \text{Das kann man nicht beweisen.}\end{array}\right.$$

It should be noted, however, that the construction of **sein** with an active infinitive can also be used as a substitute for the ideas expressed by some other modal auxiliaries with a passive infinitive. Thus, depending on the context, the sentence:

Das ist nicht *zu machen*

could be the equivalent of the following English statements:

That cannot be done.
That must not (is not to) be done.
That should not (ought not to) be done.

4. For the use of reflexive constructions as substitutes for the passive, see the previous chapter.

Special Point

Imperative of passive

The imperative of the passive voice is rare and has a literary or even poetical flavor. Its construction is unusual in that the auxiliary **werden** of the passive voice is not used. Instead, the imperative forms of **sein** (which really are forms of the subjunctive I, see Chapter 17, Section A, paragraph 3) are combined with the past participle of the verb in question:

Sei *bedankt* (*gegrüßt,* etc.)
Be thanked (greeted, etc.)

Seien Sie *versichert* (*überzeugt,* etc.), daß . . .
(You can) be assured (convinced, etc.) that . . .

English frequently handles such constructions with set phrases: Thanks, thank you (**sei bedankt**); greetings (**sei gegrüßt**).

RECOGNITION EXERCISES

A. *Translate:*

1. Sein neuer Roman wird jetzt nicht nur in England, sondern auch in Amerika populär. 2. Sein neuer Roman wird jetzt nicht nur in England, sondern auch in Amerika erscheinen. 3. Sein neuer Roman wird jetzt nicht nur in England, sondern auch in Amerika viel gelesen. 4. Die Fenster waren alle

schon geschlossen, als ich nach Hause kam. 5. Die Fenster waren wohl von meiner Mutter geschlossen worden, ehe ich nach Hause kam. 6. Ich wurde gestern, als er mir erzählte, was mein kleiner Sohn nun wieder angestellt hatte, wirklich wütend. 7. Ich wurde gestern, als ich ihm erzählte, was sein kleiner Sohn nun wieder angestellt hatte, so oft unterbrochen, daß ich schließlich wirklich wütend wurde. 8. Das, was schon geleistet worden ist, ist nichts gegen das, was noch geleistet werden muß. 9. In Amerika wird das Theater noch nicht durch die Regierung unterstützt. 10. Viele Stücke, die eigentlich gespielt werden sollten, werden nicht gegeben, weil keine Geldgeber dafür gefunden werden können. 11. Gewöhnlich werden nur die Dramen, bei denen man sicher sein kann, daß sie Geld einbringen werden, in den größeren Theatern New Yorks gespielt. 12. Durch das Feuer, das nach dem Erdbeben ausbrach, wurde fast die ganze Stadt zerstört. 13. Es sind in den letzten Tagen Gerüchte *haue been* verbreitet worden, die uns alle beunruhigt haben. 14. Auf diese Weise wird nichts Neues erfahren. 15. Auf diese Weise wird man nichts Neues erfahren. 16. Als der zweite Weltkrieg ausbrach, war die Atombombe, durch die später der Krieg so schnell beendet werden sollte, noch nicht erfunden worden. 17. Der junge Mann, der schon mit dreißig Jahren Bankdirektor geworden, dann aber bald danach wegen schwerer Unterschlagungen verhaftet worden war, wurde gestern zu fünf Jahren Zuchthaus verurteilt. *PRISON   house of CORRECTION*

B. *Translate:*

1. Dem Kind, das sich immer bei jeder Gelegenheit so angestellt hat, wurde natürlich nicht geglaubt, als es eines Tages wirklich krank wurde. 2. Mit einer so kleinen Unterstützung wird kaum jemandem geholfen. 3. Ihm ist mit dieser Unterstützung sehr geholfen worden. 4. Wir wissen nicht, ob das Projekt auf diese Weise durchgeführt werden kann, aber wir sind überzeugt, daß es durchgeführt werden muß. 5. Glaubt mir, Kinder, das ist nicht zu machen! 6. Ich habe mich sehr bemüht, ihm zu folgen, aber was er da sagt, ist einfach nicht zu verstehen. 7. Wenn das Experiment auf diese Weise nicht durchgeführt werden kann, läßt es sich vielleicht anders machen. 8. Da im ganzen Haus kein Laut zu hören war, nahmen wir an, daß niemand da war. 9. Die Quelle des von ihm beobachteten Lichts ist noch nicht festgestellt worden. 10. Sobald sich die Quelle aber eindeutig feststellen läßt, wird er sein Experiment genau beschreiben und das Ganze dann veröffentlichen lassen. 11. Als ich ins Zimmer trat, wurde laut gesprochen und gelacht. 12. Es wird in diesem Zimmer nur geheizt, wenn Gäste erwartet werden. 13. In Amerika wird vielleicht nur deswegen mehr geraucht als in Europa, weil der Tabak hier weniger hoch versteuert ist. 14. Sein Buch ist sehr interessant, aber trotzdem kann hier kaum von einer neuen literarischen Bewegung gesprochen werden. 15. Viele deutsche Redewendungen lassen sich nicht leicht ins Englische übersetzen. 16. Sie lassen sich diesen wichtigen deutschen Aufsatz über die Atomenergie von einem Experten ins Englische übersetzen. 17. Er hat die alten Volkslieder gesammelt, weil sie Gefahr liefen, vom gebildeten Publikum vergessen zu werden. 18. Wären sie nicht von ihm gesammelt worden, so wären sie sicher vergessen worden. 19. Es ist oft behauptet, daß ein guter Roman sich

nicht verfilmen läßt. 20. In Deutschland wird gewöhnlich später zu Abend gegessen als in Amerika.

C. Strong verbs. *Memorize:*

INFINITIVE	PRESENT	PAST	PAST PARTICIPLE	INFINITIVE
backen	bäckt *or* backt	(buk) [*]	gebacken	to bake
empfehlen	empfiehlt	empfahl	empfohlen	to recommend
gießen		goß	gegossen	to pour
heben		hob	gehoben	to lift, to raise
kneifen		kniff	gekniffen	to pinch
pfeifen		pfiff	gepfiffen	to whistle
raten	rät	riet	geraten	to advise
schelten	schilt	schalt	gescholten	to scold
schlagen	schlägt	schlug	geschlagen	to hit, to beat
schwingen		schwang	geschwungen	to swing
treiben		trieb	getrieben	to drive
vergleichen		verglich	verglichen	to compare

ACTIVE EXERCISES

A. *Restate the following sentences, changing the verbs first to the past tense and then to the present perfect:*

1. Er wird von seinem Vater gescholten. 2. Die Blumen werden täglich begossen. 3. Du wirst nicht gefragt. 4. Um 12 Uhr wird zum Essen gepfiffen. 5. Das wird mir von allen Leuten geraten. 6. Schiller wird oft mit Shakespeare verglichen. 7. Das kleine Mädchen wird von seinem Bruder geschlagen. 8. Heute wird hier nicht getanzt. 9. Seine Bücher werden von allen Leuten sehr empfohlen. 10. Solche Kuchen werden nur von meiner Mutter gebacken.

B. *Rewrite the following sentences in the passive voice:*

1. Er schwingt die Fahne in der Luft. 2. Der freche Junge kneift das kleine Mädchen in die Backe. 3. Er hat den Bleistift aufgehoben. 4. Dieses eine Rad treibt die ganze Maschine. 5. Mein Freund machte einen schlimmen Fehler. 6. Er hat seine Kinder prinzipiell (*on principle*) nicht gescholten. 7. Sie riet ihm, das Haus zu kaufen. 8. Nur mein Vater hat ihm dafür gedankt. 9. Wer empfiehlt dir dieses Buch? 10. Kinder hören solche Märchen gern.

C. *Translate into German:*

1. This young man was very much recommended by his superior.
2. They know that they will be scolded for it, but they will do it anyway (**trotzdem**).

[*] In modern German the weak form **backte** is preferred.

3. This excellent bread is sold in the shop around the corner, but I don't know if it is baked there too.
4. These two stories have often been compared with one another.
5. Is the door closed? Yes, it was closed by the janitor.
6. These flowers must be watered often and they should be placed in the light.
7. That cannot be explained. (*Express in four different ways.*)
8. The eggs must be beaten lightly before they are poured into the pan.
9. She was advised by her lawyer not to answer any questions.
10. The soldiers were ordered to drive the enemy from (**aus**) the village.
11. He got so furious that he was asked to leave the room.
12. That may be true but it cannot be proved.
13. The car had to be repaired before it could be used.
14. The work that was assigned for yesterday still has not been done.
15. His research is supported by the government.
16. This song, which was often sung before the war, is scarcely heard anymore (**noch**).
17. The source of (**für**) this story has not yet been established.
18. Before he became conductor of the orchestra this symphony had never been played in Berlin.
19. We looked for the book everywhere but it simply could not be found.
20. If you behave like a child you will be treated like one.

22

Prefixes

Three types of prefixes

1. Prefixes change or modify the basic meaning of a verb and thus enrich the vocabulary of the language in a variety of ways. Three groups of prefixes have to be distinguished, depending on the manner in which they are treated in conjugation and sentence construction. They either remain attached to the basic verb in all forms and positions (INSEPARABLE PREFIXES), or they are separated from it under certain conditions (SEPARABLE PREFIXES). In addition, there is a small number of prefixes which can be used either separably or inseparably (VARIABLE PREFIXES).

Inseparable prefixes

2. The inseparable prefixes consist of the following UNSTRESSED SYLLABLES:

PREFIXES	EXAMPLES
be–	streiten, to quarrel: bestreiten, to contest
emp–	finden, to find: empfinden, to feel
ent–	decken, to cover: entdecken, to discover
er–	ziehen, to pull: erziehen, to educate
ge–	fallen, to fall: gefallen, to please
miß–	handeln, to act: mißhandeln, to mistreat
ver–	stehen, to stand: verstehen, to understand
zer–	stören, to disturb: zerstören, to destroy

Accent on stem

THE WORD ACCENT IN VERBS COMBINED WITH INSEPARABLE PREFIXES IS ALWAYS ON THE STEM: entdécken, empfínden, etc. The only peculiarity of these verbs is the omission of the past participle prefix ge–: erziehen—erzogen; empfinden—empfunden; zerstören—zerstört.

Caution. Certain strong verbs with inseparable prefixes have the same form for the infinitive and the past participle. Usually the difference can easily be determined on the basis of the auxiliary verb used:

FUTURE:

> Er **wird** ihm nie **vergeben.**
> He will never forgive him.

PRESENT PERFECT:

> Er **hat** ihm nie **vergeben.**
> He never forgave him.

The future active of such verbs, however, is easily confused with the present passive:

PRESENT PASSIVE:

> Sie **werden** von uns mit Lebensmitteln **versehen.**
> They are being supplied with food by us.

FUTURE ACTIVE:

> Sie **werden** uns mit Lebensmitteln **versehen.**
> They will supply us with food.

2. Because of the omission of the past participle **ge–** in verbs with inseparable prefixes, the verbs which use the **ge–** as an inseparable prefix have the same past participle as the respective basic verb: **fallen,** *to fall* —past participle: **gefallen; gefallen,** *to please*—past participle: **gefallen; hören,** *to hear*—past participle: **gehört; gehören,** *to belong*—past participle: **gehört:**

> Es **hat** mir nicht **gefallen,** daß die Börsenpreise wieder **gefallen sind.**
> It didn't please me that the prices on the stock market fell again.

Separable prefixes

3. While there is only a small number of inseparable prefixes, a great variety of independent words, mostly prepositions and adverbs, can serve as separable prefixes:

ankommen, to arrive   aufstehen, to get up   untergehen, to go down
   weggeben, to give away   heimgehen, to go home

Prefix is accented

Note that THE WORD ACCENT IN VERBS WITH SEPARABLE PREFIXES IS ON THE PREFIX: ánkommen, aúfstehen, etc.

When separation occurs

4. Separable prefixes SEPARATE FROM THE STEM OF THE VERB IN THE

PRESENT AND PAST TENSES IN PRINCIPAL CLAUSES AND IN THE IMPERATIVE; they then stand at the end of the clause:

ausgehen, to go out

PRESENT:

Er geht nicht oft **aus.**

PAST:

Er ging nicht oft **aus.**

IMPERATIVE:

Gehen Sie nicht so oft **aus!**

In subordinate clauses the prefix is combined with the stem of the verb at the end of the clause:

Ich glaube, daß er nicht oft **ausgeht** (**ausging**).

Past participle

5. The past participle of verbs with separable prefixes is formed by placing the prefix in front of the regular past participle of the stem verb: **ausgehen—ausgegangen; aufstehen—aufgestanden:**

Er ist nicht früh **aufgestanden.**
He did not get up early.

Infinitive

6. In the infinitive of a verb with a separable prefix no separation of the prefix occurs:

Er wird nicht früh **aufstehen.**
He will not get up early.

If a **zu** must be used with such an infinitive, it is inserted BETWEEN the prefix and the stem, but the combination is still written as one word:

Er hat die Absicht, morgen sehr früh **aufzustehen.**
He intends to get up very early tomorrow.

Nouns as prefixes

7. At times nouns are also used as separable prefixes: **haushalten,** *to keep house,* **teilnehmen,** *to take part.* In many cases, such nouns are still felt to be objects of the verb and are therefore capitalized and not written together with the verb: **Abschied nehmen,** *to take leave,* **Ausdruck finden,** *to be expressed.* As far as word order is concerned, these noun objects function like separable prefixes:

Er nahm gestern von seiner Familie **Abschied.**
He took leave of his family yesterday.

Auch dieser Gedanke **fand** in seinem Roman **Ausdruck.**
Also this thought was expressed in his novel.

Prepositional phrases as prefixes

8. Certain prepositional phrases closely allied to verbs in fixed expressions also act like separable prefixes and tend to appear in final position in principal clauses in the present and past tenses: **nach Hause gehen,** *to go home,* **in Empfang nehmen,** *to receive,* and so forth:

> Er **geht** erst nach dem Mittagessen **nach Hause.**
> He is not going home until after lunch.

> Sie **nahm** das Paket auf dem Postamt selbst **in Empfang.**
> She received (accepted) the parcel herself at the post office.

Infinitives as prefixes

9. In addition to nouns and prepositional phrases, some infinitives can serve as separable prefixes: **kennenlernen,** *to get to know, become acquainted,* **spazierengehen,** *to go for a walk,* **stehenbleiben,** *to stop:*

> Nach dem Abendessen **gehen** wir immer **spazieren.**
> After dinner we always go for a walk.

> Meine Uhr **bleibt** alle fünf Minuten **stehen.**
> My watch stops every five minutes.

Caution. Since separable prefixes (and words or phrases which function as prefixes) often alter the meaning of the verb stem in an unpredictable manner, it is particularly important not to make up one's mind about the meaning of a verb form appearing in second position in a principal clause until the end of the clause has been reached. The following examples will serve as an illustration:

Er **hörte** erst kürzlich von dieser Zeitschrift.
He heard only recently about this publication.

Er **hörte** erst kürzlich **auf,** für diese Zeitschrift zu arbeiten.
Only recently did he stop working for this periodical.

Er **stellte** seine Theorie so **dar,** daß jeder sie verstehen konnte.
He presented his theory in such a fashion that everybody could understand it.

Er **stellte** seine Theorie so **auf,** daß Einwände nicht möglich waren.
He formulated his theory in such a fashion that objections were impossible.

Variable prefixes

10. The following prefixes occur both as separable and as inseparable prefixes: **durch, über, um, unter, voll, wider,** and **wieder.**

In most cases a given verb stem will combine with one of these prefixes in only one of the two ways: **überordnen,** *to place in a higher rank—*separable: Er wurde ihm **übergeordnet.** But: **überráschen,** *to surprise—*inseparable: Ich habe ihn **überrascht.**

In any case, the word accent determines how such a verb is used (if in doubt, consult a dictionary!): If the accent is on the prefix, it is separable; if the verb stem is stressed, the prefix is inseparable.

11. Whenever a variable prefix can be combined with a given stem in both ways, the verb with the separable prefix usually has a literal meaning which can often be arrived at by adding the meaning of the prefix to that of the verb stem:

überschütten, to pour over, to spill:

> Sie hat die Suppe **übergeschüttet.**
> She spilled the soup.

übertreten, to go over, convert:

> Er war zum Katholizismus **übergetreten.**
> He had converted to Catholicism.

However, if the prefix is used inseparably, the meaning of the new verb is usually figurative and often cannot be deduced immediately from its component parts:

überschütten, to overwhelm:

> Er hat seine Braut mit Geschenken **überschüttet.**
> He overwhelmed his fiancée with presents.

übertréten, to violate, transgress:

> Er hat das Gesetz immer wieder **übertreten.**
> He violated the law again and again.

Special Points

Verbs in *-ieren*

1. Verbs in **–ieren** (**studieren** and others) which regularly form their past participle without the prefix **ge–,** also omit the **ge–** when they are combined with a separable prefix: **ausprobieren,** *to try out;* **einstudieren,** *to prepare a role.*

> Sie hat ihre Kochkunst an uns **ausprobiert.**
> She tried out her culinary art on us.

In all other respects, however, they function as verbs with separable prefixes:

Warum **probiert** sie ihre Kochkunst an uns **aus?**
Why is she trying out her culinary art on us?

Er plant, die Rollen mit uns **einzustudieren.**
He plans to study the roles with us.

Verbs with two prefixes

2. Separable prefixes are sometimes added to verbs which already have an inseparable prefix: **anerkennen,** *to recognize;* **einbeziehen,** *to include;* **nacherzählen,** *to retell.* Such verbs also do not form their past participles with the prefix **ge–:**

Er war allgemein als einer der größten Violinisten **anerkannt.**
He was generally recognized as one of the greatest violinists.

In all other respects they are usually treated like verbs with separable prefixes:

Man **erkannte** seine Leistungen allgemein **an.**
One generally recognized his achievements.

RECOGNITION EXERCISES

A. *Translate:*

1. Er wird unsere Universität bei der Versammlung der Deutschlehrer vertreten. 2. Wenn er nicht selbst gehen kann, wird er von einem jüngeren Kollegen bei der Versammlung der Deutschlehrer vertreten. 3. Er wird den neuen Angestellten, der immer betrunken zur Arbeit kommt, aus dem Amt entlassen. 4. Er wird sicher bald aus dem Amt entlassen. 5. Wir haben ihm geraten, diesen fragwürdigen Leuten aus dem Wege zu gehen, aber trotzdem ist er in schlechte Gesellschaft geraten. 6. Die Schallplatte, die Sie eben gehört haben, gehört nicht mir, sondern meiner Schwester. 7. Er nahm im Laufe des Sommers zehn Pfund zu. 8. Sie nahm im Laufe des Winters zehn Pfund ab. 9. Er nahm nach einer längeren, durch eine schwere Krankheit verursachten Unterbrechung die Arbeit an seinem Experiment wieder auf. 10. Er nahm nach einer längeren, durch eine schwere Krankheit verursachten Unterbrechung an der gemeinsamen Arbeit der Gruppe wieder teil. 11. Er nahm das Paket, das von einem seiner Kollegen an die Firma geschickt worden war, selbst in Empfang. 12. Er nahm das Paket, das von einem seiner Kollegen an die Firma geschickt worden war, in Verwahrung, bis der Direktor selbst es in Empfang nehmen konnte. 13. Er nahm gestern von seinem Vater, der wieder einmal alle seine Schulden getilgt hatte, Abschied, um eine längere Reise zu unternehmen. 14. Er nahm gestern von seinem Vater, der wieder einmal alle seine Schulden getilgt hatte, das Angebot an, eine längere Reise für ihn zu unternehmen. 14. Das Mädchen, das den besten Essay für das Preisausschreiben eingereicht hatte, wird morgen von dem Bürgermeister im Rathaus empfangen.

15. Das Mädchen, das den besten Essay für das Preisausschreiben eingereicht hatte, wird morgen von dem Bürgermeister im Rathaus den Preis empfangen. 16. Der Einbrecher hatte schließlich gestanden, daß sein Kumpan an der Straßenecke Wache gestanden hatte.

B. *Translate:*

1. Er kam in seiner Heimatstadt, die er seit Jahren nicht gesehen hatte, nach einer neuntägigen Reise an. 2. Er kam in seine Heimatstadt, die er selten und dann nur ungern verließ, nach einer neuntägigen Reise wieder zurück. 3. Diese Gedanken fanden in seinem letzten, kurz vor seinem Tod erschienenen Roman ihren gültigen Ausdruck. 4. Diese Gedanken fanden aber beim Publikum, das auf so etwas nicht gefaßt war, keine günstige Aufnahme. 5. Einer der Kritiker stellt in seinem Aufsatz über den Dichter den Einfluß von dessen Vater auf ihn in den Vordergrund. 6. Ein anderer Kritiker stellt in einem ähnlichen Artikel auch den Einfluß des Vaters auf ihn dar, legt auf diese Dinge aber nicht so viel Gewicht. 7. Eine ähnliche Gestalt kommt fast in jedem seiner Romane vor. 8. Ein ähnlicher Gesichtspunkt kommt in fast jedem seiner Romane zum Ausdruck. 9. Der Professor setzte die Prüfung, die er am nächsten Tag geben wollte, erst im letzten Augenblick auf. 10. Der Professor setzte die Untersuchung, die er vor den Ferien begonnen hatte, erst in den letzten Tagen wieder fort. 11. Jedesmal, wenn der Junge den Ball für den Hund in den Garten warf, wiederholte er die Worte: „Hol' den Ball wieder, Bruno!" 12. Stellen Sie sich nur vor: dieser erzkonservative Politiker trat gestern zur demokratischen Partei über! 13. Im Mittelalter übertraten nur wenige Menschen die ihnen von der Kirche gesetzten Grenzen. 14. Der Lehrer ließ den Jungen den Aufsatz noch einmal umschreiben, weil er gewisse Dinge darin zu direkt ausgedrückt hatte, die man vorsichtig zu umschreiben hat. 15. Die Fenster des seit Jahren nicht mehr bewohnten Hauses waren so lange nicht gewaschen worden, daß es unmöglich war, durch sie durchzuschauen. 16. Er hatte ganz sicher die Absicht, uns zu beschwindeln, aber es war uns glücklicherweise möglich, ihn rechtzeitig zu durchschauen.

C. *Strong verbs. Memorize:*

INFINITIVE	PRESENT	PAST	PAST PARTICIPLE	INFINITIVE
binden		band	gebunden	to tie, bind
dringen		drang	(ist) gedrungen	to penetrate; urge
fließen		floß	(ist) geflossen	to flow
greifen		griff	gegriffen	to seize, grip
kriechen		kroch	(ist) gekrochen	to crawl
reißen		riß	gerissen	to tear
schieben		schob	geschoben	to push
schießen		schoß	geschossen	to shoot
steigen		stieg	(ist) gestiegen	to climb
stoßen	stößt	stieß	gestoßen	to push
wachsen	wächst	wuchs	(ist) gewachsen	to grow
weisen		wies	gewiesen	to point (to)

ACTIVE EXERCISES

A. *Complete the following sentences by supplying the correct form of the past tense of the German infinitive in parentheses:*

1. Meine Freundin (ankommen) gestern in New York. 2. Er (verbringen) den Sommer in den Bergen. 3. Mein Bruder (zurückbringen) das Buch zur Bibliothek. 4. Ihnen (zustoßen) ein kleiner Unfall. 5. Ich (anbieten) ihm eine Zigarette, aber er (annehmen) sie nicht. 6. Der Arzt (verbinden) den Verwundeten auf der Stelle. 7. Der Regen (eindringen) auch durch die geschlossenen Fenster. 8. Wir (erfahren) das erst gestern. 9. Zwei Jahre (verfließen), ehe man ihn (wiedersehen). 10. Der Feind (angreifen) mitten im Winter und (vordringen) langsam.

B. *Change the verbs in the following sentences to the present perfect:*

1. Der Kleine kroch auf dem Boden herum. 2. Die Merkmale wiesen eindeutig auf den Ursprung hin. 3. Er übersetzte den Brief ins Deutsche. 4. Sie zerriß seinen Brief in kleine Stücke. 5. Die Polizei drang in das Haus ein und erschoß den Räuber. 6. Ich bat ihn um das Brot und er schob es mir zu. 7. Er wuchs in einem kleinen Dorf auf, was man ihm bis ins Alter anmerkte. 8. Sie schlugen einen ganz neuen Plan vor. 9. Wir wiederholten die Anweisungen zweimal. 10. Sie stiegen in München aus und besuchten ihre Freunde.

C. *Translate into German:*

1. We aren't going out tonight because we have invited some friends.
2. From now on we must get up every morning at seven o'clock.
3. I am not coming along because I have no desire to listen to him all evening.
4. He doesn't like (*use* **gefallen**) the plan she has proposed.
5. I do not understand why he insists on getting up so early.
6. We are still assuming that he will take part in the conference.
7. He said good-bye to (*took leave of*) his family at the railroad station.
8. I met (*became acquainted with*) a very interesting girl on (*in*) the train to New York.
9. He is translating these sentences as fast as he can.
10. After he had accepted the invitation it occurred to him that he had to work that evening.
11. I never understood (*use* **begreifen**) how he passed the examination.
12. We want to keep the letter we received today because it contains something which we consider important.
13. I was not disappointed that he did not repeat that terrible remark.
14. We were completely surprised by the news which arrived this morning.
15. After he had left the house he remembered (*use* **einfallen**) that he had forgotten the keys in the kitchen.
16. He was very busy and completely forgot that he hadn't eaten anything all day.
17. I really cannot stand it when girls wear pants.

18. He introduced me to the speaker after he had sat down again.
19. His suggestion to produce (*perform*) the new play next winter cannot be carried out.
20. They called me up in order to inform me that my suggestion had been rejected.

Strong and Irregular Weak Verbs

Forms for the second and third person singular present are listed only for those verbs with vowel changes or other irregularities. If not otherwise indicated the last column lists irregularities in the formation of the present subjunctive II.

INFINITIVE	PRESENT	PAST	PAST PARTICIPLE	IRREGULARITIES
backen, *to bake*	bäckst bäckt (*also, without umlaut*)	(*now rare:* buk), backte	gebacken	büke *or* backte
befehlen, *to command*	befiehlst befiehlt	befahl	befohlen	beföhle *or* befähle
beginnen, *to begin*		begann	begonnen	begönne *or* begänne
beißen, *to bite*		biß	gebissen	
beklemmen, *to depress, oppress*		beklomm	beklommen	
bergen, *to hide*	birgst birgt	barg	geborgen	
bersten, *to burst*	birst birst	barst	ist geborsten	
betrügen, *to deceive*		betrog	betrogen	
biegen, *to bend*		bog	hat ist } gebogen	
bieten, *to offer*		bot	geboten	
binden, *to bind, tie*		band	gebunden	
bitten, *to ask, request*		bat	gebeten	
blasen, *to blow*	bläst bläst	blies	geblasen	

213

Infinitive	Present	Past	Past Participle	Irregularities
bleiben, *to remain, stay*		blieb	ist geblieben	
bleichen, *to bleach*		blich	geblichen	
braten, *to roast*	brätst brät	briet	gebraten	
brechen, *to break*	brichst bricht	brach	gebrochen	
brennen, *to burn*		brannte	gebrannt	brennte
bringen, *to bring*		brachte	gebracht	brächte
denken, *to think*		dachte	gedacht	dächte
dreschen, *to thrash, thresh*	drischst drischt	drosch	gedroschen	
dringen, *to penetrate*		drang	ist gedrungen	
erlöschen, *to become extinguished*	erlischst erlischt	erlosch	ist erloschen	
erschrecken, *to be startled* (weak when transitive, meaning *to frighten*)	erschrickst erschrickt	erschrak	ist erschrocken	
essen, *to eat*	ißt ißt	aß	gegessen	
fahren, *to drive, travel, go*	fährst fährt	fuhr	hat⎫ ist⎭gefahren	
fallen, *to fall*	fällst fällt	fiel	ist gefallen	
fangen, *to catch*	fängst fängt	fing	gefangen	
fechten, *to fence, fight*	fichst ficht	focht	gefochten	*Imperative:* ficht!
finden, *to find*		fand	gefunden	
flechten, *to plait, braid*	flichst flicht	flocht	geflochten	*Imperative:* flechte! *or* flicht!
fliegen, *to fly*		flog	hat⎫ ist⎭geflogen	
fliehen, *to flee*		floh	ist geflohen	
fließen, *to flow*		floß	ist geflossen	
fressen, *to eat* (of animals)	frißt frißt	fraß	gefressen	

Infinitive	Present	Past	Past Participle	Irregularities
frieren, *to freeze,* *be cold*		fror	hat⎱ ist⎰ gefroren	
gären, *to ferment*		gor (*also* *weak:* *gärte*)	ist gegoren (*also weak:* *gegärt*)	
gebären, *to give* *birth to*	gebierst gebiert	gebar	geboren	
geben, *to give*	gibst gibt	gab	gegeben	
gedeihen, *to thrive*		gedieh	ist gediehen	
gehen, *to go*		ging	ist gegangen	
gelingen, *to succeed*		gelang	ist gelungen	
gelten, *to be valid*	giltst gilt	galt	gegolten	*Imperative:* gelte!
genesen, *to recover*		genas	ist genesen	*Imperative:* genese!
genießen, *to enjoy*		genoß	genossen	
geschehen, *to* *happen* (impersonal only)	geschieht	geschah	ist geschehen	
gewinnen, *to win*		gewann	gewonnen	gewönne *or* gewänne
gießen, *to pour*		goß	gegossen	
gleichen, *to* *resemble*		glich	geglichen	
gleiten, *to glide,* *slide*		glitt	ist geglitten	
glimmen, *to glow*		glomm	geglommen	
greifen, *to grasp,* *grip*		griff	gegriffen	
graben, *to dig*	gräbst gräbt	grub	gegraben	
halten, *to hold*	hältst hält	hielt	gehalten	
hängen (hangen), *to hang*	hängst hängt	hing	gehangen	
hauen, *to beat, hit*		hieb	gehauen	
helfen, *to help*	hilfst hilft	half	geholfen	hülfe *or* hälfe
kennen, *to know*		kannte	gekannt	kennte
klimmen, *to climb*		klomm	ist geklommen	
klingen, *to sound*		klang	geklungen	
kneifen, *to pinch*		kniff	gekniffen	
kommen, *to come*		kam	ist gekommen	

Infinitive	Present	Past	Past Participle	Irregularities
kriechen, *to creep, crawl*		kroch	ist gekrochen	
laden, *to load, invite*	lädst lädt	lud	geladen	
lassen, *to let*	läßt läßt	ließ	gelassen	
laufen, *to run*	läufst läuft	lief	ist gelaufen	
leiden, *to suffer*		litt	gelitten	
leihen, *to lend*		lieh	geliehen	
lesen, *to read*	liest liest	las	gelesen	
liegen, *to lie*		lag	gelegen	
lügen, *to tell a lie*		log	gelogen	
mahlen, *to grind*		(*only weak:* mahlte)	gemahlen	
meiden, *to avoid*		mied	gemieden	
melken, *to milk* (also weak)	milkst milkt	molk	gemolken	
messen, *to measure*	mißt mißt	maß	gemessen	
nehmen, *to take*	nimmst nimmt	nahm	genommen	
nennen, *to call*		nannte	genannt	nennte
pfeifen, *to whistle*		pfiff	gepfiffen	
preisen, *to praise*		pries	gepriesen	
quellen, *to flow from, spring from*	quillst quillt	quoll	ist gequollen	
raten, *to advise, guess*	rätst rät	riet	geraten	
reiben, *to rub*		rieb	gerieben	
reißen, *to tear*		riß	gerissen	
reiten, *to ride* (on horseback)		ritt	ist geritten	
rennen, *to run*		rannte	ist gerannt	rennte
riechen, *to smell*		roch	gerochen	
ringen, *to struggle, wrestle*		rang	gerungen	
rinnen, *to trickle*		rann	ist geronnen	
rufen, *to call*		rief	gerufen	
salzen, *to salt*		(*only weak:* salzte)	gesalzen (*also weak:* gesalzt)	

Infinitive	Present	Past	Past Participle	Irregularities
saufen, *to drink* (of animals)	säufst säuft (*also without umlaut*)	soff	gesoffen	
saugen, *to suck* (also weak)		sog	gesogen	
schaffen, *to create* (weak when meaning *to do*)		schuf	geschaffen	
schallen, *to sound* (also weak)		scholl	geschollen	
scheiden, *to separate, depart*		schied	hat ist } geschieden	
scheinen, *to shine, seem*		schien	geschienen	
schelten, *to scold*	schiltst schilt	schalt	gescholten	schölte
scheren, *to shear*	schierst schiert (*also without vowel change*)	schor	geschoren	
schieben, *to push*		schob	geschoben	
schießen, *to shoot*		schoß	geschossen	
schinden, *to flay*		schund	geschunden	
schlafen, *to sleep*	schläfst schläft	schlief	geschlafen	
schlagen, *to hit*	schlägst schlägt	schlug	geschlagen	
schleichen, *to creep*		schlich	ist geschlichen	
schleifen, *to sharpen*		schliff	geschliffen	
schließen, *to close*		schloß	geschlossen	
schlingen, *to tie, wind, twist*		schlang	geschlungen	
schmeißen, *to throw*		schmiß	geschmissen	
schmelzen, *to melt*	schmilzt schmilzt	schmolz	hat ist } geschmolzen	
schnauben, *to snort* (also weak)		schnob	geschnoben	
schneiden, *to cut*		schnitt	geschnitten	

Infinitive	Present	Past	Past Participle	Irregularities
schreiben, *to write*		schrieb	geschrieben	
schreien, *to scream*		schrie	geschrie(e)n	
schreiten, *to step*		schritt	ist geschritten	
schweigen, *to be silent*		schwieg	geschwiegen	
schwellen, *to swell* (also weak)	schwillst schwillt	schwoll	ist geschwollen	
schwimmen, *to swim*		schwamm } hat ist	geschwommen	schwämme *or* schwömme
schwinden, *to dwindle, disappear*		schwand	ist geschwunden	
schwingen, *to swing*		schwang	geschwungen	
schwören, *to swear* (also weak)		schwor, schwur	geschworen	
sehen, *to see*	siehst sieht	sah	gesehen	
senden, *to send*		sandte *or* sendete	gesandt *or* gesendet	sendete
sieden, *to boil* (also weak)		sott	gesotten	
singen, *to sing*		sang	gesungen	
sinken, *to sink*		sank	ist gesunken	
sinnen, *to think*		sann	gesonnen	sänne *or* sönne
sitzen, *to sit*		saß	gesessen	
speien, *to spit*		spie	gespie(e)n	
spinnen, *to spin*		spann	gesponnen	spönne
sprechen, *to speak*	sprichst spricht	sprach	gesprochen	
springen, *to jump*		sprang	ist gesprungen	
stechen, *to prick, sting*	stichst sticht	stach	gestochen	
stehen, *to stand*		stand	gestanden	stünde *or* stände
stehlen, *to steal*	stiehlst stiehlt	stahl	gestohlen	stähle *or* stöhle
steigen, *to climb*		stieg	ist gestiegen	
sterben, *to die*	stirbst stirbt	starb	ist gestorben	stürbe
stinken, *to stink*		stank	gestunken	
stoßen, *to push*	stößt stößt	stieß	gestoßen	

INFINITIVE	PRESENT	PAST	PAST PARTICIPLE	IRREGULARITIES
streichen, *to stroke*		strich	gestrichen	
streiten, *to quarrel*		stritt	gestritten	
tragen, *to carry,* *wear*	trägst trägt	trug	getragen	
treffen, *to hit, meet*	triffst trifft	traf	getroffen	
treiben, *to drive*		trieb	getrieben	
treten, *to kick, step*	trittst tritt	trat	hat ist } getreten	
triefen, *to drip* (usually weak)		troff	getroffen	
trinken, *to drink*		trank	getrunken	
tun, *to do*		tat	getan	
verderben, *to spoil*	verdirbst verdirbt	verdarb	verdorben	verdürbe
verdrießen, *to vex*		verdroß	verdrossen	
vergessen, *to forget*	vergißt vergißt	vergaß	vergessen	
verlieren, *to lose*		verlor	verloren	
verzeihen, *to* *forgive*		verzieh	verziehen	
wachsen, *to grow*	wächst wächst	wuchs	ist gewachsen	
waschen, *to wash*	wäschst wäscht	wusch	gewaschen	
weben, *to weave* (also weak)		wob	gewoben	
weichen, *to yield*		wich	ist gewichen	
weisen, *to show*		wies	gewiesen	
wenden, *to turn*		wandte *or* wendete	gewandt *or* gewendet	wendete
werben, *to recruit,* *enlist*	wirbst wirbt	warb	geworben	würbe
werfen, *to throw*	wirfst wirft	warf	geworfen	würfe
wiegen, *to weigh*		wog	gewogen	
winden, *to wind*		wand	gewunden	
wissen, *to know*	weiß weißt weiß	wußte	gewußt	wüßte
ziehen, *to pull, go,* *move*		zog	hat ist } gezogen	
zwingen, *to force*		zwang	gezwungen	

German-English Vocabulary

This vocabulary lists all words appearing in the Recognition Exercises. Only obvious cognates and the basic forms of the **der**-words, **ein**-words, and personal pronouns have been omitted.

der **Abend,** –s, –e evening
das **Abendessen,** –s, – supper, dinner, evening meal
    abends in the evening
    aber but, however
    abfahren (fährt ab, fuhr ab, ist abgefahren) to depart
    abgestanden stale
    abhängig (von) dependent (on)
    abholen to pick up
    ablehnen to reject
    abnehmen (nimmt ab, nahm ab, abgenommen) to take off, remove
die **Abreise,** –, (*no plural*) departure
    abreisen to leave, depart
die **Absage,** –, –n refusal
der **Abschied,** –s, (*no plural*) leave; **Abschied nehmen,** to take leave, to say good-bye
    abschließen (schloß ab, abgeschlossen) to lock
die **Absicht,** –, –en intention
    acht eight
    achtgeben (gibt acht, gab acht, achtgegeben) to pay attention to, to watch out for
    achtzehnt– eighteenth

    ähnlich similar; **einem ähnlich sehen** to look like someone
    allein (*conjunction*) but, yet, however; (*adverb*) alone
das **Alleinsein,** –s, (*no plural*) being alone
    alles everything
die **Alpen** (*plural*) the Alps
    als as; (*conjunction*) when; (*after comparative*) than
    alt old
das **Alter,** –s, – age, old age
das **Amt,** –es, ⁼er office, job
    amüsant amusing
sich **amüsieren** to have a good time
    an up to, to; on; at, by; alongside of
    anbetteln (um) to beg (for)
    anbieten (bot an, angeboten) to offer
    ander– other; **andere** others
    anders different(ly), in a different way; **irgendwo anders** somewhere else
der **Anfang,** –s, ⁼e beginning
    anfangen (fängt an, fing an, angefangen) to begin
    anführen to cite, to quote

das **Angebot,** –s, –e   offer
der **Angestellte,** –n, –n   employee
angreifen (griff an, angegrif-
   fen)   to attack
die **Angst,** –, –e   fear
anhaben   to have on, to wear
anklagen   to accuse
Anklang finden   to meet with
   approval, to be approved,
   supported
ankommen (kam an, ist angekommen)   to arrive
die **Ankunft,** –, –e   arrival
anlächeln   to smile at
anmerken   to notice, to tell by
   looking at
annehmbar   acceptable
annehmen (nimmt an, nahm
   an, angenommen)   to accept; to assume; **sich annehmen** (*with genitive object*)   to take care of
anrufen (rief an, angerufen)
   to call up (on the phone)
anscheinend   apparently
sich **anschließen** (schloß sich an,
   sich angeschlossen)   to join,
   go along with
ansehen (sieht an, sah an, angesehen)   to look at
die **Ansicht,** –, –en   view, opinion
anstatt (*or:* **statt**)   instead of
anstellen   to do; **sich anstellen**
   to make a fuss
anstößig   offensive, indecent
anstrengend   tiring, strenu-
   ous
antreffen (trifft an, traf an,
   angetroffen)   to find, to
   meet
die **Antwort,** –, –en   answer
die **Anweisung,** –, –en   instruction, direction
anziehen (zog an, angezogen)
   to put on; **sich anziehen**
   to get dressed
der **Anzug,** –s, –e   suit

der **Apfel,** –s, –   apple
das **Aquarell,** –s, –e   watercolor
die **Arbeit,** –, –en   work; paper,
   essay
arbeiten   to work
ärgern   to annoy, vex; **sich
   ärgern** (**über**)   to be annoyed (at *or* about)
arm   poor
die **Armbanduhr,** –, –en   wrist
   watch
der **Artikel,** –s, –   article
die **Arznei,** –, –en   medicine
der **Arzt,** –es, –e   doctor of medicine
der **Assistent,** –en, –en   assistant
die **Atombombe,** –, –n   atomic
   bomb
die **Atomenergie,** –   atomic
   energy
auch   also, too; **auch noch**
   also, in addition; **wenn . . .
   auch**   even if, even though,
   although
auf   on; to; in, at; for
aufbrechen (bricht auf, brach
   auf, ist aufgebrochen) to de-
   part, to set out
aufdringlich   "pushy," impor-
   tunate
die **Aufenthaltserlaubnis,** –, –se
   residence permit
die **Auffassung,** –, –en   view,
   concept
aufführen   to perform (*as,* a
   play)
die **Aufgabe,** –, –n   task, job, assignment, lesson
aufgeben (gibt auf, gab auf,
   aufgegeben)   to give up
aufgeregt   excited
aufheben (hob auf, aufgehoben)   to pick up
aufhören   to stop, cease
die **Aufnahme,** –, –n   reception;
   Aufnahme finden   to be
   received

aufnehmen (nimmt auf, nahm auf, aufgenommen) to resume

aufpassen to pay attention

der Aufsatz, –es, ⁼e essay, paper

aufsetzen to set up, to compose

aufstellen to set up, to draw up, to propound

aufwachen to wake up

aufwachsen (wächst auf, wuchs auf, ist aufgewachsen) to grow up

das Auge, –s, –n eye

der Augenblick, –s, –e moment

aus from, out of; (made) of

ausbilden to train

ausbrechen (bricht aus, brach aus, ist ausgebrochen) to break out

der Ausdruck, –s, ⁼e expression; Ausdruck finden to be expressed; zum Ausdruck kommen to be expressed

ausdrücken to express

ausführen to carry out, to execute

die Ausführung, –, –en execution, carrying out

ausgehen (ging aus, ist ausgegangen) to go out

ausgezeichnet excellent

die Auskunft, –, ⁼e information

auslachen to laugh at

die Ausrede, –, –n excuse

sich ausruhen to rest

ausschneiden (schnitt aus, ausgeschnitten) to cut out

aussehen (sieht aus, sah aus, ausgesehen) to look (to appear)

außer except, but, besides; out of; beyond

außerhalb (preposition with genitive) outside

äußerst extremely

ausstehen (stand aus, ausgestanden) to stand, to bear, to tolerate

aussteigen (stieg aus, ist ausgestiegen) to climb out, to get out (or off)

die Backe, –, –n cheek

backen (buk or backte, gebacken) to bake

das Badezimmer, –s, – bathroom

der Bahnhof, –s, ⁼e railroad station; am Bahnhof at the railroad station

bald soon; bald danach soon afterwards

der Band, –es, ⁼e volume

bangen (um) to be afraid (of losing)

die Bank, –, –en bank

die Baracke, –, –n barracks

bauen to build

der Bauer, –n (or –s), –n peasant, farmer

der Baum, –es, ⁼e tree

der Beamte, –n, –n (government) official

beantworten to answer

sich bedanken to thank, to say thank you

bedauern to regret, to feel sorry about (or for)

bedeuten to mean, to signify, to be

bedeutend important, significant

sich bedienen to make use of (with genitive object)

bedürfen (bedarf, bedurfte, bedurft) (with genitive object) to need, to require

beenden to end, to conclude

befehlen (befiehlt, befahl, befohlen) to order, to command

sich befinden (befand sich, sich befunden) to be, to be found

begabt talented, gifted

sich **begeben** (begibt sich, begab sich, sich begeben) to go

begegnen to meet (by chance)

begehen (beging, begangen) to commit (a crime, *etc.*)

begehren to desire

begeistern to fill with enthusiasm, to make enthusiastic; **sich begeistern für** to be enthusiastic about

begießen (begoß, begossen) to water

der **Beginn,** –s, (*no plural*) beginning

begrüßen to greet

behandeln to treat

behaupten to assert, to claim

die **Behauptung,** –, –en assertion, claim

bei near, with, at; upon; while; in the case of; considering; in view of

beibringen (brachte bei, beigebracht) to teach

das **Bein,** –es, –e leg

das **Beispiel,** –s, –e example

beiwohnen to attend

bekannt known, well known

bekommen (bekam, bekommen) to get, to obtain

beliebt popular

bellen to bark; das **Bellen,** –s (*no plural*) barking

sich **bemächtigen** (*with genitive object*) to take possession of

die **Bemerkung,** –, –en remark

sich **bemühen** to try hard, to take great pains; **sich bemühen um etwas** to endeavor, to strive to achieve something

sich **benehmen** (benimmt sich, benahm sich, hat sich benommen) to behave, to act

benutzen to use

beobachten to observe

berauben to rob

bereit ready

der **Berg,** –es, –e mountain

der **Bericht,** –es, –e report

der **Beruf,** –es, –e profession, occupation

berühmt famous

sich **beschäftigen** (**mit**) to occupy oneself (with), to be busy (with)

beschreiben (beschrieb, beschrieben) to describe

beschwindeln to cheat, swindle

besonder– special; **besonders** especially

besorgen to fetch, to get; to take care of

besprechen (bespricht, besprach, besprochen) to discuss; to review (a book, *etc.*)

besser better

best– best

bestätigen to confirm

bestehen (bestand, bestanden) to pass (an exam, *etc.*); **bestehen auf** to insist on

bestimmt definite(ly)

der **Besuch,** –s, –e visit; company; **bei jemand zu Besuch sein** to be visiting someone

besuchen to visit

betreffend in question

betreten (betritt, betrat, betreten) to enter

betrügen (betrog, betrogen) to cheat, to deceive

betrunken drunk

das **Bett,** –es, –en bed

der **Bettler,** –s, – beggar

die **Bettzeit,** –, –en bedtime, time one goes to bed

beunruhigen to disturb

bevor before

die **Bewegung,** –, –en movement

beweisen (bewies, bewiesen) to prove

bewohnen   to live in, to occupy

bewundern   to admire

bewußt (*with genitive object*) aware of, conscious of; **sich einer Sache bewußt sein** to be aware of something

bezahlen   to pay

sich beziehen auf (bezog sich, sich bezogen)   to refer to

die Bibliothek, –, –en   library

das Bier, –es, –e   beer

das Bild, –es, –er   picture

bis (*conjunction*) until; (*preposition*) until, up to, as far as, by; **bis vor kurzem** until recently

bitten (bat, gebeten)   to ask, to request; **bitten um** to ask for, to request

blau   blue

bleiben (blieb, ist geblieben) to remain, to stay

blicken (nach)   to look (at)

die Blondine, –, –n   blond girl (*or* woman)

bloß   only, merely

blühen   to bloom

die Blume, –, –n   flower

der Boden, –s, ⁓   floor, ground

der (*or* das) Bonbon, –s, –s   piece of candy

borgen   to borrow

brauchen   to need, to have to; to use

braun   brown

brechen (bricht, brach, gebrochen)   to break

der Brief, –es, –e   letter

der Briefträger, –s, –   mailman

bringen (brachte, gebracht) to bring, to take

das Brot, –es, –e   bread

die Brücke, –, –n   bridge

der Bruder, –s, ⁓   brother

das Buch, –es, ⁓er   book

die Buchhandlung, –, –en   book store, book shop

der Bürgermeister, –s, –   mayor

das Büro, –s, –s   office

der Chef, –s, –s   boss, chief

der Chirurg, –en, –en   surgeon

da (*adverb*) then, there; here; (*conjunction*) since; when, that

dahin   there

damals   then, at that time

die Dame, –, –n   lady

damit (*conjunction*)   so that

dankbar   thankful, grateful

danken   to thank

darstellen   to portray, to present

die Darstellung, –, –en   portrayal

daß (*conjunction*)   that

demonstrieren   to demonstrate

denken (dachte, gedacht)   to think; **sich denken** to imagine; **denken an** to think of

das Denkmal, –s, ⁓er   monument, statue

denn (*conjunction*)   for

derselbe, dieselbe, dasselbe the same

deswegen   for this reason

deutlich   clear(ly)

deutsch   German

(das) Deutschland, –s   Germany

der Deutschlehrer, –s, –   German teacher (i.e., teacher of German)

der Dichter, –s, –   poet

dick   fat

der Dieb, –es, –e   thief

der Diebstahl, –s, ⁓e   theft, robbery

der Dienst, –es, –e   service

der Dienstag, –s, –e   Tuesday

diesmal   this time

das Ding, –es, –e   thing

diskutieren   to discuss
doch   after all; but; still, nevertheless
dort   there
das **Drama, –s, Dramen**   drama, play
draußen   outside
drei   three
dringen (drang, ist gedrungen) to penetrate, to enter into
dringend   urgent(ly)
dumm   stupid, dumb
der **Dummkopf, –es, ⸚e**   stupid person
dunkel   dark
dünn   thin
durch (preposition)   through; by
durchdenken (dachte durch/ durchdachte, durchgedacht/ durchdacht) (*either separable or inseparable, without change of meaning*) to think through, to consider carefully
durchfallen (fällt durch, fiel durch, ist durchgefallen) to flunk, to fail; **durchfallen lassen** to flunk (someone), to fail
durchführen   to conduct, to carry out, to perform
durch′schauen   to look through; **durchschau′en** to see through
dürfen (darf, durfte, gedurft) to be allowed (permitted) to; may, might

eben   just
die **Ecke, –, –n**   corner
ehe (*conjunction*)   before
die **Ehe, –, –n**   marriage
die **Ehre, –, –n**   honor
das **Ei, –es, –er**   egg
der **Eierbecher, –s, –**   egg-cup
eigen   own

eigenartig   special, peculiar
eigentlich   real(ly)
sich **einbilden**   to imagine
der **Einbrecher, –s, –**   burglar
einbringen (brachte ein, eingebracht) to bring in, to earn
eindeutig   clearly
eindringen (drang ein, ist eingedrungen) to enter, to penetrate
der **Eindruck, –s, ⸚e**   impression
eindrucksvoll   impressive
einfach   simple, simply
der **Einfall, –s, ⸚e**   idea
einfallen (fällt ein, fiel ein, ist eingefallen) to occur to
der **Einfluß, Einflusses, ⸚e**   influence
eingebildet   conceited
eingeführt   introduced
einige   a few, several
das **Einkommen, –s, –**   income
einladen (lädt ein, lud ein, eingeladen) to invite
einmal   once; ever
einreichen   to hand in, to submit
einschlafen (schläft ein, schlief ein, ist eingeschlafen) to fall asleep
eintreten (tritt ein, trat ein, ist eingetreten) to enter, to step into
einverstanden sein (mit) to agree (with)
einzeln   individual, single
das **Eis, –es,** (*no plural*)   ice cream; ice
elf   eleven
die **Eltern** (*plural*)   parents
der **Empfang, –es, ⸚e**   reception; **in Empfang nehmen** to receive
empfangen (empfängt, empfing, empfangen) to receive

empfehlen (empfiehlt, empfahl, empfohlen) to recommend; **sich empfehlen** to be advisable

endgültig final(ly)

endlich finally

enterben to disinherit

die **Entfernung**, –, –en distance

enthalten (enthält, enthielt, enthalten) to contain; **sich enthalten** (*with genitive*) to refrain from

entkommen (entkam, ist entkommen) to escape, to get away

entlang along

entlassen (entläßt, entließ, entlassen) to dismiss, to fire

die **Entscheidung**, –, –en decision; **eine Entscheidung treffen** to make a decision

entschlossen determined

sich **entschuldigen** to apologize

die **Entstehung**, –, –en origin

enttäuschen to disappoint

entweder . . . oder either . . . or

sich **entwickeln** to develop

die **Entwicklung**, –, –en development

das **Erdbeben**, –s, – earthquake

die **Erde**, –, (*no plural*) earth

erfahren (erfährt, erfuhr, erfahren) to learn, to find out

erfinden (erfand, erfunden) to invent

erfolgreich successful

erhalten (erhält, erhielt, erhalten) to receive, to get

sich **erholen** to recover

erinnern to remind; **sich erinnern** (**an**) to remember

sich **erkälten** to catch cold

erkennen (erkannte, erkannt) to recognize

erklären to explain, to declare

sich **erkundigen** (**nach**) to enquire (about)

erleben to experience

ermüden to tire out

ernst serious

erscheinen (erschien, ist erschienen) to appear

erschießen (erschoß, erschossen) to kill by shooting, to shoot dead

ersehnen to long for

erst first; (*with expressions of time*) only, not until

erwähnen to mention

erwarten to expect

erweisen (erwies, erwiesen) to show, to bestow

erzählen to tell, to narrate

die **Erzählung**, –, –en story

erzkonservativ extremely conservative

essen (ißt, aß, gegessen) to eat; **das Essen**, –s, – meal

etwas something, anything; some (*e.g.*, **etwas Geld** some money); **so etwas** such a thing, something like that

die **Ewigkeit**, –, –en eternity

das **Exemplar**, –s, –e copy

die **Fabrik**, –, –en factory

fähig capable of (*with genitive*)

die **Fahne**, –, –n banner, flag

fahren (fährt, fuhr, ist gefahren) to go, to travel, to ride; (*used transitively*) to operate, to drive

der **Fahrer**, –s, – driver

der **Fall**, –es, ⸚e case

fallen (fällt, fiel, ist gefallen) to fall; **einem leicht fallen** to be easy for someone

falls (*conjunction*) in case, if

falsch wrong, false

die **Familie**, –, –n family

fangen (fängt, fing, gefangen) to catch

farbenblind color-blind

fast almost

faul lazy

die **Faustlegende**, –, –n   Faust legend

die **Feder**, –, –n   pen

der **Federhalter**, –s, –   fountain pen; pen holder

fehlen to be wrong with; to be missing (absent, lacking); **es fehlt mir (dir, ihm,** *etc.*) **an** I (you, he, *etc.*) lack(s)

der **Fehler**, –s, –   mistake

der **Feind**, –es, –e   enemy

das **Feld**, –es, –er   field

das **Fenster**, –s, –   window

die **Ferien** (*plural*)   vacation

der **Fernseher**, –s, –   television (set)

fertig finished; **fertig sein** to be finished; **mit etwas fertig werden** to finish (something), to handle, to manage (something)

feststellen to determine, to establish

fett fat

das **Feuer**, –s, –   fire

der **Film**, –es, –e   picture, movie

finden (fand, gefunden) to find; **sich finden** to be found, to be located

die **Firma**, –, **Firmen**   firm, company

flach flat

die **Flasche**, –, –n   bottle

das **Fleisch**, –es, (*no plural*)   meat

die **Fliege**, –, –n   fly

fliegen (flog, ist geflogen) to fly

fliehen (floh, ist geflohen) to flee

fließen (floß, ist geflossen) to flow, to stream

das **Flugzeug**, –s, –e   airplane

der **Fluß, Flusses,** ⸚e   river

flüstern to whisper

die **Folge**, –, –n   consequence, result

folgen to follow

der **Forscher**, –s, –   researcher

die **Forschung**, –, –en   research

fortsetzen to continue

die **Frage**, –, –n   question

fragen to ask

fragwürdig questionable

(das) **Frankreich**, –s   France

französisch French

die **Frau**, –, –en   woman; wife

frech fresh, impudent

frei free

die **Freude**, –, –n   joy, pleasure

freuen to please; **es freut mich (dich, ihn,** *etc.*) I (you, he, *etc.*) am pleased; **sich freuen** to be pleased; **sich freuen auf** to look forward to

der **Freund**, –es, –e   friend

die **Freundin**, –, –nen   girl friend

freundlich friendly, in a friendly way

frieren (fror, gefroren) to freeze; **mich (dich, ihn,** *etc.*) **friert** I (you, he, *etc.*) am (are, is, *etc.*) freezing

die **Frucht**, –, ⸚e   fruit

früher earlier, before

der **Frühling**, –s, –e   spring (*season of year*)

das **Frühstück**, –s, –e   breakfast; **zum Frühstück** for breakfast

führen to lead

fünf five

fünfzig fifty

für (*preposition*) for

der **Fußball**, –s, ⸚e   football

ganz whole, entire; quite; very

gar nicht not at all; **gar nichts** nothing at all

der **Garten, –s, ∸** garden, yard

die **Gasgesellschaft, –, –en** gas company

der **Gast, –es, ∸e** guest

das **Gebäude, –s, –** building

gebären (gebar, geboren) to give birth to

geben (gibt, gab, gegeben) to give; **es gibt** there is (are)

gebildet educated

der **Gebrauch, –s, ∸e** use

gebrauchen to use

der **Gedanke, –ns, –n** thought, idea

gedenken (gedachte, gedacht) to remember, to think of (*with genitive object*)

das **Gedicht, –(e)s, –e** poem

die **Gefahr, –, –en** danger; **(die) Gefahr laufen** to run the risk, to be in danger (of)

gefallen (gefällt, gefiel, gefallen) to please

der **Gefallen, –s, –** favor

der **Gefangene, –n, –n** prisoner

das **Gefängnis, –ses, –se** prison

gefaßt composed; **auf etwas gefaßt sein** to be ready for something

gegen (*preposition*) against, toward; compared with; about

der **Gegenstand, –s, ∸e** object, subject

gegenüber (*preposition with dative*) opposite; toward; with respect to

die **Gegenwart, –,** (*no plural*) presence; present

gehen (ging, ist gegangen) to go; **es geht mir gut (schlecht)** I am fine (terrible); **einem zu Herzen gehen** to bother, to disturb

gehorchen to obey

gehören to belong to

gelb yellow

das **Geld, –es, –er** money

der **Geldgeber, –s, –** sponsor, backer

gelegen situated, located

die **Gelegenheit, –, –en** opportunity

der **Gelehrte, –n, –n** scholar

gelingen (gelang, ist gelungen) to succeed; **es gelingt mir** I succeed

gemein common, vulgar, base

gemeinsam common

gemütlich comfortable(-bly), pleasant(ly)

genau precise(ly), exact(ly)

genießen (genoß, genossen) to enjoy

genug enough

genügen to be enough (sufficient)

gerade just, just now, at the moment; exactly, precisely

geraten (gerät, geriet, ist geraten) to come into, to fall into, to get into

gering small; **nicht im geringsten** not at all, not in the least

gern(e) gladly, willingly; **ich esse gern** I like to eat; **ich trinke gern** I like to drink, *etc.*

das **Gerücht, –(e)s, –e** rumor

das **Geschäft, –(e)s, –e** store; business

der **Geschäftsmann, –es, Geschäftsleute** businessman

geschehen (geschieht, geschah, ist geschehen) to happen

das **Geschenk, –(e)s, –e** present, gift

die **Geschichte, –, –n** story; history

die **Geschwister** (*plural*) brothers and sisters

die **Gesellschaft, –, –en** company, society; party; **in Gesellschaft** when other people are around

das **Gesetz, –es, –e** law

das **Gesicht, –(e)s, –er** face

der **Gesichtspunkt, –es, –e** point of view

das **Gespenst, –(e)s, –er** ghost

die **Gestalt, –, –en** figure, form; character

gestehen (gestand, gestanden) to admit, to confess

gestern yesterday; **gestern abend** last evening

gewachsen (*past participle of* wachsen, to grow) up to, equal to, a match for

gewahr werden (*with genitive object*) to become aware of, to notice

das **Gewicht, –(e)s, –e** weight

gewöhnlich usual, ordinary

sich **gewöhnen (an)** to get used (to)

gewöhnt (an) used (to), accustomed (to)

glauben to believe, to think

gleich (sogleich) right (away), immediately

gleichen (glich, geglichen) to be like, to resemble

gleichgültig indifferent(ly), a matter of indifference

glücklicherweise fortunately

graben (gräbt, grub, gegraben) to dig

gratulieren to congratulate

greifen (griff, gegriffen) to grasp; **greifen (nach)** to reach (for)

die **Grenze, –, –n** border, boundary line, limit

die **Großmutter, –, –̈** grandmother

grün green

grüßen to greet

der **Gulden, –s, –** florin (*old monetary unit*)

gültig valid

günstig favorable (to *or* for)

die **Gurke, –, –n** pickle, cucumber

das **Haar, –es, –e** hair

haben (hatte, gehabt) to have

halten (hält, hielt, gehalten) to hold; **halten für** to consider; **halten von** to think of

die **Haltung, –, –en** attitude

die **Hand, –, –̈e** hand

handeln to act; to deal; **es handelt sich um** it is a question of (a matter of)

der **Handschuh, –s, –e** glove

die **Handtasche, –, –n** pocketbook

hängen (hing, gehangen) to hang

hassen to hate

der **Haufen, –s, –** pile

das **Haupt, –es, –̈er** head

die **Hauptstraße, –, –n** main street

das **Haus, –es, –̈er** house; **nach Hause** home; **zu Hause** at home

die **Hausaufgabe, –, –n** homework

heben (hob, gehoben) to lift, to raise; **einen Schatz heben** to unearth (discover) a treasure

heilen to cure, to heal

die **Heimat, –,** (*no plural*) home (*referring to the region a person comes from*)

das **Heimatdorf, –es, –̈er** home village (*or* town)

die **Heimatstadt, –, –̈e** home

town, city where one was born

heiraten to marry

heiß machen to bother, to worry

heißen (hieß, geheißen) to be called; to be

heizen to heat

helfen (hilft, half, geholfen) to help

hereinkommen (kam herein, ist hereingekommen) to come in

hereinlassen (läßt herein, ließ herein, hereingelassen) to let in

der **Herr, –n, –en** Mr.; gentleman

herstellen to make, to manufacture

(**herum**) **um . . . herum** around, about

herumkriechen (kroch herum, ist herumgekrochen) to crawl around

das **Herz, –ens, –en** heart; **auf dem Herzen haben** to have on one's mind; **einem zu Herzen gehen** to bother, to disturb

das **Heu, –es,** (*no plural*) hay

heute today; **heute abend** this evening; **heute morgen** this morning; **heute nachmittag** this afternoon

hier here

die **Hilfe, –,** (*no plural*) help, aid, assistance

hinauswerfen (wirft hinaus, warf hinaus, hinausgeworfen) to throw out

hindurch through (out)

hinfahren (fährt hin, fuhr hin, ist hingefahren) to go, to travel

hingehen (ging hin, ist hingegangen) to go (there)

hinhalten (hält hin, hielt hin, hingehalten) to hold out to

hinter behind, in back of

hinweisen (**auf**) (wies hin, hingewiesen) to point to

die **Hitze, –,** (*no plural*) heat, hot spell

hoch high

hocherfreut very pleased, delighted

die **Hochschule, –, –n** university, academy (of music, art, *etc.*)

höchst very, extremely

hoffen (**auf**) to hope (for)

hoffentlich hopefully; I (we) hope

das **Holz, –es, ⸚er** wood

hören to hear; **hören** (**auf**) to listen (to), to obey

der **Hörsaal, –s, Hörsäle** lecture hall

hübsch pretty

der **Hund, –es, –e** dog

hungrig hungry

der **Hut, –es, ⸚e** hat

die **Idee, –, –n** idea

immer always; **immer noch** still

imstande sein to be able

in in, into; to; at

indem (*conjunction*) while, as; by . . . –ing

infolge (*preposition with genitive*) as a result of

der **Ingenieur, –s, –e** engineer

innerhalb (*preposition with genitive*) inside, within

interessieren to interest; **sich interessieren** (**für**) to be interested in

irgendein any (at all)

irgendwo (**anders**) somewhere (else)

die **Jacke, –, –n** jacket

das **Jahr, –es, –e** year; **mit dreißig
Jahren** at the age of thirty
jahrelang for years
die **Jahreszeit, –, –en** season
das **Jahrhundert, –s, –e** century
jahrzehntelang for decades
je ever; **je . . . desto, je
. . . um so, je . . . je** the
. . . the
jemand someone
jenseits (*preposition with genitive*) on the other side of,
beyond
jetzt now
jung young
der **Junge, –n, –n** boy

der **Kaiser, –s, –** emperor
kalt cold
kämmen to comb
das **Kapitel, –s, –** chapter
(der) **Karlsplatz, –es** Charles'
Square
die **Karte, –, –n** card
das **Kätzchen, –s, –** kitten
die **Katze, –, –n** cat
kaufen to buy
der **Kaufmann, –es, Kaufleute**
merchant
kaum hardly, scarcely; **kaum
noch** hardly . . . anymore
keineswegs by no means
der **Keller, –s, –** cellar
kennen (kannte, gekannt) to
know, to be acquainted with
kennenlernen to meet, to
make the acquaintance of
das **Kind, –es, –er** child
der **Kinderspielplatz, –es, –̈e**
playground
die **Kindheit, –,** (*no plural*)
childhood
das **Kino, –s, –s** movie theater;
ins Kino gehen to go to
the movies
die **Kirche, –, –n** church
klagen to complain

die **Klasse, –, –n** class
das **Kleid, –es, –er** dress
klein small, little
die **Kleinigkeit, –, –en** trifle,
insignificant thing
kneifen (kniff, gekniffen) to
pinch
kochen to cook, to boil
der **Kollege, –n, –n** colleague
komisch funny, humorous
kommen (kam, ist gekommen)
to come
die **Komödie, –, –n** comedy
kompliziert complicated
der **Komponist, –en, –en** composer
können (kann, konnte, gekonnt) to be able to; can;
may
die **Konzertkarte, –, –n** concert
ticket
die **Konzertreise, –, –n** concert
tour
der **Konzertsaal, –es, Konzertsäle**
concert hall
der **Kopf, –es, –̈e** head
kosten to cost
krank sick
kränken to offend, to hurt
das **Krankenhaus, –es, –̈er**
hospital
die **Krankheit, –, –en** sickness,
disease
kriechen (kroch, ist gekrochen)
to crawl, to creep; **herumkriechen** to crawl around
der **Krieg, –es, –e** war
die **Kritik, –, –en** criticism;
review; the critics
der **Kritiker, –s, –** critic
der **Kuchen, –s, –** cake
sich **kümmern** (um) to be concerned (about)
der **Kumpan, –s, –e** companion
der **Kunde, –n, –n** customer
die **Kunst, –, –̈e** art
die **Kunstakademie, –, –n** art
academy

der **Künstler,** –s, – artist

kurieren to cure

die **Kurzgeschichte,** –, –n short story

kürzlich recently

lächeln to smile

das **Lachen,** –s, (*no plural*) laughing, laughter

der **Laden,** –s, ⸚ shop, store

das **Land,** –es, ⸚er country; **aufs Land gehen** to go to the country; **auf dem Lande sein** to be in the country

lang long

lange a long time, long

die **Lang(e)weile,** –, (*no plural*) boredom

langsam slow(ly)

langweilig boring

der **Lärm,** –(e)s, (*no plural*) noise

lassen (läßt, ließ, gelassen) to let, to allow; to have (something done)

(das) **Latein,** –s Latin

der **Lauf,** –es, ⸚e course

laufen (läuft, lief, ist gelaufen) to run

die **Laune,** –, –n mood

der **Laut,** –es, –e sound, noise

leben to live

das **Leben,** –s, (*no plural*) life

die **Lebensmittel** (*plural*) food, provisions

die **Leberwurst,** –, ⸚e liverwurst

das **Leder,** –s, – leather

leer empty

legen to put, to place

der **Lehrer,** –s, – teacher; **die Lehrerin,** –, –nen (female) teacher

die **Lehrtätigkeit,** –, (*no plural*) teaching

leicht easy

leid: es tut mir (dir, ihm, *etc.*) I (you, he, *etc.*) am sorry

leiden (litt, gelitten) to suffer, to stand, to tolerate

leider unfortunately

leihen (lieh, geliehen) to lend

leise gentle, soft(ly)

leisten to perform, to achieve, to accomplish, to do

lernen to learn

lesen (liest, las, gelesen) to read

lesenswert worth reading

letzt last, past; **in den letzten Tagen** in the past few days

die **Leute** (*plural*) people

das **Licht,** –es, –er light

lieb dear; **mir ist es lieb** I like it

die **Liebe,** –, (*no plural*) love

lieber (*comparative of* **gern**) rather

liebst– (*superlative of* **gern**) best

das **Lied,** –es, –er song

loben to praise

los: was ist los? what's up, what is going on?

lösen to solve

sich **lossagen** (**von**) to disown, to reject

lossein to be rid of

die **Lösung,** –, –en solution

loswerden (wird los, wurde los, ist losgeworden) to get rid of

die **Luft,** –, ⸚e air; **als wäre ich Luft** as if I didn't exist

die **Lungenentzündung,** –, –en pneumonia

die **Lust,** –, ⸚e desire; **Lust haben** to desire, to want to, to feel like

machen to make, to do; **einen Spaziergang machen** to take a walk; **sich machen (an)** to begin

das **Mädchen,** –s, – girl

der **Magen,** –s, ∸ stomach
malen to paint
die **Malerei,** –, –en painting
man one, people, they, we
manchmal sometimes
mangelhaft deficient
der **Mann,** –es, ∸er man; husband
die **Mannschaft,** –, –en team
der **Mantel,** –s, ∸ coat
das **Märchen,** –s, – fairy-tale
die **Masern** (*plural*) measles
die **Mauer,** –, –n wall
mehr more; **nicht mehr** no more, no longer; **um so mehr** all the more
die **Mehrheit,** –, (*no plural*) majority
meinen to mean; to say, to think
die **Meinung,** –, –en opinion; **einem seine Meinung sagen** to tell someone what one really thinks
meist– most
meistens mostly, usually
die **Menge,** –, –n quantity, amount; crowd
der **Mensch,** –en, –en man, human being
merken to notice
das **Merkmal,** –s, –e characteristic, characteristic feature
die **Metzgerei,** –, –en butcher's shop
die **Milch,** –, (*no plural*) milk
mit with; by
mitbringen (brachte mit, mitgebracht) to bring along
mitgehen (ging mit, ist mitgegangen) to go along
mitkommen (kam mit, ist mitgekommen) to come along
mitleidig sympathetic(ally), compassionate(ly)
mitnehmen (nimmt mit, nahm mit, mitgenommen) to take along

der **Mittag,** –s, –e midday, noon; **zu Mittag essen** to eat lunch
die **Mitte,** –, –n middle
mitteilen to tell, to inform (someone of something)
das **Mittel,** –s, – means
das **Mittelalter,** –s, (*no plural*) the Middle Ages
mittelalterlich medieval
mittels (*preposition with genitive*) by means of
mitten in the middle (of)
die **Mitternacht,** –, ∸e midnight
der **Mittwoch,** –s, –e Wednesday
möchte (*subjunctive of* **mögen**) would like to
mögen (mag, mochte, gemocht) to like to, to care to, to wish to; may
möglich possible
der **Monat,** –s, –e month
morgen tomorrow; **morgen früh** tomorrow morning
das **Morgen,** –s, – tomorrow
morgens in the morning
müde (*with genitive or accusative*) tired, tired of
die **Mühe,** –, –n effort; **sich Mühe mit etwas geben** to take great pains with something, to expend effort or energy on something
mündlich oral
die **Münze,** –, –n coin
die **Musik,** –, (*no plural*) music
müssen (muß, mußte, gemußt) to have to; must
der **Mut,** –es, (*no plural*) courage
die **Mutter,** –, ∸ mother
die **Mütze,** –, –n cap

nach to, toward; after; according to
der **Nachbar,** –n (*or* –s), –n neighbor

das **Nachbarskind, –es, –er**
neighbor's child
nachdem (*conjunction*) after
nachdenken (dachte nach,
nachgedacht) to think
over (about), to consider
nachgehen (ging nach, ist
nachgegangen) to be (run)
slow (of a watch or clock)
der **Nachhauseweg, –es, –e** way
home
nachholen to make up, to
catch up
die **Nachlässigkeit, –, –en** carelessness
der **Nachmittag, –s, –e** afternoon
nachmittags in the afternoon
die **Nachricht, –, –en** news
nächst– next; **in den nächsten Wochen** (**Tagen,** *etc.*)
in the next few weeks (days,
etc.)
nagelneu brand new
nähen to sew
der **Name, –ns, –n** name
neben next to, along side of;
in addition to
nennen (nannte, genannt) to
name, to call; to mention
nett nice(ly), pleasant(ly)
neu new
neulich recently
neuntägig nine-day
neunzehnt– nineteenth
neunzig ninety
die **Nibelungensage, –, (–n)** saga
(*or* story) of the Nibelungen
nicht not; **nicht einmal** not
even; **nicht mehr** no longer;
**nich nur . . . , sondern
auch** not only . . . but
also
die **Nichte, –, –n** niece
nichts nothing; **gar nichts**
nothing at all
nie never
niedrig low

niemand no one, nobody
noch still, yet, in addition;
even; **noch ein** another
(one more); **noch einmal**
once more, again; **noch nie**
never before; **immer noch**
still
die **Novelle, –, –n** "novella,"
short story
nur only
nützen to be useful to

ob if, whether
obgleich (*conjunction*)
although
obwohl (*conjunction*)
although
der **Ofen, –s, ⸚** stove
der **Offizier, –s, –e** officer
öffnen to open
oft often
ohne without
das **Ohr, –es, –en** ear
der **Onkel, –s, –** uncle
die **Oper, –, –n** opera; **in die
Oper gehen** to go to the
opera
der **Ort, –es, –e** place, spot,
locality

ein paar (a) few, several
das **Paket, –s, –e** package
das **Papier, –s, –e** paper
die **Partei, –, –en** party
passend fitting, suitable
persönlich personal(ly)
pfeifen (pfiff, gepfiffen) to
whistle
der **Pfennig, –s, –e** penny
das **Pferd, –es, –e** horse
pflegen to cultivate, to take
care of
pflücken to pick
das **Pfund, –es, –e** pound
das **Phänomen, –s, –e** phe-
nomenon
der **Photoapparat, –s, –e** camera

der **Photograph, –en, –en**
photographer
planen to plan
der **Platz, –es, ⸚e** square
die **Politik, –,** (*no plural*) policy,
politics
der **Politiker, –s, –** politician
die **Polizei, –,** (*no plural*) police
der **Polizist, –en, –en** policeman
das **Postamt, –s, ⸚er** post office
die **Praxis, –,** (*no plural*) practice
der **Preis, –es, –e** prize; price
das **Preisausschreiben, –s, –**
contest
das **Prinzip, –s, –ien** principle
die **Prüfung, –, –en** test,
examination
das **Publikum, –s,** (*no plural*)
public, audience
das **Pulver, –s, –** powder
der **Punkt, –es, –e** point; **um
Punkt 10 Uhr** at 10 o'clock
sharp, at exactly 10 o'clock
der **Psychiater, –s, –** psychiatrist

die **Quelle, –, –n** source

das **Rad, –es, ⸚er** wheel
der **Rat, –es, Ratschläge** advice
raten (rät, riet, geraten) to
advise
das **Rätsel, –s, –** puzzle, riddle
der **Räuber, –s, –** robber
rauchen to smoke
recht right; **recht haben** to
be right
der **Rechtsanwalt, –s, ⸚e** lawyer
rechtzeitig on time, in time
reden to talk, to speak
die **Redewendung, –, –en** idiom,
expression
der **Redner, –s, –** speaker
das **Referat, –s, –e** report, paper
der **Regen, –s, –** rain
der **Regenschirm, –s, –e** umbrella

die **Regierung, –, –en** government
regnen to rain
reich rich, wealthy
die **Reihe, –, –n** row
rein pure
die **Reise, –, –n** trip, journey;
eine Reise machen to take
a trip
reisen to travel
der **Reiseplan, –s, ⸚e** travel plan
reizend charming
rennen (rannte, ist gerannt)
to run
reparieren to repair
das **Rezept, –s, –e** recipe
der **Rhein, –s** the Rhine
richtig correct
die **Richtigkeit, –,** (*no plural*)
correctness
der **Ring, –es, –e** ring
der **Roman, –s, –e** novel
der **Römer, –s, –** Roman
rot red
rufen (rief, gerufen) to call
die **Ruhe, –,** (*no plural*) peace,
quiet

die **Sache, –, –n** thing, matter,
affair
die **Säge, –, –n** saw
sagen to say, to tell
sammeln to collect; **sich sammeln** to gather
die **Sammlung, –, –en** collection
der **Samstag, –s, –e** Saturday
der **Sänger, –s, –** singer; **die
Sängerin, –, –nen** (female)
singer
satt (*with genitive or accusative*) sick (of), tired (of)
der **Satz, –es, ⸚e** sentence
sauer sour
schade (that's) too bad
schaden to hurt, to do damage to

die **Schallplatte, –, –n** phono-
graph record

sich **schämen** (*with genitive object*)
to be ashamed

der **Schatz, –es, ⸚e** treasure

schätzen to appreciate, to
value

die **Schauspielerin, –, –nen** actress

der **Scheck, –s, –s(–e)** check

scheinen (schien, geschienen)
to seem, to appear

schelten (schilt, schalt, gescholten) to scold

schicken to send

schlafen (schläft, schlief, geschlafen) to sleep

das **Schlafzimmer, –s, –** bedroom

schlagen (schlägt, schlug, geschlagen) to beat; to hit,
to strike

die **Schlagsahne, –,** (*no plural*)
whipped cream

schlecht bad, awful, poor

schleichen (schlich, ist ge-
schlichen) to creep, to
sneak, to prowl

schließen (schloß, geschlossen)
to close; to conclude

schließlich finally

schlimm bad

das **Schloß, Schlosses, ⸚er** castle

schluchzen to sob

das **Schlußexamen, –s, –** final
exam

schmecken to taste

schneiden (schnitt, geschnitten)
to cut

der **Schneider, –s, –** tailor

schnell fast

schon already; don't worry,
you can be sure (*as in* **ich
werde es schon finden**);
schon wieder again

schön beautiful, handsome,
nice

schrecklich terrible (–ly)

schreiben (schrieb,
geschrieben) to write

die **Schreibmaschine, –, –n**
typewriter

der **Schreibtisch, –es, –e** desk

schüchtern shy

der **Schuh, –(e)s, –e** shoe

die **Schulaufgabe, –, –n** (school)
homework, assignment

die **Schulden** (*plural*) debts

die **Schule, –, –n** school; **in die
Schule gehen** to go to
school

der **Schüler, –s, –** pupil

der **Schulkamerad, –en, –en**
school comrade, friend

der **Schullehrer, –s, –** school-
teacher

der **Schultag, –s, –e** school day

schwach weak

die **Schwalbe, –, –n** swallow

schwänzen to cut (class)

schwarz black

schweigen (schwieg, geschwiegen) to be silent

schwer heavy; hard, difficult;
serious

die **Schwester, –, –n** sister

schwierig difficult, hard

die **Schwierigkeit, –, –en**
difficulty

schwimmen (schwamm, ist
geschwommen) to swim

schwingen (schwang, ge-
schwungen) to swing,
to wave

der **See, –s, –n** lake

sehen (sieht, sah, gesehen)
to see; **sehen nach** to look
after

sich **sehnen** (**nach**) to long (for)

sehr very, very much

sein (ist, war, ist gewesen)
to be

seit (*preposition with dative*) since; for; **seit langem** for a long time

seitdem (*conjunction*) since; (*adverb*) since then, since that time

die **Seite**, –, –n page; side

die **Sekretärin**, –, –nen (female) secretary

selbst myself, himself, themselves, *etc.;* even

selten seldom, rarely

die **Seminararbeit**, –, –en seminar paper

senken to lower, to bend, to bow

servieren to serve

setzen to put, to place; **sich setzen** to sit down

sicher sure; (*with genitive*) certain of; safe, secure; surely, certainly

singen (sang, gesungen) to sing

sitzen (saß, gesessen) to sit

so thus, that (this) way; then (*after a subordinate clause, beginning a main clause*); **so etwas** such a thing, something like that; **so . . . wie** as . . . as

sobald (*conjunction*) as soon as

soeben just, just now

sofort immediately, right away

sogar even

sogleich immediately, right away

der **Sohn**, –es, ⁻e son

solange (*conjunction*) as long as

der **Soldat**, –en, –en soldier

sollen to be to, to be supposed to; to be said to

die **Sonate**, –, –n sonata

sondern but; **nicht nur . . . , sondern auch** not only . . . but also

sonst otherwise

sooft (*conjunction*) as often as

die **Sorge**, –, –n worry, care; **sich Sorgen machen** to worry

sorgen (**für**) to take care (of)

sorgfältig careful(ly)

spannend exciting, thrilling

der **Spaß**, –es, ⁻e fun, joke; **das macht mir Spaß** that's fun, I like it; **zum Spaß** for a joke

spät late

spazierengehen (ging spazieren, ist spazierengegangen) to take a walk, to go for a walk

der **Spaziergang**, –s, ⁻e walk; **einen Spaziergang machen** to take a walk

der **Spiegel**, –s, – mirror

spielen to play

das **Spielzeug**, –, (*no plural*) toy

der **Spitzbube**, –n, –n rogue, rascal

sprechen (spricht, sprach, gesprochen) to speak, to talk; to speak to (with)

das **Staatstheater**, –s, – state theater

die **Stadt**, –, ⁻e city; **in die (der) Stadt** downtown

die **Stadtgrenze**, –, –n city limits (boundary)

stammen (**aus**) to stem (from), to come (from)

stattfinden (fand statt, stattgefunden) to take place

stecken to put, to place

stehen (stand, gestanden) to stand, to be situated

stehlen (stiehlt, stahl, gestohlen) to steal

steinalt ancient, very old

die **Stelle, –, –n** place, passage, spot; job, position; **auf der Stelle** on the spot
stellen to put, to place; **eine Frage stellen** to ask a question
die **Stellung, –, –en** job, position
stellungslos unemployed, without a job
sterben (stirbt, starb, ist gestorben) to die
stimmen to be right (correct)
stören to disturb
die **Straße, –, –n** street
die **Straßenecke, –, –n** street corner
der **Streik, –s, –s** strike
streng strict
das **Stück, –es, –e** piece, play
der **Student, –en, –en** student; die **Studentin, –, –nen** (female) student
die **Studienzeit, –, –en** period of study, time at the university
studieren to study
das **Studium, –s, Studien** study
stundenlang for hours
suchen to look for
(das) **Südamerika, –s** South America
die **Suppe, –, –n** soup
die **Symphonie, –, –n** symphony

der **Tabak, –s, –e** tobacco
tadellos excellent(ly), perfect(ly)
der **Tag, –es, –e** day
täglich daily
die **Tante, –, –n** aunt
der **Tanz, –es, –̈e** dance
tanzen to dance
die **Tasche, –, –n** pocket
die **Tasse, –, –n** cup
die **Tat, –, –en** deed, act
tatsächlich actually, really
tausend thousand

der **Teil, –es, –e** part
teilnehmen (nimmt teil, nahm teil, teilgenommen) to take part, to participate
teuer expensive
der **Teufel, –s, –** devil
das **Theater, –s, –** theater; **ins Theater gehen** to go to the theater
das **Thema, –s, Themen** theme, topic, subject
das **Tier, –es, –e** animal
tilgen to pay off (a debt)
die **Tinte, –, –n** ink
der **Titel, –s, –** title
die **Tochter, –, –̈** daughter
der **Tod, –es, (–e)** death
tot dead
tragen (trägt, trug, getragen) to wear; to carry
die **Träne, –, –n** tear
treffen (trifft, traf, getroffen) to meet
treiben (trieb, getrieben) to drive, to run, to operate
treten (tritt, trat, ist getreten) to step; (used transitively) to kick
trinken (trank, getrunken) to drink
die **Tropen** (plural) the tropics
trösten to console
trotz inspite of, despite
trotzdem nevertheless; (as conjunction) in spite of the fact that, although
tüchtig capable; industrious
tun (tat, getan) to do; to act
die **Tür, –, –en** door

übel sick; **mir wird übel** I am getting sick
üben to practice
über over, above; across; about; more than; via
überall everywhere

überhaupt in general; at all

überhören not to hear; to miss

die **Überlegung, –, –en** consideration, deliberation

übermorgen the day after tomorrow

übernehmen (übernimmt, übernahm, übernommen) to take over

überraschen to surprise

übersetzen to translate

ü´bertreten (tritt über, trat über, ist übergetreten) to go over to; **übertre´ten** (übertritt, übertrat, übertreten) to overstep, violate

überzeugen to convince; **überzeugt** convinced

üblich usual, customary

das **Ufer, –s, –** bank (of a river)

die **Uhr, –, –en** clock, watch; **ein** (**zwei, drei,** *etc.*) **Uhr** one (two, three, *etc.*) o'clock

um around; at; by; **um . . . willen** for the sake of

umgeben (umgibt, umgab, umgeben) to surround

die **Umgebung, –, –en** environment, vicinity, surroundings

um´schreiben (schrieb um, umgeschrieben) to rewrite; **umschrei´ben** to paraphrase, to express indirectly

um so (*with comparative*) all the . . .

der **Umstand, –s, ⸚e** circumstance

unangenehm unpleasant

unbekannt unknown

die **Undankbarkeit, –,** (*no plural*) ingratitude

der **Unfall, –s, ⸚e** accident

die **Unfreundlichkeit, –,** (*no plural*) unfriendliness

ungern unwillingly

ungeschickt clumsy

unglaublich unbelievable(–ly)

unglücklich unhappy

unmöglich impossible; not possibly

unschuldig innocent

unter under; among

unterbrechen (unterbricht, unterbrach, unterbrochen) to interrupt

die **Unterbrechung, –, –en** interruption

unterhalten (unterhält, unterhielt, unterhalten) to entertain; **sich unterhalten** to converse

unternehmen (unternimmt, unternahm, unternommen) to undertake

das **Unternehmen, –s, –** undertaking

der **Unterricht, –s,** (*no plural*) instruction

unterrichten to instruct

die **Unterschlagung, –, –en** embezzlement

unterstützen to support

die **Unterstützung, –, –en** support

untersuchen to examine, to investigate

die **Untersuchung, –, –en** investigation

ununterbrochen uninterrupted(ly)

die **Unvorsichtigkeit, –, –en** carelessness

der **Ursprung, –s, ⸚e** origin

das **Vakzin, –s, –e** vaccine

der **Vater, –s, ⸚** father

veranschaulichen to illustrate, to make clear

verantwortlich responsible

verbergen (verbirgt, verbarg, verborgen) to hide, to conceal

verbinden (verband, verbunden) to bandage; to join, to connect

das **Verbrechen, –s, –** crime; **ein Verbrechen begehen** to commit a crime

der **Verbrecher, –s, –** criminal

verbreiten to spread

verbrennen (verbrannte, verbrannt) to burn up

verbringen (verbrachte, verbracht) to spend (time)

verdienen to earn

die **Vereinigten Staaten** (*plural*) the United States

verfilmen to make into a movie, to make a movie out of

verfließen (verfloß, ist verflossen) to flow by, to pass by

die **Verfügung, –, –en** disposition; **einem zur Verfügung stehen** to be at one's disposal

vergeben (vergibt, vergab, vergeben) to forgive

vergessen (vergißt, vergaß, vergessen) to forget

vergleichen (verglich, verglichen) to compare

das **Vergnügen, –s, –** pleasure

verhaften to arrest

verheiraten to marry (off); **sich verheiraten** (**mit**) **to** marry, to get married (to)

verhungern to starve

verkaufen to sell

verkünden to announce

verlangen to ask, to demand

verlassen (verläßt, verließ, verlassen) to leave; **sich verlassen** (**auf**) to rely (on)

der **Verleger, –s, –** publisher

verletzen to hurt, to wound

verlieren (verlor, verloren) to lose; **aus den Augen verlieren** to lose sight of

vermeiden (vermied, vermieden) to avoid

vermieten to rent (out)

vermißt missing

das **Vermögen, –s, –** fortune

veröffentlichen to publish

verrückt crazy

der **Vers, –es, –e** verse

die **Versammlung, –, –en** meeting, gathering

verschaffen to get, to obtain

verschieden different, various

das **Versehen, –s, –** mistake, oversight; **aus Versehen** by mistake

versichern to assure

die **Versicherungsgesellschaft, –, –en** insurance company

versprechen (verspricht, versprach, versprochen) to promise; **sich etwas versprechen** (**von**) to expect something from

das **Versprechen, –s, –** promise

verstecken to hide, to conceal

verstehen (verstand, verstanden) to understand

versteuern to tax

versuchen to try, to attempt

der **Versuchsapparat, –s, –e** apparatus for an experiment

vertreten (vertritt, vertrat, vertreten) to represent

verursachen to cause

verurteilen to condemn, to sentence

die **Verwahrung, –,** (*no plural*) keeping, custody; **in Verwahrung nehmen** to take into custody

der **Verwandte, –n, –n** relative

der **Verwundete, –n, –n** wounded (person)

die **Verwundung, –, –en** wound

die **Verzeihung, –,** (*no plural*) forgiveness

der **Vetter, –s, –** (male) cousin

viel much, a lot of; **viele**

many; **vieles** many things, a lot

vielleicht perhaps

vier four

vierzig forty

die **Villa, –, Villen** villa, country house

das **Volkslied, –(e)s, –er** folk song

voll, voller full (of)

völlig complete(ly)

vollkommen complete(ly)

von from; about; by; of

vor before, in front of; ago

voraussehen (sieht voraus, sah voraus, vorausgesehen) to predict, to foresee

vorbeigehen (ging vorbei, ist vorbeigegangen) to go by, to pass by

vorbeikommen (kam vorbei, ist vorbeigekommen) to come by, to pass

vorbereiten to prepare; **sich vorbereiten (auf)** to prepare (for), to get ready (for)

die **Vorbereitung, –, –en** preparation

der **Vordergrund, –s, –̈e** foreground

vordringen (drang vor, ist vorgedrungen) to push forward

vorgestern the day before yesterday

vorher (*adverb*) before that, previously

vorig– past, last, previous

vorkommen (kam vor, ist vorgekommen) to seem, to appear; to occur, to happen

der **Vorort, –(e)s, –e** suburb

der **Vorschlag, –s, –̈e** proposal, suggestion

vorschlagen (schlägt vor, schlug vor, vorgeschlagen) to suggest, to propose

vorsichtig careful(ly)

vorstellen to introduce; **sich vorstellen** (*with dative*) to imagine

die **Vorstellung, –, –en** performance

der **Vortrag, –s, –̈e** lecture

die **Wache, –, –n** watch, guard; **Wache stehen** to stand guard

wachsen (wächst, wuchs, ist gewachsen) to grow

wagen to dare

der **Wagen, –s, –** car, automobile

wählen to choose, to select

wahr true

während (*conjunction*) while; whereas; (*preposition*) during

die **Wahrheit, –, –en** truth

wahrscheinlich probably

der **Wald, –es, –̈er** forest, woods

die **Wand, –, –̈e** wall

wann (*interrogative*) when

das **Warenhaus, –es, –̈er** department store

warten to wait; **warten (auf)** to wait (for)

der **Wartesaal, –s, Wartesäle** waiting room (in public building)

das **Wartezimmer, –s, –** waiting room

warum why

was what; **was für (ein)** what kind of (a)

waschen (wäscht, wusch, gewaschen) to wash

das **Wasser, –s, –** water

weder . . . noch neither . . . nor

der **Weg, –es, –e** way, road; **einem aus dem Weg gehen** to avoid someone

wegen because of, on account of

wehtun (tat weh, weh getan) to hurt, to harm

weichgekocht soft-boiled

weil because

der **Wein, –s, –e** wine

weinen to cry

die **Weinflasche, –, –n** wine bottle

die **Weise, –, –n** way, manner; **auf diese Weise** in this way

weiß white

weiterreiten (ritt weiter, ist weitergeritten) to ride on (farther)

die **Welt, –, –en** world

der **Weltkrieg, –s, –e** world war

sich **wenden (an)** (wandte sich an, sich [an] gewandt) to turn to

wenig little; **ein wenig** a little; **weniger** less

wenigstens at least

wenn if, when; **wenn . . . auch** even if, even though

werden (wird, wurde, ist geworden) to become, to get, to grow

werfen (wirft, warf, geworfen) to throw

das **Werk, –es, –e** work

das **Werkzeug, –s, –e** tool

wert worth

das **Wetter, –s, –** weather

der **Wetterbericht, –s, –e** weather report

wichtig important

wider against

widersprechen (widerspricht, widersprach, widersprochen) to contradict

wie how

wieder again

wiederfinden (fand wieder, wiedergefunden) to find again

wiederho'len to repeat; **wie'-**

derholen to fetch, to get again

wiederkommen (kam wieder, ist wiedergekommen) to return, to come again

wiedersehen (sieht wieder, sah wieder, wiedergesehen) to see again

wiegen (wog, gewogen) to weigh

wild wild

die **Wildente, –, –n** wild duck

willkommen welcome

wirklich real(ly)

wissen (weiß, wußte, gewußt) to know

der **Wissenschaftler, –s, –** scientist

die **Witwe, –, –n** widow

wo where

die **Woche, –, –n** week

wohl well, very well; probably, undoubtedly

wohlhabend wealthy

wohnen to live, to reside

das **Wohnzimmer, –s, –** living room

wollen (will, wollte, gewollt) to want to, to intend to, to wish to; to claim

das **Wort, –es, ⸚er** (*or* –e) word

das **Wunder, –s, –** miracle

wunderbar wonderful

sich **wundern** to be surprised

wunderschön lovely, very beautiful

wünschen to wish

würdig (*with genitive*) worthy of

wütend furious

zart tender, delicate

der **Zaun, –es, ⸚e** fence

zehn ten

zeigen to show, to reveal; **sich zeigen** to be shown, to be revealed

die **Zeit**, –, –en time; **zu allen
Zeiten** at all times
die **Zeitschrift**, –, –en periodical
die **Zeitung**, –, –en newspaper
die **Zensur**, –, –en grade, mark
zerreißen (zerriß, zerrissen)
to tear up
zerstören to destroy
ziehen (zog, ist gezogen) **to**
move
das **Ziel**, –es, –e goal
ziemlich rather
die **Zigarette**, –, –n cigarette
das **Zimmer**, –s, – room
zitieren to quote
zu (*preposition*) to; at; for;
(*with infinitive*) to; (*adverb*) too
das **Zuchthaus**, –es, –er prison,
imprisonment (at hard labor)
zuerst at first, first
zufrieden satisfied
der **Zug**, –es, –e train
zuhören (*with dative object*)
to listen
der **Zuhörer**, –s, – listener
zunächst first
zunehmen (nimmt zu, nahm
zu, zugenommen) to put
on, to gain

zurückgeben (gibt zurück, gab
zurück, zurückgegeben) to
return, to give back
zurückgehen (ging zurück, ist
zurückgegangen) to go
back, to return
zurückkehren to return
zurückkommen (kam zurück,
ist zurückgekommen) to
come back
zurücklegen to put aside
zurückwerfen (wirft zurück,
warf zurück, zurückgewor-
fen) to throw back
zusammen together
zuschicken to send (to)
zuschieben (schob zu, zuge-
schoben) to push to-
ward
zustoßen (stößt zu, stieß zu,
ist zugestoßen) to happen
to, to befall
zwanzig twenty
zwei two
der **Zweifel**, –s, – doubt
zweimal twice
die **Zwillinge** (plural) twins
zwingen (zwang, gezwungen)
to force, to compel
zwischen between

English-German Vocabulary

This vocabulary lists all English words appearing in the active exercises, with the exception of the definite article, the indefinite article, the possessive adjectives, the personal pronouns, and the relative pronouns.

to **be able to** können (kann, konnte, gekonnt)

about (*preposition*) (**around**) um (*with acc.*); (**concerning**) von (*with dat.*), über (*with acc.*)

absolutely unbedingt

to **accept** annehmen (nimmt an, nahm an, angenommen)

to **accompany** begleiten

according to nach (*with dat., preposition after noun it modifies*)

to **accuse** (**of**) anklagen (*with gen. of thing and acc. of person*)

acquainted (*see:* to become acquainted)

across über (*with acc.*)

to **act** (**as if**) (so) tun (als ob)

advice der Rat, –es, Ratschläge

to **advise** raten (rät, riet, geraten) (*with dat.*)

to **be afraid** Angst haben

after (*conjunction*) nachdem; (*preposition*) nach (*with dat.*)

afternoon der Nachmittag, –s, –e; **this afternoon** heute nachmittag; **tomorrow afternoon** morgen nachmittag

again wieder; (*in the sense of:* once more) noch einmal

against gegen (*with acc.*)

ago vor (*with dat.*)

all (*plural*) alle

almost fast

alone allein

along (*see:* to come along)

already schon

also auch

although obgleich

always immer

among unter (*with dat. or acc.*)

to **be angry** (**with**) böse sein (mit, *with dat.*)

to **be annoyed** (**at**) sich ärgern (über, *with acc.*)

another ein anderer (eine andere, ein anderes); **with one another** miteinander

to **answer** (**a person**) antworten (*with dat.*); (**a question or thing**) beantworten (*with acc.*) *or* antworten auf (*with acc.*)

answer (**to**) die Antwort, –, –en (auf, *with acc.*)

245

anthology   die Anthologie, –,
–n

(*not*) **any**   kein

(*not*) **anyone**   niemand, keiner

(*not*) **anything**   nichts

apartment   die Wohnung, –,
–en

April   der April, –s

around (*preposition*)   um (*with
acc.*)

arrival   die Ankunft, –, ⸚

to **arrive** (**of people**)   ankommen
(kam an, ist angekommen);
(**of news,** *etc.*)   eintreffen
(trifft ein, traf ein, ist ein-
getroffen)

article   der Aufsatz, –es, ⸚e;
der Artikel, –s, –

artist   der Künstler, –s, –

as (*conjunction*)   während; **as
a**   als; **as . . . as**   so . . .
wie; **as far as** (*conjunction*)
soweit, (*preposition*)   bis; **as
if** (*conjunction*)   als ob; **as
long as** (*conjunction*)   solange; **as soon as** (*conjunction*)   sobald; **as well as**   so
gut wie

to be **ashamed** (**of**)   sich schämen
(*with gen. or with* für)

to **ask** (**about**)   fragen (nach,
with dat.); to **ask questions**
Fragen stellen; (**request:** bitten [bat, gebeten])

asleep (*see:* to fall asleep)

to **assign**   aufgeben (gibt auf, gab
auf, aufgegeben)

assignment   die Aufgabe, –, –n
(*usually in the plural*); **to do
an assignment**   die Auf-
gabe(n) machen

to **assume**   annehmen (nimmt an,
nahm an, angenommen)

at (**the home of**)   bei (*with
dat.*); (**next to, near**)   an
(*with dat. or acc.*); (**in,** *as in*
at the station, post office,

etc.)   auf (*with dat. or acc.*);
at all (*see:* not at all); **at
home**   zu Hause; **at . . .
o'clock**   um . . . Uhr

to **attend**   beiwohnen (*with dat.*)

aunt   die Tante, –, –n

to **avoid**   vermeiden (vermied,
vermieden)

to be **aware** (**of**)   sich (*dat.*) einer
Sache (*gen.*) bewußt sein

bad   schlimm; **badly**   schlecht

to **bake**   backen (buk *or* backte,
gebacken)

to **beat**   schlagen (schlägt, schlug,
geschlagen)

beautiful   schön

because   weil, da; **because of**
(*preposition*)   wegen (*with
gen.*)

to **become**   werden (wird, wurde,
ist geworden); **to become acquainted** (**with**)   kennenlernen (*with acc.*)

bed   das Bett, –es, –en; **to go
to bed**   zu Bett gehen

beer   das Bier, –es, –e

before (*conjunction*)   bevor,
ehe; (*preposition*)   vor (*with
dat. or acc.*)

to **begin**   anfangen (fängt an, fing
an, angefangen), beginnen
(begann, begonnen)

beginning   der Anfang, –s, ⸚e

to **behave**   sich benehmen (benimmt sich, benahm sich,
sich benommen)

behind   hinter (*with dat. or
acc.*)

to **believe**   glauben (*with dat. of
person and acc. of thing*)

to **belong** (**to**)   gehören (*with
dat.*)

best   der (die, das) Beste; am
besten; **best of all**   am
liebsten

better besser
between zwischen (*with dat. or acc.*)
big groß
to bite beißen (biß, gebissen)
blond(e) blond
blue blau
book das Buch, –es, –̈er
bottle die Flasche, –, –n
boy der Junge, –n, –n
bread das Brot, –es, –e
bridge die Brücke, –, –n
to bring bringen (brachte, gebracht); to bring (to) mitbringen (brachte mit, mitgebracht)
brother der Bruder, –s, –̈
bus der Autobus, –ses, –se
businessman der Geschäftsmann, –s, Geschäftsleute
busy beschäftigt
but aber; (but rather) sondern
to buy kaufen
by (*means of transportation*) mit (*with dat.*); (*referring to authorship*) von (*with dat.*)

cab das Taxi, –s, –s
to call nennen (nannte, genannt); to call up anrufen (rief an, angerufen); to be called heißen (hieß, geheißen)
(ñe) can (er) kann (*see also:* to be able to)
candy die Süßigkeiten (*plural*), der Bonbon, –s, –s
capable (of) fähig (*with gen.*)
car das Auto, –s, –s
care (*see:* to take care of)
careful(ly) sorgfältig
to carry out durchfüh'ren
case der Fall, –es, –̈e; in case falls
cat die Katze, –, –n
to catch fangen (fängt, fing, gefangen); to catch cold sich erkälten
century das Jahrhundert, –s, –e
chair der Stuhl, –es, –̈e
chapter das Kapitel, –s, –
charming reizend
child das Kind, –es, –er
childhood die Kindheit, –, (*no plural*)
church die Kirche, –, –n; church steeple der Kirchturm, –s, –̈e
cigar die Zigarre, –, –n
cigarette die Zigarette, –, –n
city die Stadt, –, –̈
to claim behaupten; to claim (to be, have, etc.) wollen
class die Klasse, –, –n
to close schließen (schloß, geschlossen), zumachen
clothes die Kleidung, –, –en; die Kleider (*plural*)
coat der Mantel, –s, –̈
coffee der Kaffee, –s, (*no plural*)
cold kalt
to come (to) kommen (kam, ist gekommen) (nach); to come along mitkommen (kam mit, ist mitgekommen)
to compare vergleichen (verglich, verglichen)
complaint die Klage, –, –n
complete(ly) vollkommen
concert das Konzert, –s, –e
conductor der Dirigent, –en, –en
conference die Konferenz, –, –en
to consider halten (hält, hielt, gehalten) für (*with acc.*)
to contain enthalten (enthält, enthielt, enthalten)
to convince überzeu'gen; convincing überzeugend
cool kühl

corner die Ecke, –, –n
correct(ly) richtig
to **cost** kosten
(he) **could** (er) konnte (*see also:* to be able to)
country das Land, –es, ⸚er; **in the country** auf dem Land
courage der Mut, –es, (*no plural*)
course der Kurs, –es, –e
criminal der Verbrecher, –s, –
to **criticize** kritisieren
curtain der Vorhang, –s, ⸚e
to **cut** schneiden (schnitt, geschnitten)

dance der Tanz, –es, ⸚e
to **dare** wagen
daughter die Tochter, –, ⸚
day der Tag, –es, –e; **all day** den ganzen Tag; **every day** jeden Tag; **one day** eines Tages
to **deserve** verdienen
desire die Lust, –, ⸚e
difficult schwer
difficulty die Schwierigkeit, –, –en
dinner das Essen, –s, –
directly direkt, sofort, gleich
disappointed enttäuscht
to **disturb** stören
to **do** machen; tun (tat, getan)
doctor der Arzt, –es, ⸚e
dog der Hund, –es, –e
dollar der Dollar, –s, –
door die Tür, –, –en
downtown in die Stadt
dress das Kleid, –es, –er
to **drink** trinken (trank, getrunken)
to **drive** (*in a vehicle*) fahren (fährt, fuhr, ist gefahren); (**to force to go**) treiben (trieb, getrieben)
during während (*with gen.*)

early früh
to **earn** verdienen
easy, easily leicht
to **eat** essen (ißt, aß, gegessen)
egg das Ei, –es, –er
either . . . or entweder . . . oder; **not . . . either** auch nicht
elegant elegant
empty leer
enemy der Feind, –es, –e
to be **engaged** verlobt sein
enough genug
to **enter** betreten (*transitive only*) (betrat, betreten)
essay der Aufsatz, –es, ⸚e
to **establish** feststellen
eternal ewig
even selbst; **even if** selbst wenn, wenn . . . auch; **even though** wenn . . . auch, obgleich
evening der Abend, –s, –e; **all evening** den ganzen Abend; **in the evening** abends; **last evening** gestern abend; **this evening** heute abend; **that evening** an diesem Abend; **tomorrow evening** morgen abend
ever je(mals)
every jeder, jede, jedes
everything alles (*neuter*)
exam(ination) das Examen, –s, –; die Prüfung, –, –en
excellent ausgezeichnet
except außer (*with dat.*)
to **expect** erwarten
expensive teuer
experiment das Experiment, –s, –e
to **explain** erklären
extremely äußerst, höchst
eye das Auge, –s, –n

fact die Tatsache, –, –n

fall der Herbst, –es, –e

to **fall asleep** einschlafen (schläft ein, schlief ein, ist eingeschlafen)

family die Familie, –, –n

famous berühmt

far weit

fast schnell

father der Vater, –s, –

to **feel** (**well,** *etc.*) sich (gut, *etc.*) fühlen

few wenige (*plural*)

finally endlich

to **find** finden (fand, gefunden); **to be found** sich befinden (befand sich, sich befunden), sein

to **finish** (**with**) fertig sein (*or* werden) (mit, *with dat.*)

first (*adj.*) erst–; (*adverb*) zuerst

to **flatter** schmeicheln (*with dat.*)

flower die Blume, –, –n

to **fly** fliegen (flog, ist geflogen)

to **follow** folgen (*with dat.*)

for (*conjunction*) denn; (*preposition*) für (*with acc.*); (*time*) seit (*with dat.*)

to **force** zwingen (zwang, gezwungen)

forefathers die Vorfahren (*plural*)

to **forget** vergessen (vergißt, vergaß, vergessen)

the former jener, jene, jenes

formerly früher

to **be found** sich befinden (befand sich, sich befunden), sein

to **freeze** frieren (fror, gefroren); kalt sein (*impersonal, with dat.*)

French französisch

friend der Freund, –es, –e

from von (*with dat.*); aus (*with dat.*); **from . . . on** von . . . an

in front of vor (*with dat. or acc.*)

full of voller (*with gen.*)

fur coat der Pelzmantel, –s, –

furious wütend

game das Spiel, –es, –e

garage die Garage, –, –n

garden der Garten, –s, –

German deutsch; Deutsch (*language*)

Germany (das) Deutschland, –s

to **get** (**obtain**) bekommen (bekam, bekommen); (*in the meaning of* **grow, become**) werden (wird, wurde, ist geworden); **to get up** aufstehen (stand auf, ist aufgestanden)

girl das Mädchen, –s, –

girl friend die Freundin, –, –nen

to **give** geben (gibt, gab, gegeben); **to give a name** (**to**) nennen (nannte, genannt)

glass das Glas, –es, –er

to **go** gehen (ging, ist gegangen); **to go along** mitgehen (ging mit, ist mitgegangen), mitkommen (kam mit, ist mitgekommen); **to go out** ausgehen (ging aus, ist ausgegangen)

good gut

government die Regierung, –, –en

grade die Zensur, –, –en, die Note, –, –n

grateful dankbar (*with dat. of person and with* für *referring to object*)

gray grau

great groß

hair das Haar, –es, –e (*normally in plural*)

to **hammer** hämmern
hand die Hand, –, –̈e
to **hand in** einhändigen
to **hang** hängen (hing, gehangen) (*intransitive*); (*weak: transitive*)
to **happen** geschehen (geschieht, geschah, ist geschehen), passieren
happy glücklich
to **harm** schaden (*with dat.*)
hat der Hut, –es, –̈e
to **have** (**done**, *etc.: causation*) lassen (läßt, ließ, gelassen); **to have to** müssen (muß mußte, gemußt)
to **hear** hören
to **help** helfen (hilft, half, geholfen) (*with dat.*)
help die Hilfe, –, (*no plural*)
here hier
to **hide** sich verstecken, sich verbergen (verbirgt sich, verbarg sich, sich verborgen)
high hoch
holiday der Feiertag, –es, –e
home nach Hause; **at home** zu Hause
homework die Hausarbeit, –, –en
to **hope** hoffen
hot heiß
hotel das Hotel, –s, –s
hour die Stunde, –, –n
house das Haus, –es, –̈er
hundred hundert
to **hurry** sich beeilen
husband der Mann, –es, –̈er

if wenn
illness die Krankheit, –, –en
to **imagine** sich (*dat.*) vorstellen
immediately sofort, sogleich
to **inform** mitteilen (*with dat. of the person and acc. of the thing*)

information die Nachricht, –, –en, die Information, –, –en
to **insist** (**on**) bestehen (bestand, bestanden) **auf** (*with dat.*)
instead of (*preposition*) anstatt (*with gen.*); (**instead of . . . ing**) anstatt . . . zu + *inf.*
instruction die Anweisung, –, –en
intelligent intelligent
to **intend** (**to**) beabsichtigen
intention die Absicht, –, –en
to be **interested** (**in**) sich interessieren (für, *with acc.*)
interesting interessant
to **introduce** vorstellen
to **invite** einladen (lädt ein, lud ein, eingeladen)
invitation die Einladung, –, –en

janitor der Verwalter, –s, –; der Pedell, –s, –e (*in a school*)
July der Juli, –s
June der Juni, –s
just gerade

to **keep** behalten (behält, behielt, behalten), aufbewahren
key der Schlüssel, –s, –
what kind of was für ein
kitchen die Küche, –, –n
to **knock** (**on**) anklopfen (an, *with acc.*)
to **know** (*i.e.,* **to be acquainted with**) kennen (kannte, gekannt); **to know** (**for a fact**) wissen (wußte, gewußt); **known** (**for**) bekannt (für, *with acc.*)

to **lack** fehlen (*impersonal, with dat. of person:* es fehlt mir, **I lack,** *etc.*)
large groß

last letzt, last night gestern abend

late spät, later später

the latter dieser, diese, dieses

to laugh lachen

lawyer der Rechtsanwalt, –s, ⁼e

to learn lernen

to leave verlassen (verläßt, verließ, verlassen)

leave der Abschied, –s, (–e)

to lend leihen (lieh, geliehen)

letter der Brief, –es, –e

library die Bibliothek, –, –en

to lie liegen (lag, gelegen); (to tell a lie) lügen (log, gelogen)

light das Licht, –es, –er

light(ly) leicht

to be lightning blitzen

to like (to) mögen (mag, mochte, gemocht); gern (with a verb)

like wie

to listen to zuhören (with dat.)

little klein

to live leben

long lang; longer länger; no longer nicht mehr

to look (to appear) aussehen (sieht aus, sah aus, ausgesehen); to look at ansehen (sieht an, sah an, angesehen); to look for suchen

a lot of viel, viele (plural)

love die Liebe, –, (no plural)

to love lieben

loyally treu

loyalty die Treue, –, (no plural)

to be lucky Glück haben

lunch das Mittagessen, –s, –

man der Mann, –es, ⁼er

many viele; many a mancher, manche, manches

mark die Zensur, –, –en; die Note, –, –n

to marry heiraten

May der Mai, –es

may (i.e., to be allowed to) dürfen (darf, durfte, gedurft); können (kann, konnte, gekonnt); may be mag . . . sein

means das Mittel, –s, –

meat das Fleisch, –es, (no plural)

to meet treffen (trifft, traf, getroffen)

meeting die Versammlung, –, –en

message die Botschaft, –, –en

middle die Mitte, –, –n

milk die Milch, –, (no plural)

mist der Nebel, –s, –

mistake der Fehler, –s, –

Monday der Montag, –s, –e

money das Geld, –es, –er

month der Monat, –s, –e

mood die Laune, –, –n; to be in a good (etc.) mood guter (etc.) Laune sein

more mehr

morning der Morgen, –s, –; in the morning morgens; this morning heute morgen

Moslem der Mohammedaner, –s, –

most die meisten

mother die Mutter, –, ⁼

mountain der Berg, –es, –e

to move out ausziehen (zog aus, ist ausgezogen)

movie der Film, –s, –e; movie theater das Kino, –s, –s; to go to the movies ins Kino gehen

much viel

Munich (das) München, –s

music die Musik, –, (no plural)

must (*see:* to have to); (**I**)
must (ich) muß
myself (**yourself,** *etc.*) selbst

nail der Nagel, –s, ∸
name der Name, –ns–, –n
to **need** bedürfen (bedarf, bedurfte, bedurft) (*with gen.*)
never nie(mals)
new neu
news die Nachrichten (*plural*)
newspaper die Zeitung, –, –en
next nächst; **next to** (*preposition*) neben (*with dat. or acc.*)
nice (**to**) nett (zu, mit *with dat.*)
night die Nacht, –, ∸e; **all night** die ganze Nacht; **at night** nachts, abends; **last night** gestern abend
ninety neunzig
no! nein!; **no longer** nicht mehr; **no one** niemand, keiner
nobody, no one niemand, keiner
not nicht; **not at all** gar nicht; **not yet** noch nicht
novel der Roman, –s, –e
now jetzt, nun

to **occupy oneself** (**with**) sich beschäftigen (mit, *with dat.*)
to **occur** (**to**) einfallen (fällt ein, fiel ein, ist eingefallen) (*with dat. of person*)
ocean der Ozean, –s, –e
at . . . o'clock um . . . Uhr; **since . . . o'clock** seit . . . Uhr
to **offer** anbieten (bot an, angeboten)
official der Beamte, –n, –n
often oft
old alt

on (**on top of**) auf (*with dat. or acc.*); (**about, concerning**) über (*with acc.*)
once einmal
one ein(s); (*impersonal pronoun*) man
only nur
to **open** öffnen
opera die Oper, –, –n; **to go to the opera** in die Oper gehen
opinion die Meinung, –, –en
orchestra das Orchester, –s, –
to **order** befehlen (befiehlt, befahl, befohlen) (*with dat. of person*)
in order to um . . . zu + *infinitive*
original das Original, –s, –e
other ander–
out of aus (*with dat.*)
outside (*adverb*) draußen
over über (*with dat. or acc.*)

package das Paket, –(e)s, –e
pan die Pfanne, –, –n
pants die Hose, –, –n
park der Park, –s, –s
to **pass** (**an** *or* **the examination**) (ein *or* das Examen) bestehen (bestand, bestanden)
pen der Federhalter, –s, –
pencil der Bleistift, –es, –e
pension die Pension, –, –en
people die Leute (plural)
to **perform** aufführen
physicist der Physiker, –s, –
picture das Bild, –es, –er
to **place** stellen, rücken; (*see also:* to take place)
to **plan** vorhaben, planen
plan der Plan, –es, ∸e
to **play** spielen
play das Stück, –es, –e
to **please** gefallen (gefällt, gefiel, gefallen) (*with dat. of person*); **please** (**!**) bitte

pocket die Tasche, –, –n
pocketbook die Handtasche, –, –n
poem das Gedicht, –(e)s, –e
police die Polizei, –, (*collective noun; no plural*)
polite höflich
poor arm; (*of quality*) schlecht
popular beliebt
possible möglich
pound das Pfund, –es, –e
to **pour** gießen (goß, gegossen)
Prague (das) Prag, –s
to **prefer (to)** lieber (*with verb*)
to **prepare oneself (for)** sich vorbereiten (auf, *with acc.*)
present das Geschenk, –(e)s, –e
pretty hübsch, niedlich
price der Preis, –es, –e
prize der Preis, –es, –e
probably wahrscheinlich
problem das Problem, –s, –e
professor der Professor, –s, –en
to **promise** versprechen (verspricht, versprach, versprochen) (*with dat. of person*)
to **propose** vorschlagen (schlägt vor, schlug vor, vorgeschlagen)
to **prove** beweisen (bewies, bewiesen)
to **publish** veröffentlichen
pupil der Schüler, –s, –

to **quarrel** sich streiten (stritt sich, sich gestritten)
question die Frage, –, –n; **to ask questions Fragen stellen**
quick(ly) schnell

railroad station der Bahnhof, –s, –̈e

to **rain** regnen
rain der Regen, –s, –
rarely selten
to **read** lesen (liest, las, gelesen)
reader der Leser, –s, –
ready fertig
really wirklich
to **receive** erhalten (erhält, erhielt, erhalten)
to **recommend** empfehlen (empfiehlt, empfahl, empfohlen)
red rot
to **refer (to)** sich beziehen (bezog sich, sich bezogen) (auf, *with acc.*)
to **refuse** sich weigern
to **reject** ablehnen
to **rely (on)** sich verlassen (verläßt sich, verließ sich, sich verlassen) (auf, *with acc.*)
remark die Bemerkung, –, –en
to **remember** sich erinnern (*with gen. or with* an + *acc.*)
to **remind (of)** erinnern (an, *with acc.*)
to **repair** reparieren
to **repeat** wiederho′len
to **reply** antworten, erwidern
to **report** berichten
report der Bericht, –es, –e
research die Forschung, –, –en
to **resemble** ähneln (*with dat.*); ähnlich sehen (*with dat.*)
restaurant das Restaurant, –s, –s
to **return (something)** zurückgeben (gibt zurück, gab zurück, zurückgegeben)
to **rob (someone of something)** berauben (*with gen. of the thing and acc. of the person*)
rock der Stein, –es, –e
room das Zimmer, –s, –
rule die Regel, –, –n
to **run** laufen (läuft, lief, ist ge-

laufen), rennen (rannte, ist gerannt)

to be said sollen (soll, sollte, gesollt)

salesman der Verkäufer, –s, –

(the) same derselbe, dieselbe, dasselbe

satisfied zufrieden

to say sagen

scarcely kaum

school die Schule, –, –n; to school in die Schule

to scold ausschimpfen

to scream schreien (schrie, geschrieen)

second zweit–

secretary der Sekretär, –s, –e; die Sekretärin, –, –nen

to see sehen (sieht, sah, gesehen)

to seem scheinen (schien, geschienen)

to sell verkaufen

semester das Semester, –s, –

to send schicken, senden (sandte or sendete, gesandt or gesendet)

sentence der Satz, –es, ⸚e

September der September, –s

to serve dienen (with dat.)

seven sieben

seventeenth siebzehnt–

several verschiedene (plural)

shoe der Schuh, –es, –e

shop der Laden, –s, ⸚

to show zeigen

sick krank; to be sick (of) müde (or: satt) sein (with gen. or acc.).

to be silent schweigen (schwieg, geschwiegen)

since (preposition) seit (with dat.); (conjunction) da

to sing singen (sang, gesungen)

sister die Schwester, –, –n

to sit sitzen (saß, gesessen); to sit down sich hinsetzen

slow(ly) langsam

small klein

to smell riechen (roch, gerochen)

to smile (at) anlächeln (with acc.)

to smoke rauchen

to snow schneien

snow der Schnee, –s, (no plural)

so so; so that so daß

sofa das Sofa, –s, –s

soldier der Soldat, –en, –en

to solve lösen

some einige

somebody, some one jemand

something etwas

son der Sohn, –es, ⸚e

song das Lied, –es, –er

soon bald

to be sorry leid tun (tat leid, leid getan) (impersonal with dat. of person, es tut mir leid, I am sorry, etc.)

soup die Suppe, –, –n

source die Quelle, –, –n

to speak (about) sprechen (spricht, sprach, gesprochen) (über, with acc.), reden (über, with acc.)

speaker der Redner, –s, –

spinach der Spinat, –s, (no plural)

in spite of trotz (with gen.)

spring der Frühling, –s, –e

to stand stehen (stand, gestanden); (something) ertragen (erträgt, ertrug, ertragen), leiden können

to starve verhungern

to stay bleiben (blieb, ist geblieben)

to steal stehlen (stiehlt, stahl, gestohlen)

steel der Stahl, –es, (no plural)

to step up (to) treten (tritt, trat, ist getreten) (an, with acc.)

still noch

store das Geschäft, –(e)s, –e
story die Geschichte, –, –n
street die Straße, –, –n
strict streng
student der Student, –en, –en
to study studieren
to succeed gelingen (gelang, ist gelungen) (*impersonal, with dat. of person*, es gelingt mir, **I succeed**, *etc.*)
successful erfolgreich
such solcher, solche, solches; **such a** ein solcher, eine solche, ein solches
to suffer leiden (litt, gelitten)
suggestion der Vorschlag, –s, ∸e
suitcase der Koffer, –s, –
summer der Sommer, –s, –; **this summer** diesen Sommer
Sunday der Sonntag, –s, –e
superior der Vorgesetzte, –n, –n
supper das Abendessen, –s, –
to support unterstützen
support die Hilfe, –, (*no plural*), die Unterstützung, –, –en
to be supposed (to) sollen (soll, sollte, gesollt)
to be sure (of) sicher sein (*with gen.*)
surely sicher
to surprise überraschen
Switzerland die Schweiz, –
symphony die Symphonie, –, –n

table der Tisch, –es, –e
to take nehmen (nimmt, nahm, genommen); **to take away** wegnehmen (nimmt weg, nahm weg, weggennommen) (*with dat. of the person and acc. of the thing*); **to take care (of)** sich annehmen (nimmt sich an, nahm sich

an, sich angenommen) (*with gen.*); **to take leave (of)** Abschied nehmen (nimmt Abschied, nahm Abschied, Abschied genommen) (von, *with dat.*); **to take part (in)** teilnehmen (nimmt teil, nahm teil, teilgenommen) (an, *with dat*); **to take place** stattfinden (fand statt, stattgefunden)
talented begabt
to talk (about) reden (über, *with acc.*), sprechen (spricht, sprach, gesprochen) (über, *with acc.*); **to talk (to)** reden (mit, *with dat.*)
tall groß
teacher der Lehrer, –s, –
to tell (*i.e.*, **give information**) sagen; (**tell a story**) erzählen; **to tell the truth** die Wahrheit sagen
ten zehn
tennis das Tennis, –, (*no plural*); **tennis player** der Tennisspieler, –s, –
terrible schrecklich
than (*after comparative*) als
to thank danken (*with dat.*)
that (*pronoun*) das; (*conjunction*) daß
the . . . the je . . . desto
theater das Theater, –s, –
theft der Diebstahl, –s, ∸e
then dann
theory die Theorie, –, –n
there da, dort
think denken (dachte, gedacht); (**believe**) glauben; **to think of** denken an (*with acc.*), (**to have an opinion about**) halten von (*with dat.*)
this dieser, diese, dieses
thought der Gedanke, –ns, –n
three drei

through durch (*with acc.*)

to **throw** werfen (wirft, warf, geworfen)

to **thunder** donnern

time (*by clock*) die Zeit, –, –en; (*enumerative*) das Mal, –es, –e; **to have a good time** sich (gut) amüsieren; **for a long time** lange; **on time** pünktlich

to zu (*with dat.*); (*with place names*) nach (*with dat.*); **to the movies** ins Kino; **to the theater** ins Theater; **to the opera** in die Oper; **to school** in die Schule, zur Schule

today heute

together zusammen

tomorrow morgen; **tomorrow evening** morgen abend

tonight heute abend

too zu; (*in the meaning of also*) auch

town die Stadt, –, –e

train der Zug, –es, –e

to **translate** überse'tzen

to **travel** reisen, fahren (fährt, fuhr, ist gefahren)

to **treat** behandeln

trip die Reise, –, –n; **to take a** (*or* **the**) **trip** eine (*or* die) Reise machen

true wahr

to **trust** trauen, vertrauen (*with dat. of person*)

truth die Wahrheit, –, –en

to **try** versuchen

two zwei, beide (*after a der-word*); **two hundred** zweihundert

uncle der Onkel, –s –

under unter (*with dat. or acc.*)

to **understand** verstehen (verstand, verstanden), begreifen

(begriff, begriffen)

unemployed stellungslos, arbeitslos

university die Universität, –, –en

unknown unbekannt

unsatisfactory ungenügend

until bis

up to an (*with acc.*)

to **use** gebrauchen

usual(ly) gewöhnlich

vacation die Ferien (*plural*)

veranda die Veranda, –, Veranden

very sehr; **very much** sehr

via über (*with acc.*)

Vienna (das) Wien, –s

village das Dorf, –es, –er

visible sichtbar

to **visit** besuchen

to **wait** (**for**) warten (auf, *with acc.*)

walk der Spaziergang, –s, –e

wall (**of a room**) die Wand, –, –e; (*a structure as such, as a wall of a house, around a garden or city*) die Mauer, –, –n

to **want** (**to**) wollen (will, wollte, gewollt)

war der Krieg, –es, –e

warm warm

to **wash** waschen (wäscht, wusch, gewaschen)

watch die Uhr, –, –en

to **water** begießen (begoß, begossen)

way der Weg, –es, –e; **by way of** über (*with acc.*)

to **wear** tragen (trägt, trug, getragen)

weather das Wetter, –s, –

week die Woche, –, –n; **a week** (*adverbial phrase*) die

Woche; **all week**   die ganze Woche

week-end   das Wochenende, –s, –n

well   gut; **well known** bekannt

what?   was?

when (*interrogative*)   wann; (*action in future or repeated action*)   wenn; (*single occurrence in past*)   als

where   wo

whether   ob

while   während

who?   wer?; **whoever**   wer

whole   ganz

whom?   wem? (*dative*); wen? (*accusative*)

whose?   wessen?

why?   warum? weshalb?

wife   die Frau, –, –en

to **win**   gewinnen (gewann, gewonnen)

window   das Fenster, –s, –

wine   der Wein, –es, –e

winter   der Winter, –s, –

to **wish**   wünschen; **I wish**   ich möchte

with   mit (*with dat.*); (**at the home of**)   bei (*with dat.*)

without   ohne (*with acc.*)

woman   die Frau, –, –en

word   das Wort, –es, –e (or ̈er)

to **work** (**on**)   arbeiten (an, *with dat.*)

work   die Arbeit, –, –en

worthy (**of**)   wert (*with gen. or acc.*), würdig (*with gen.*)

to **write**   schreiben (schrieb, geschrieben)

year   das Jahr, –es, –e; **for years**   jahrelang

yes   ja

yesterday   gestern

yet   noch; **no one . . . yet** niemand . . . noch; **not yet** noch nicht

young   jung

Index